Beyond
the
Magic
Bullet

Kumarian Press Books on International Development

Selected Titles

Beyond the Magic Bullet:
NGO Performance and
Accountability in the
Post–Cold War World
*Michael Edwards and
David Hulme, editors*

The Two Faces of Civil Society:
NGOs and Politics in Africa
Stephen N. Ndegwa

Intermediary NGOs:
The Supporting Link in
Grassroots Development
Thomas F. Carroll

Getting to the 21st Century:
Voluntary Action and the
Global Agenda
David C. Korten

Democratizing Development:
The Role of Voluntary
Organizations
John Clark

Promises Not Kept:
The Betrayal of Social Change in
the Third World, Third Edition
John Isbister

The New World of
Microenterprise Finance:
Building Healthy Financial
Institutions for the Poor
*María Otero and Elisabeth Rhyne,
editors*

Down to Earth:
Community Perspectives on
Health, Development, and the
Environment
*Bonnie Bradford and
Margaret Gwynne, editors*

Women at the Center:
Development Issues and Practices
for the 1990s
*Gay Young, Vidyamali
Samarasinghe and Ken Kusterer,
editors*

Kumarian Press Books for a World that Works

Selected Titles

When Corporations Rule
the World
David C. Korten

The Human Farm:
A Tale of Changing Lives and
Changing Lands
Katie Smith

The Immigration Debate:
Remaking America
John Isbister

HIV & AIDS:
The Global Inter-Connection
Elizabeth Reid, editor

Beyond the Magic Bullet

NGO Performance and Accountability in the Post–Cold War World

editors
Michael Edwards
David Hulme

*Published under the auspices of
The Save the Children Fund–U.K.*

Save the Children Y

*The Save the Children Fund–U.K. is a member of
the International Save the Children Alliance*

Kumarian Press

*Beyond the Magic Bullet: NGO Performance and Accountability
in the Post–Cold War World.*

Published 1996 in the United States of America by Kumarian Press, Inc.,
14 Oakwood Avenue, West Hartford, Connecticut 06119-2127 USA.

Production supervised by Jenna Dixon
Copyedited by Linda Lotz   Proofread by Barbara Ames
Text designed by Jenna Dixon   Typeset by Ultragraphics
Index prepared by Mary Neumann

Printed in the United States of America on recycled acid-free paper
by Thomson-Shore, Inc. Text printed with soy-based ink.

Library of Congress Cataloging-in-Publication Data
Beyond the magic bullet : NGO performance and accountability in the post cold war
world / editors, Michael Edwards, David Hulme.
       p.   cm. — (Kumarian Press books on international development)
    Includes bibliographical references and index.
    ISBN 1-56549-052-5 (cloth : alk. paper). — ISBN 1-56549-051-7 (paper : alk.
paper)
    1. Nonprofit organizations—Evaluation—Congresses. 2. Non-governmental
organizations—Evaluation—Congresses. 3. Non-governmental organizations—
Developing countries—Congresses. I. Edwards, Michael, 1957–   . II. Hulme,
David. III. Series.
    HD2769.15.B48   1996
    338.6'2'091724—dc20   95-20653

05 04 03 02 01 00 99   10 9 8 7 6 5 4 3 2   1st Printing 1996

Contents

Illustrations

Preface

In 1992, The Save the Children Fund–U.K. and the Institute for Development Policy and Management (IDPM) at Manchester University cosponsored an international workshop called "Scaling Up NGO Impact: Learning from Experience," the outcome of which was published in the book *Making a Difference: NGOs and Development in a Changing World* (Edwards and Hulme 1992). *Making a Difference* has been reprinted three times, but growing concerns have been expressed about the causes and consequences of nongovernmental organization (NGO) growth and what appears to be an increasingly close relationship between NGOs and official aid agencies. To investigate these concerns, The Save the Children Fund–U.K. and IDPM organized a second international workshop in Manchester in June 1994 entitled "NGOs and Development: Performance and Accountability in the 'New World Order.'" which provided the basis for this volume.

When we reread the papers that had been presented at the second Manchester workshop, it became clear that there were two overlapping themes of concern. The first involved issues of NGO performance and accountability and how these processes were being reshaped by changing roles and funding arrangements. *Beyond the Magic Bullet* presents a detailed review of those concerns. The second theme involved the broader relationships between NGOs, governments, and official donor agencies and how these changing relationships were affecting state-society relations, the future of development cooperation, and the interests of poor people. These concerns are explored in another book entitled *Too Close for Comfort?* (Hulme and Edwards forthcoming).

Inevitably, this book is the result of contributions from a large number of people, not all of whom are credited in the text. In particular, we would like to acknowledge the contributions of all those who presented papers and took part in discussion groups at the second Manchester workshop. They helped shape our own thinking and the thinking of the other contributors. We should stress, however, that none of the contributors speaks on behalf of or represents any constituency; all write as individuals with their own personal points of view. No collection of essays can claim to be truly comprehensive, but we endeavored to include as wide a range of views and experiences as possible from different regions of the world and from contrasting organizations.

We would also like to acknowledge the financial support of a number of institutions that helped make the workshop and the resulting publication possible. These include the NGO Unit of the Swedish International Development Authority (SIDA), the Government and Institutions Department and the Economic and Social Research Department (ESCOR) in the U.K. Overseas Development Administration (ODA), Save the Children Fund–U.K., and IDPM at Manchester University. A number of other NGOs also sponsored participants at the workshop, and our thanks go to them, especially to Save the Children field offices in Sudan, Uganda, Bangladesh, Peru, India, Pakistan, Thailand, Ghana, Colombia, and Honduras.

At the University of Manchester, special thanks go to Debra Whitehead and Jayne Hindle for sweating blood to make the workshop a success; Catherine Williams and Marcia Doyle undertook similar responsibilities for Save the Children Fund–U.K. The same teams spent long hours hunched in front of computer screens in order to prepare the manuscript in record time. Our sincere thanks go to them and to all the other individuals and agencies who helped us see this book through to a successful conclusion.

References

Edwards, Michael, and David Hulme, eds. 1992. *Making a difference: NGOs and development in a changing world.* London: Earthscan.

Hulme, David, and Michael Edwards, eds. Forthcoming. *Too close for comfort? NGOs, states and donors.* London: Macmillan.

Introduction

NGO Performance and Accountability

Michael Edwards and David Hulme

By any standards, the 1980s and 1990s brought an explosion in the number of nongovernmental organizations (NGOs) and grassroots organizations (GROs) active in relief and development.[1] The number of development NGOs registered in the Organization for Economic Cooperation and Development (OECD) countries of the industrialized North grew from 1,600 in 1980 to 2,970 in 1993 (Smillie and Helmich 1993). Over the same period, the total spending of these NGOs rose from US$2.8 billion to US$5.7 billion in current prices (OECD 1994). The 176 international NGOs of 1909 had blossomed into 28,900 by 1993 (Commission on Global Governance 1995). Similar figures have been reported in most countries in the South where political conditions have been favorable, with a particularly rapid increase over the last five years. For example, the number of NGOs registered with the government of Nepal rose from 220 in 1990 to 1,210 in 1993 (Rademacher and Tamang 1993, 34); in Bolivia, the figure increased from around 100 in 1980 to 530 twelve years later (Arellano-Lopez and Petras 1994, 562); and in Tunisia, there were 5,186 NGOs registered in 1991, compared with only 1,886 in 1988 (Marzouk forthcoming).

Paralleling this increase in overall numbers has been the growth of some individual NGOs to cover the provision of health, education, and credit services to millions of people in thousands of communities, especially in South Asia. For example, the Bangladesh Rural Advancement Committee (BRAC) now has more than 12,000 staff and has plans to work with over 3 million people (Aga Khan Foundation/NOVIB 1993); in India, the Self-Employed Women's Association (SEWA) has over 1 million clients in its credit programs; and Sarvodaya in Sri Lanka works in 7,000 villages (Perera forthcoming). NGOs' access to decision makers in both North and South is greater than ever before; their advocacy role continues to expand, and they are courted in debates over policy and practice. GROs have a lower public profile, but they have also experienced considerable growth over the last decade and are beginning to organize

1

themselves at the international level (Korten 1990; CIVICUS 1994). Clearly, something significant is happening in the world of international development. Lester Salamon (1993, 1) goes so far as to say that "a veritable associational revolution now seems underway at the global level that may constitute as significant a social and political development of the latter twentieth century as the rise of the nation state was of the nineteenth century."

Whether or not Salamon's conclusion is justified by current trends, the rise of NGOs and GROs on the world scene is an important phenomenon that has implications for the development prospects of poor people, for the future of these organizations themselves, and for the wider political economy of which they form a small but growing part. But what lies behind these trends? This book takes the view that the rise of NGOs is not an accident; nor is it solely a response to local initiative and voluntary action. Equally important is the increasing popularity of NGOs with governments and official aid agencies,[2] which is itself a response to recent developments in economic and political thinking. Over the last fifteen years, and particularly since the end of the Cold War, development policy and aid transfers have come to be dominated by what Robinson (1993) calls a "New Policy Agenda." This agenda is not monolithic—its details vary from one official aid agency to another—but in all cases, it is driven by two basic sets of beliefs organized around the two poles of neoliberal economics and liberal democratic theory (Moore 1993).

First, markets and private initiative are seen as the most efficient mechanisms for achieving economic growth and providing most services to most people (Colclough and Manor 1991). Governments "enable" private provision but should minimize their direct role in the economy; because of their supposed cost-effectiveness in reaching those who are poorest, official agencies support NGOs in providing welfare services to those who cannot be reached through markets (Fowler 1988; Meyer 1992). Of course, NGOs have always provided welfare services to poor people in countries where governments lacked the resources to ensure universal coverage in health and education; the difference is that now they are seen as the *preferred channel* for service provision, in *deliberate substitution* for the state.

Second, under the New Policy Agenda, NGOs and GROs are seen as vehicles for democratization and as essential components of a thriving civil society, which in turn are seen as essential to the success of the agenda's economic dimension (Moore 1993). NGOs and GROs are supposed to act as a counterweight to state power—protecting human rights, opening up channels of communication and participation, providing training grounds for activists, and promoting pluralism. The rise of citizens' movements around the world documented by Korten (1990) and crystallized most recently in the establishment of CIVICUS—the World Alliance for Citizen Participation—is not merely (or perhaps even primarily) a result of developments in official aid; but it cannot be separated entirely from the political ideals of the New Policy Agenda.

As a result of these developments, governments are prepared to channel increasing amounts of official aid to and through NGOs. Although accurate and comprehensive data are hard to come by, there is a good deal of evidence to suggest that the rise and growth of NGOs (and less so of GROs) are directly related to the increasing availability of official funding under the New Policy Agenda. NGOs are seen as effective vehicles for the delivery of the agenda's economic and political objectives, even though these roles are potentially incompatible, at least within the same organization (a proposition that is explored later). The proportion of total aid from OECD countries channeled through NGOs increased from 0.7 percent in 1975 to 3.6 percent in 1985 to *at least* 5.0 percent in 1993–94 (US$2.3 billion in absolute terms). This figure is certainly an underestimate, since it omits multilateral agency funding to NGOs and NGO funding from the U.S. government, which represented over half the Development Assistance Committee (DAC) total in all previous years (OECD 1988, 1994, 1995). Figures vary greatly among countries, donors, and NGOs; but in general, bilateral agencies are spending a steadily increasing proportion of their aid budgets through NGOs (including directly through NGOs in the South). Most NGOs (especially the largest ones in both North and South) depend on these donors for an increasing slice of their total budgets, partly as a result of a flattening out in voluntary income over the last year or two.[3] NGOs that are not dependent on official aid for the majority of their budgets are now the exception rather than the rule. As Smillie (Chapter 14 of this volume) says, "when CIDA [the Canadian International Development Agency] sneezes, Canadian NGOs reach for their vitamin C."

Although both the economic and the political dimensions of the New Policy Agenda are important to official agencies, aid to NGOs has gone primarily to finance welfare services. Some authors have criticized what they see as a fundamental change in the *function* of NGOs as a result of official funding, with service delivery and contracting replacing support to GROs and institutional development (Arellano-Lopez and Petras 1994). The increasing numbers of NGOs in many countries, a growth in the size of individual NGOs, an increasing concentration on service provision, and rising reliance on official funding all seem to be related, but this is not universally true (see Chapter 4).

The overall picture is one in which NGOs are seen as the "favored child" of official agencies and as something of a panacea for the problems of development. As Vivian (1994) puts it, official agencies (and the supporters of Northern NGOs) often see NGOs as a "magic bullet" that can be fired off in any direction and will still find its target, though often without leaving much evidence. Clearly, the increasing availability of official funding for NGOs, the popularity they enjoy, and the increasing access they are offered to centers of national and international decision making represent both an opportunity and a danger. NGOs can scale up their operations using official funds and use the New Policy Agenda to make their voices heard more loudly and more often through lobbying and advocacy; at the same time, by becoming more dependent on governments, NGOs run the risk of being co-opted into the agendas of others and seeing their independent social base eroded. As far back as 1988, Jan Pronk (in Hellinger, Hellinger, and O'Rogan 1988) warned that "the corruption of NGOs will be the political game in the years ahead." Pronk saw "corruption" not simply in terms of financial scandal but also more broadly, as the deviation of NGOs from their mission for social transformation. The only way that NGOs can avoid "corruption" in this sense is to develop systems for performance monitoring, accountability, and strategic planning that "ensure that a line remains drawn between transparent compromise and blind co-option" (Eade 1993, 161). That is why the central themes of this book—performance and accountability—are so important.

Strong accountability systems can help NGOs take advantage of the opportunities offered by the New Policy Agenda while ensuring that any warning signals are identified, listened to, and addressed. Of course, performance and accountability would be crucial subjects for debate whether NGOs were growing closer to governments or not. Performing effectively and accounting transparently are essential components of responsible practice, on which the legitimacy of development intervention ultimately depends. Moving beyond the magic bullet means taking accountability much more seriously than has so far been the case among most NGOs, Northern or Southern. But the New Policy Agenda complicates the issue of accountability considerably; as the chapters in this book demonstrate, dependence on official aid and the models of planning and intervention that underlie it could make an already unsatisfactory situation significantly worse.

NGO Performance

For reasons that are explained later in this introduction, assessing NGO performance is a difficult and messy business. In any case, the absence of a large body of reliable evidence on the impact and effectiveness of NGOs and GROs makes it difficult to generalize about this subject, despite claims that NGOs are "cost-effective" or that GROs are "close to the poor" (Fowler 1988). Most studies of NGO and GRO impact are based on small samples and are often restricted to agencies working in a particular sector (often economic development) or context (usually favorable), which makes measurement easier. Internal evaluations are rarely released, and what *is* released comes closer to propaganda than rigorous assessment.

Nevertheless, there is increasing evidence that NGOs and GROs do not perform as effectively as had been assumed in terms of poverty reach, cost-effectiveness, sustainability, popular participation (including gender), flexibility, and innovation.[4] In terms of service provision, there is certainly evidence that NGOs are able to provide some services more cost-effectively than governments. For example, the Orangi Pilot Project in Pakistan has developed sanitation systems at less than one-third of the equivalent cost in the commercial or government sector (Hasan 1993); similar cost advantages have been claimed for BRAC in primary education and credit provision (Aga Khan Foundation/NOVIB 1993). However, evidence from other studies contradicts this conclusion (Tendler 1989), and there is no empirical study that demonstrates a general case that NGO provision is cheaper than public provision. Even when NGO service provision is low-cost, it usually fails to reach the poorest people, though it may still reach a wider cross section of the population than government or commercial agencies (Hashemi and Schuler 1992; Farrington and Bebbington 1993; Hulme and Mosley 1995). The sustainability of large-scale service provision by NGOs has also been called into question by those who cite the large subsidies granted to NGOs (and denied to governments), which make the gap between private and public provision a "self-perpetuating reality" (Farrington and Lewis 1993, 333). There are also worries about a "patchwork quilt" of social services developing in which only certain regions are supplied by well-resourced NGOs, leaving others to fend for themselves under weak central oversight (Robinson 1993; Edwards and Hulme 1994). In all cases, careful management is needed to avoid a falloff in quality when NGOs scale up service provision to cover large populations, though as Howes and Sattar (1992) and Wils (Chapter 4) show, there is not necessarily a trade-off.

Evidence on the performance of NGOs and GROs in democratization is more difficult to come by, except in the area of micropolicy reform, where a growing number of case studies demonstrate that NGOs and GROs can influence governments and official agencies, especially when they come together to form a united front (Edwards and Hulme 1992). On occasion (as in Bangladesh, with the fall of President Ershad, or in the Philippines in the case of President Marcos), such united action can exert an influence on the position of governments as a whole. However, there is little evidence that NGOs or even GROs are engaging in the formal political process successfully without becoming embroiled in partisan politics and the distortions that accompany the struggle for state power. In both Latin America and Africa, evidence shows that NGOs have had little impact on political reform, partly because states are adept at containing such a possibility, and partly because NGOs themselves (as nonrepresentative organizations) have failed to develop effective strategies to promote democratization

(Lehmann 1990; Fowler 1991; Bratton 1990). The failure of many NGOs (and even GROs) to democratize their own structures makes them less effective in this process and, as the chapters in this book show, poses a particular problem for "downward" accountability to members and beneficiaries (Carroll 1992; Bebbington and Thiele 1993). Nevertheless, NGOs and GROs can be proud of their achievements in helping to cement human and political rights in many societies and in democratizing the informal political process by training grassroots activists, building stronger local institutions, promoting micropolicy reform, and undertaking education for citizenship (Friedmann 1992; Ghai and Vivian 1992).

A particular area of concern here is the contradiction that may exist between effective performance in the two dimensions of the New Policy Agenda—economic and political—an issue to which little attention has been paid thus far. Large-scale service provision requires standardized delivery mechanisms (to reduce unit costs), structures that can handle large amounts of external funding, and systems for speedy—and often hierarchical—decision making; effective performance as an agent of democratization rests on organizational independence, closeness to the poor, representative structures, and a willingness to spend large amounts of time in consciousness-raising and dialogue (Edwards and Hulme 1994). It is difficult to combine these characteristics within the same organization, and there is little evidence that alliances of different organizations (which could enable the two to go together) have developed very far. The fear is that, because service delivery tends to attract more official funding, there will be a growing rift between well-resourced service providers and poorly funded social mobilization agencies, a danger already identified by Pearce (1993) in Chile and Central America. The tendency of Northern NGOs to base their strategic plans on the easy availability of funding for humanitarian emergencies poses similar problems for their longer-term work in institutional development and development education. Some critics (including Hashemi in Chapter 9 of this volume) cite the switch from consciousness-raising to service delivery by NGOs such as BRAC in Bangladesh as evidence that they have retreated from any serious role in addressing structural facets of poverty and injustice. However, recent attacks on BRAC and other large NGOs by religious fundamentalists, citing their success in empowering women, suggest that such pessimism is misplaced, or at least that the real situation is more complex than is suggested by the supposed dichotomy between service delivery and consciousness-raising, an issue that is explored further in Chapter 19.

As NGOs become more involved in large-scale service delivery (or grow for other reasons) and become more reliant on official funding, one might expect some falloff in their flexibility, speed of response, and ability to innovate. Although organizational growth can be managed successfully, bureaucratization poses problems for any agency, as do the complex appraisal and reporting requirements that accompany official aid (Edwards and Hulme 1992, 1994). When official agencies finance service delivery, they expect contracted outputs to be achieved and are less interested in a learning process (Voorhies 1993; Perera forthcoming). Time and space for reflection may be reduced, and the ability of NGOs to articulate approaches, ideas, language, and values that run counter to official orthodoxies may also be compromised. These issues are discussed later in this introduction. A further concern is that the willingness of NGOs to speak out on issues that are unpopular with governments will be diluted by their growing dependence on official aid. There is evidence from Africa that NGOs that depend on external funding (not just official funding) are more likely to be ignored as "illegitimate" by their own governments in policy debates (Bratton 1989). In the United States, the largest operational NGOs (which are all heavily dependent on the U.S. Agency for International Development) tend to avoid a campaigning role, no doubt fearful of the consequences if they spoke out too sharply against government policy (Smith 1990; Salamon and Anheier 1993; Smith and Lipsky 1993). And a context in which NGOs compete with one another for government grants seems unlikely to foster the collaborative relationships on which effective policy alliances are built (Fowler 1992; Edwards 1993; Covey, Chapter 15 of this volume).

Finally, NGOs that depend on official funding often perform poorly in the crucial task of local institutional development (Esman and Uphoff 1984), the gradual strengthening of capacities and capabilities among GROs to enable them to play a more effective and independent role in development. This is so because many official agencies are unwilling to support the long time horizons, careful nurturing, and gradual qualitative results that characterize successful institutional development (Carroll 1992; Fowler 1992). Such work is difficult to "sell" to politicians and their constituents, on whom aid bureaucracies depend for their budgets (LaFond 1995).

The point of presenting this evidence is not to claim that NGOs perform less effectively than other organizations (public or private) in these various tasks, but simply to point out that they often perform less well than their popular image suggests. A comparative analysis of the performance of NGOs, governments, and commercial operators is beyond the scope of this book, but there is reason to believe that any differences that do emerge have less to do with inherent traits and more to do with factors that cut across the public-private divide (Tendler 1983). In any case, comparisons with other types of organizations that perform less well are not grounds for arguing that current NGO performance is satisfactory: NGOs should always be striving to serve others better.

NGO Accountability

Accountability is generally interpreted as the means by which individuals and organizations report to a recognized authority (or authorities) and are held responsible for their actions (Edwards and Hulme 1994). Accountability is a complex and abstract concept, however, and relatively little research has been conducted on this topic with regard to NGOs and GROs (Brett 1993). Although accountability is viewed as a desirable organizational characteristic, empirical studies commonly indicate that both leaders and subordinates in public and private organizations seek to avoid accountability (Fox 1992).[5] The common perception that somewhere there are organizations that are perfectly accountable must be dismissed. However, there is clearly a level at which the absence of accountability begins to make the likelihood of ineffective or illegitimate actions by an organization much more probable.

Effective accountability requires a statement of goals (whether in adherence to certain rules or based on achievement of identified performance levels), transparency of decision making and relationships, honest reporting of resource use and achievements, an appraisal process for the overseeing authorities to judge whether results are satisfactory, and concrete mechanisms for holding accountable (rewarding or penalizing) those responsible for performance. GRO and NGO accountability may be formal (for example, an evaluation of whether agreed-on objectives in a program have been met) or informal (for example, ongoing discussions between partners). It may emphasize the honesty and efficiency with which resources are used (commonly referred to as probity) or the impact and effectiveness of the work (commonly called performance). Avina (1993) distinguishes between short-term *functional accountability* (accounting for resources, resource use, and immediate impacts) and *strategic accountability* (accounting for the impacts that an NGO's actions have on the actions of other organizations and the wider environment).

Crucially, GROs and NGOs have multiple accountabilities—"downward" to their partners, beneficiaries, staff, and supporters; and "upward" to their trustees, donors, and host governments. Multiple accountability presents any organization with problems, particularly the possibilities of having to "overaccount," because of multiple demands, or being able to "underaccount," because each overseeing authority assumes that another authority is taking a close look at actions and results. Legally, most NGOs, as nonmembership organizations, are accountable to their trustees, who often exercise only a light hand in governance (see Chapter 3). NGOs cannot be formally accountable to their beneficiaries, however much they may want to be (see Chapter 1). By contrast, GROs are accountable to their members. Both usually have an obligation to account to the governments of the countries in which they operate, though in practice, this often means only brief annual reports and occasional audits. Morally (in accordance with values of participation and empowerment), and in terms of their wider claims to legitimacy, NGOs are accountable to other constituencies, most obviously beneficiaries and contributors. But of course, equal accountability to all at all times is an impossibility. Many of the concerns expressed about the weak accountability of NGOs relate to the difficulties they face in prioritizing and reconciling these multiple accountabilities (see Table I.1).

Although the accountability of GROs (to their members) may seem more straightforward, there is surprisingly little evidence that they perform better than NGOs in this respect. Indeed, Carroll (1992, 89) finds the opposite to be true in Latin America. These conclusions are confirmed by Bebbington and Thiele (1993, 21), who state, "we cannot say *a priori* that any one type of organisation is inherently more or less responsive to, or representative of, the needs of the rural poor." In GROs, problems of accountability often arise due to social and political factors (such as interest-group manipulation), whereas among NGOs, economic factors (and particularly links to donors) are likely to be more influential (Pearce 1993). Indeed, it is NGOs, especially those based in the North, that receive the most damning criticisms. Lehmann (1990, 201) calls their lack of accountability "extraordinary," and Smillie (Chapter 14 of this volume) finds that "Northern NGO survival has been almost completely delinked from performance," since they appear under little obligation to tell the truth to their supporters (Edwards 1994). Although NGOs may contest these assertions, we can find no evidence that the contemporary accountability of NGOs is satisfactory.

Measuring Impact and Effectiveness in an Uncertain World: Interpretative Accountability

A great part of the dilemma faced by GROs and NGOs lies in the nature of the work they do and the messy and complex world in which they do it. Measuring performance in relation to the kind of development subscribed to by most NGOs is an extraordinarily difficult task, particularly in relation to empowerment and other qualitative changes. As Drucker (1990) points out, the ultimate objective of nonprofit agencies is "changed human beings." There are few agreed-on performance standards for NGOs in this realm, beyond probity and some quantifiable impact indicators in certain types of NGO activities, such as service provision and economic development. Nor is there any obvious bottom line against which progress can be measured. Unlike businesses (which must make a profit) and governments (which must face elections), the bottom line for NGOs shifts according to the situation at hand (see Chapter 13). Organizational (as opposed to project) indicators are even more difficult to find, especially given the seeming obsession of many NGO managers

Table I.1 Accountability Matrix for a Hypothetical Southern NGO

Constituent	Functional Accountability[1]			Strategic Accountability[2]		
	Capacity to Demand Reports and Information	Capacity to Appraise Reports and Information	Capacity to Operate Sanctions	Capacity to Demand Reports and Information	Capacity to Appraise Reports and Information	Capacity to Operate Sanctions
Beneficiaries/members	Low[3]	Low	Low	Low	Nil	Nil
Trustees	Medium	Low	Medium	Low	Low	Low
Private contributors	Medium	Low	Low	Medium	Low	Low
NGO network	Low	Low	Low	Low	Low	Nil
National government	Medium	Low	High	Low	Low	Low
Official donors	High	Medium	High	Low	Low	Nil
Northern NGOs	High	Medium	Medium	Medium	Low	Low

[1] Accounting for resources, resource use, and immediate impacts.
[2] Accounting for impacts on other organizations and the wider environment on a medium- to long-term basis.
[3] Alternatively, the matrix could include short statements on the capacity of different authorities at different stages rather than using nil, low, medium, and high ratings.
Source: Edwards and Hulme (1994, 37).

with size and growth as indicators of success. Indicators of the *quality* of organizational performance are rare (with the exception of the "social audit" described by Zadek and Gatward in Chapter 17), and the general lack of satisfactory evaluative mechanisms is a serious drawback when it comes to GRO and NGO accountability. Because so few fixed, absolute standards exist, NGO evaluation (even more than evaluation in other organizations) is inevitably a matter of judgment and interpretation. This is the line of argument developed by Guba and Lincoln (1989) and applied specifically to social development by Marsden, Oakley, and Pratt (1994). The same line of reasoning is employed by Uphoff, Biggs and Neame, Fowler, and others in this volume to emphasize the nonlinear and "open-systems" nature of NGO work and the need to adapt concepts of performance measurement and accountability accordingly.

In addition, NGOs and GROs are rarely able to control all (or even most) of the factors that influence the outcome of their work; macroeconomic performance, state policy, and the actions of other agencies are obvious examples. Handy (1993, 15) lists at least sixty variables that influence the effectiveness of any organization. Uphoff (see Chapter 1) points to the "second- and third-order effects" of NGO actions, which are essential for sustainable development but are ignored in most evaluations. When positive long-term results are achieved, it is not because of one organization or project acting in isolation, but because a whole series of forces and actors came together to produce (for example) a sustainable change in agricultural production or the development of a strong grassroots federation. This makes measuring "strategic" accountability in its most fundamental sense almost impossible. No organization can be held accountable for the impact of forces that are beyond its control, though of course NGOs can and should be able to account for the way they use their resources within the framework set by these forces. As Rondinelli (1993, 12) puts it in the context of CIDA, the question becomes whether agencies use their resources "effectively, efficiently and prudently to achieve reasonable progress toward worthwhile development objectives," including how well they learn from experience and judge the costs and benefits of using resources for different purposes. This still leaves a great deal of room for interpretation, which is why accountability must be a process of negotiation among stakeholders rather than the imposition of one definition or interpretation of effectiveness over another.

For some NGOs and GROs, however, there is also a political dilemma related to accountability. If the organization's overt or covert goal is empowerment (making those who have little power more powerful), then transparency on this issue will, at best, make it easier for vested interests to identify what is happening and thus more effectively oppose it or, at worst, lead to the deregistration and closure of the organization for being subversive (and perhaps subject staff to violence).

Negotiating Performance and Impact among Stakeholders:
Multiple Accountability

Since there are few absolute performance measures in NGO evaluation and no single "bottom line," negotiation among stakeholders is the
essence of accountability in this area. All NGOs and most GROs have,
as mentioned above, multiple accountabilities. Therefore, definitions of
objectives, interpretations of results, and decisions on what response may
be appropriate all have to be negotiated among a wide range of actors.
For example, are higher NGO overheads an indicator of effective performance (since they are essential for improved research, learning, monitoring, and dissemination), or a sign of inefficiency? Presumably, the
answer to this question varies according to circumstance and opinion.
As the contributors to this book show, NGOs and GROs in the South are
often more interested in the wider questions of where NGOs "fit" in
relation to society and politics, rather than the narrower question of
how inputs and outputs are related at the project level, which is of
prime concern to donors. Biekart's analysis of NGO accountability in
Central America (Chapter 5) and Béjar and Oakley's description of current evaluation trends in Latin America (Chapter 6) both show how
understandings of performance vary greatly over time and between different partners. The questions posed by Karim in Chapter 10 are relevant
here—*who* defines accountability, *for whom*, and *why*?

Impact of the New Policy Agenda and Official Aid:
Distorting Accountability

An already complex situation is made even more difficult by official
aid to NGOs and the demands imposed by the New Policy Agenda. Given
the financial and political muscle of official agencies, there is an obvious fear that donor funding may reorient accountability upward, away
from the grassroots, and bias performance measurement toward criteria
defined by donors (Edwards and Hulme 1994; Fisher 1994; Tandon 1994).
Many of the chapters in this book provide evidence of this problem,
though it is difficult to disentangle the influence of official funding from
preexisting weaknesses in downward accountability (see Chapter 7, 9,
12, and 16). Fox and Hernandez (1989) and Fisher (1994) provide some
evidence that GRO leaders can be further distanced from their members
by foreign influence and assistance, though this can be mitigated by the
deliberate encouragement of new generations of leaders from within the
organization. Given that GROs are membership organizations, the reorientation of accountability away from the grassroots is a particular threat
to them, as it turns members into customers.

The type of appraisal, monitoring, and evaluation procedures insisted
on by donors, especially their heavy reliance on "logical framework"

approaches and bureaucratic reporting, may also distort accountability by overemphasizing short-term quantitative targets, standardizing indicators, focusing attention exclusively on individual projects or organizations, and favoring hierarchical management structures—a tendency to "accountancy," rather than "accountability," audit rather than learning. This is perhaps an inevitable consequence of the pressure for short-term visible results in order to keep Parliament or Congress happy. Accountability may focus too much on control functions (is the money being spent properly?) rather than on learning and sharing, something criticized by Smillie (see Chapter 14) in relation to NGO evaluation procedures adopted by CIDA in Canada. Compressed project planning cycles often leave little time to learn the lessons of experience, let alone *use them*. In this process, there is a particular danger that women will be penalized as qualitative changes in gender relations are inadequately monitored and women are excluded from senior positions in large, growing, hierarchical institutions.[6] The competitive nature of contracting also fosters an orientation toward treating information as a public-relations activity (that is, releasing the good and hiding the bad), and this compromises transparency. The contemporary self-management of the external images of international NGOs and large NGOs in South Asia provides evidence of this. As Chambers (see Chapter 18) states, the "self-deceiving NGO" is already a reality. There is, however, some evidence that donor funding may strengthen some forms of accountability by increasing external pressures for accurate reporting and more sophisticated monitoring (Tendler 1989; Bebbington and Riddell forthcoming).

The sheer volume of donor funds made available to GROs and NGOs may result in problems of probity, especially when internal management and financial systems are originally based on informality and trust. The example of Sarvodaya in Sri Lanka provides a good illustration of this (Perera forthcoming). The organization's accounting and reporting systems were adequate for a small and later medium-sized organization with an energetic leader and a highly personalized management style. However, rapid growth led to the breakdown of these systems and confusion on the part of the organization and donors as to whether functional accounting was simply weak or whether it was hiding improprieties.

Closer links with donors (and the suspicion of foreign influence that this creates in government) may result in a move away from self-regulation to regulation from above by the state. Self-regulation is not sufficient to ensure accountability, but the informal consultative processes and codes of ethics that characterize the voluntary sector in many countries (North and South) have maintained a balance between "room to maneuver" and regulation (Carroll 1992; Constantino-David 1992; International Council of Voluntary Agencies [ICVA] 1991; InterAction 1993). Formal accountability procedures may discourage innovation and speed of response and promote politicization and patronage (Brown and

Tandon 1992; Farrington and Bebbington 1993; Rademacher and Ta-mang 1993). Government coordinating mechanisms may also provide avenues for the state to gain access to NGO funding and information on organizations it considers subversive. Possible avenues for government influence over NGOs include legislation, taxation, public consultation, coordination, and official support, with the balance between monitor-ing, co-optation, and outright repression varying according to political context (Bratton 1989; Clark forthcoming; Farrington and Lewis 1993). Not surprisingly, "government-NGO relations are likely to be most con-structive where a confident and capable government with populist policies meets an NGO that works to pursue mainstream development programmes . . . and most conflictual where a weak and defensive gov-ernment with a limited power base meets an NGO that seeks to promote community mobilization" (Bratton 1989, 585). Most examples lie some-where in between these two extremes, and the overall conclusion drawn by Brown and Tandon (1992) is that government-NGO coordinating mecha-nisms would perform best if changed from a hierarchical link to a "bridge" between the two that can balance necessary accountability with essen-tial independence.

The message that must come out of this section is that little is known about the changing nature of GRO and NGO accountability. This is a serious matter, given that GRO and NGO claims to legitimacy are pre-mised at least in part on the strength of their accountability, particularly to the poor. Indeed, the New Policy Agenda thrusts the question of legitimacy into center stage, for if NGOs are becoming more responsive to external concerns, what is happening to the links—to their values and mission, and to their supporters and others—through which they claim their right to intervene in development? NGOs do not have to be mem-ber controlled to be legitimate, but they do have to be accountable for what they do if their claims to legitimacy are to be sustained. Recent doubts expressed by Southern NGOs about the advocacy role of NGOs in the North (speaking "on behalf of the poor") provide one illustration of this difficult issue (Edwards 1993). Although poorly understood and often ignored, questions of legitimacy and identity are crucial to the future of NGOs, and we return to these questions in Chapter 19.

The Structure of this Book

Part I of this volume provides the conceptual background for the case studies that follow. Norman Uphoff clarifies the distinctions that exist in terms of accountability between public, private, and "third-sector" institutions and goes on to question the value of formal evaluation unless this is seen used in "open systems." Similar themes are addressed by Stephen Biggs and Arthur Neame, who focus on the consequences of "linear thinking" for NGO accountability and emphasize the need to move away from evaluating the performance of individual NGOs and NGO projects. Part I is completed by Rajesh Tandon's survey of "board games"—the neglected territory of NGO governance and its relationship to accountability.

Part II contains a series of case studies from different regions that describe and analyze what happens to NGO and GRO performance and accountability under different conditions. There are case studies from Africa, South Asia, and Central and Latin America.

The chapters in Part III all represent ways forward in the debate over performance and accountability. Alan Fowler's chapter is both a critique of current approaches to performance assessment and a description of one possible solution to the dilemmas they present—engaging stakeholders in "combined social judgment." On the basis of experience in Canada, Ian Smillie dissects current attempts by official agencies to strengthen NGO evaluation and makes a strong case that NGOs need to put their houses in order by investing in their own research and learning. Next comes a detailed analysis by Jane Covey of these issues in the context of international policy alliances, which demonstrates that effectiveness and accountability can be successfully combined when certain conditions are met. Parmesh and Meera Shah, and Simon Zadek and Murdoch Gatward, concentrate on innovative techniques to strengthen multiple accountability (participatory monitoring and evaluation, and the "social audit," respectively). Both chapters show that concrete progress is possible in NGO accountability given vision, imagination, and openness to change. This leads to Robert Chambers's account of the personal dimension of accountability and the absolute necessity for conscious action by individuals if NGOs and GROs are to improve their record in this respect. The final chapter in the book reviews the experience of all the other contributions and relates the lessons learned about performance and accountability to the future of NGOs on the world stage.

Notes

1. Throughout this book, a distinction is made between nongovernmental organizations (NGOs), which are intermediary organizations engaged in funding or offering other forms of support to communities and other organizations, and grassroots organizations (GROs), which are membership organizations of various kinds. Other authors make the same distinction but use different terms. For example, Carroll (1992) distinguishes between grassroots support organizations (which are NGOs) and membership support organizations; GROs are also sometimes called community-based organizations (CBOs). The most important difference between the two groups lies in their accountability structures: GROs are formally

accountable to their members, whereas NGOs are not. However, many other authors use the term "NGOs" to cover all forms of nonprofit organization.

2. Official aid agencies are those that are funded by Northern governments either directly (bilateral agencies such as the British Overseas Development Administration [ODA] or the Swedish International Development Authority [SIDA]) or indirectly (multilateral agencies such as the World Bank and the European Union).

3. The figures here vary considerably, as do methods of calculating aid transfers to and through NGOs and NGO dependency on official agencies. For example, the proportion of SIDA funds channeled through NGOs increased from 9 percent in 1990–91 to 30 percent in 1994: SIDA funds over 2,000 NGO projects. The British ODA is already funding over 450 Indian NGOs directly, and a similar number in Bangladesh. All five of the largest NGOs in the United Kingdom show a significantly increasing level of financial dependence on ODA; in other countries (such as Canada, the United States, Germany, the Netherlands, and Norway), dependency ratios of between 50 and 90 percent are common. In the South, the large South Asian NGOs such as BRAC receive most of their funding from external sources, though it is difficult to specify how much of this is coming from official agencies rather than traditional Northern NGO sources. The availability of official aid under "social compensation funds" in adjusting economies has been an important source of support for NGOs in countries such as Bolivia and Uganda (Arellano-Lopez and Petras 1994). For details of these trends, see Smillie and Helmich (1993), Good (1994), Bebbington and Riddell (forthcoming), Edwards and Hulme (1994), and German and Randel (1994).

4. Early work on this subject was carried out by Judith Tendler (1982, 1983); more recent studies include Fowler (1991, 1993), Lehmann (1990), Carroll (1992), Riddell and Robinson (1992), Farrington and Lewis (1993), Bebbington and Thiele (1993), Wellard and Copestake (1993), Vivian (1994), and Hashemi and Schuler (1992).

5. For a discussion of the weakness of accountability in private sector corporations, see Survey of corporate governance (1994).

6. Some participants at the workshop from which this book emerged criticized us for not paying explicit attention to gender issues in the discussion of NGO performance and accountability. This remains an important area for further research, as we could locate no specific analysis of the many ways in which the definitions of performance and accountability may be male biased.

References

Aga Khan Foundation Canada/NOVIB. 1993. *Going to scale: the BRAC experience 1972–1992 and beyond.* The Hague: Aga Khan/NOVIB.

Arellano-Lopez, S., and J. Petras. 1994. NGOs and poverty alleviation in Bolivia. *Development and Change* 25(3):555–68.

Avina, J. 1993. The evolutionary life cycle of non-governmental development organisations. *Public Administration and Development* 13(5):453–74.

Bebbington, A., and R. Riddell. Forthcoming. New agendas and old problems: Issues, options and challenges in direct funding of Southern NGOs. In *Too close for comfort? NGOs, states and donors*, edited by D. Hulme and M. Edwards. London: Macmillan.

Bebbington, A., and G. Thiele, eds., with P. Davies, M. Prager, and H. Riveros. 1993. *NGOs and the state in Latin America: Rethinking roles in sustainable agricultural development*. London: Routledge.

Bratton, M. 1989. The politics of government-NGO relations in Africa. *World Development* 17(4):569–87.

———. 1990. Non-governmental organisations in Africa: Can they influence government policy? *Development and Change* 21:87–118.

Brett, E. 1993. Voluntary agencies as development organisations: Theorizing the problems of efficiency and accountability. *Development and Change* 24:87–118.

Brown, D., and R. Tandon. 1992. *Public-NGO financing institutions in India: An exploratory study*. Washington, D.C.: World Bank.

Carroll, T. 1992. *Intermediary NGOs: The supporting link in grassroots development*. West Hartford, Conn.: Kumarian Press.

CIVICUS. 1994. *Citizens strengthening global civil society*. Washington, D.C.: CIVICUS.

Clark, J. Forthcoming. NGO-state relations: A review of the principle policy issues. In *Too close for comfort? NGOs, states and donors*, edited by D. Hulme and M. Edwards. London: Macmillan.

Colclough, C., and J. Manor. 1991. *States or markets? Neo-liberalism and the development policy debate*. Oxford: Clarendon Press.

Commission on Global Governance. 1995. *Our common neighbourhood: The report of the Commission on Global Governance*. Oxford: Oxford University Press.

Constantino-David, K. 1992. The Philippine experience in scaling up. In *Making a difference: NGOs and development in a changing world*, edited by M. Edwards and D. Hulme. London: Earthscan.

Drucker, P. 1990. *Managing the nonprofit organization: Principles and practices*. New York: HarperCollins.

Eade, D. 1993. Editorial. *Development in Practice* 3(3):161–62.

Edwards, M. 1993. Does the doormat influence the boot? Critical thoughts on UK NGOs and international advocacy. *Development in Practice* 3(3):163–75.

———. 1994. NGOs in the age of information. *IDS Bulletin* (spring).

Edwards, M., and D. Hulme, eds. 1992. *Making a difference: NGOs and development in a changing world*. London: Earthscan.

———. 1994. NGOs and development: Performance and accountability in the "new world order." Background paper for the SCF/IDPM Workshop on NGOs and Development, Manchester, June 27–29.

Esman, M., and N. Uphoff. 1984. *Local organizations: Intermediates in rural development*. Ithaca, N.Y.: Cornell University Press.

Farrington, J., and A. Bebbington, with K. Wells and D. Lewis. 1993. *Reluctant partners? NGOs, the state and sustainable agricultural development*. London: Routledge.

Farrington, J., and D. Lewis, eds., with S. Satish and A. Miclat-Teves. 1993. *NGOs and the state in Asia: Rethinking roles in sustainable agricultural development*. London: Routledge.

Fisher, J. 1994. Is the iron law of oligarchy rusting away in the third world? *World Development* 22(2):129–43.

Fowler, A. 1988. *NGOs in Africa: Achieving comparative advantage in relief and micro-development.* IDS Discussion Paper 249. Sussex: Institute of Development Studies.

———. 1991. The role of NGOs in changing state-society relations: Perspectives from eastern and southern Africa. *Development Policy Review* 9:53–84.

———. 1992. *Distant obligations: Speculations on NGO funding and the global market.* Paper presented to the annual conference of the Development Studies Association, Nottingham, September.

———. 1993. NGOs as agents of democratisation: An African perspective. *Journal of International Development* 5(3):325–39.

Fox, J. 1992. Democratic rural development: Leadership accountability in regional peasant organizations. *Development and Change* 23(2):1–36.

Fox, J., and L. Hernandez. 1989. Offsetting the iron law of oligarchy: The ebb and flow of leadership accountability in a regional peasant organization. *Grassroots Development* 13(2):8–15.

Friedmann, J. 1992. *Empowerment: The politics of alternative development.* Oxford: Blackwell.

German, T., and J. Randel. 1994. Trends in official aid and the implications for NGOs. Paper presented to the SCF/IDPM Workshop on NGOs and Development, Manchester, June 27–29.

Ghai, D., and J. Vivian, eds. 1992. *Grassroots environmental action: People's participation in sustainable development.* London: Routledge.

Good, A. 1994. Paying the piper, calling the tune? Present and future relationships among northern NGOs, southern NGOs, and the ODA. Paper presented to the SCF/IDPM Workshop on NGOs and Development, Manchester, June 27–29.

Guba, E., and Y. Lincoln. 1989. *Fourth generation evaluation.* London: Sage.

Handy, C. 1993. *Understanding organisations.* 4th ed. Harmondsworth: Penguin.

Hasan, A. 1993. *Scaling-up the OPP's low-cost sanitation programme.* Karachi: Orangi Pilot Project.

Hashemi, S., and S. Schuler. 1992. *State and NGO support networks in rural Bangladesh: Concepts and coalitions for control.* Copenhagen: Centre for Development Research.

Hellinger, D., S. Hellinger, and F. O'Rogan. 1988. *Aid for just development.* Boulder, Colo.: Lynne Rienner.

Howes, M., and M. G. Sattar. 1992. Bigger and better? Scaling-up strategies pursued by BRAC 1972–1991. In *Making a difference: NGOs and development in a changing world,* edited by M. Edwards and D. Hulme. London: Earthscan.

Hulme, D., and M. Edwards. eds. Forthcoming. *Too close for comfort? NGOs, states and donors.* London: Macmillan.

Hulme, D., and P. Mosley. 1995. *Finance against poverty.* Vols. 1 and 2. London: Routledge.

ICVA. 1991. *Relations between Southern and Northern NGOs: Policy guidelines.* Geneva: ICVA.

InterAction. 1993. *InterAction private voluntary agencies (PVOs) standards.* Washington, D.C.: InterAction.

Korten, D. 1990. *Getting to the 21st century: Voluntary action and the global agenda*. West Hartford, Conn.: Kumarian Press.

LaFond, A. 1995. *Sustaining primary health care*. London: Earthscan/Save the Children Fund.

Lehmann, D. 1990. *Democracy and development in Latin America: Economics, politics and religion in the post war period*. Cambridge: Polity Press.

Marsden, D., P. Oakley, and B. Pratt. 1994. *Measuring the process: Guidelines for evaluating social development*. Oxford: International NGO Training and Research Centre.

Marzouk, M. Forthcoming. The associative phenomenon in the Arab world: Engine of democratization or witness to the crisis? In *Too close for comfort? NGOs, states and donors*, edited by D. Hulme and M. Edwards. London: Macmillan.

Meyer, C. 1992. A step back as donors shift institution building from the public to the "private" sector. *World Development* 20(8):1115–26.

Moore, M. 1993. Good government? Introduction. *IDS Bulletin*, 24(1):1–6.

OECD. 1988. *Development assistance committee report 1987*. Paris: OECD.

———. 1994. *Development assistance committee report 1993*. Paris: OECD.

———. 1995. *Development assistance committee report 1994*. Paris: OECD.

Pearce, J. 1993. NGOs and social change: Agents or facilitators? *Development in Practice* 3(3):222–27.

Perera, J. Forthcoming. Unequal dialogue with donors: The Sarvodaya experience. In *Too close for comfort? NGOs, states and donors*, edited by D. Hulme and M. Edwards. London: Macmillan.

Rademacher, A., and D. Tamang. 1993. *Democracy, development and NGOs*. Kathmandu: SEARCH.

Riddell, R., and M. Robinson. 1992. *The impact of NGO poverty-alleviation projects: Results of the case study evaluations*. ODI Working Paper 68. London: Overseas Developmental Institute.

Robinson, M. 1993. Governance, democracy and conditionality: NGOs and the new policy agenda. In *Governance, democracy and conditionality: What role for NGOs?* edited by A. Clayton. Oxford: International NGO Training and Research Centre.

Rondinelli, D. 1993. Strategic and results-based management in CIDA: Reflections on the process (mimeo). Ottawa: Canadian International Development Agency.

Salamon, L. 1993. *The global associational revolution: The rise of the third sector on the world scene*. Occasional Paper 15. Baltimore: Institute for Policy Studies, Johns Hopkins University.

Salamon, L., and H. Anheier. 1993. *The third route: Subsidiarity, third-party government and the provision of social services in the United States and Germany*. Report to OECD, Paris.

Smillie, I., and H. Helmich. 1993. *Non-governmental organisations and governments: Stakeholders for development*. Paris: OECD.

Smith, B. 1990. *More than altruism: The politics of private foreign aid*. Princeton, N.J.: Princeton University Press.

Smith, S., and M. Lipsky. 1993. *Non-profits for hire: The welfare state in the age of contracting*. Cambridge, Mass.: Harvard University Press.

A survey of corporate governance. 1994. *The Economist*, January 29, special supplement.

Tandon, R. 1994. Civil society, the state and the role of NGOs. In *Civil society in the Asia-Pacific region*, edited by I. Serrano. Washington, D.C.: CIVICUS.

Tendler, J. 1982. *Turning private voluntary organizations into development agencies: Questions for evaluation*. Evaluation Discussion Paper no. 10. Washington, D.C.: U.S. Agency for International Development.

———. 1983. *Ventures in the informal sector and how they worked out in Brazil*. Evaluation Special Study no. 12. Washington, D.C.: U.S. Agency for International Development.

———. 1989. Whatever happened to poverty alleviation? *World Development* 17(7):1033–44.

Vivian, J. 1994. NGOs and sustainable development in Zimbabwe: No magic bullets. *Development and Change* 25:181–209.

Voorhies, S. 1993. *Working with government using World Bank funds*. World Vision International Staff Working Paper no. 16.

Wellard, K., and J. Copestake, eds. 1993. *NGOs and the state in Africa: Rethinking roles in sustainable agricultural development*. London: Routledge.

Part I
Conceptual Frameworks

———— 1 ————

Why NGOs Are Not a Third Sector

A Sectoral Analysis with Some Thoughts on Accountability, Sustainability, and Evaluation

Norman Uphoff

Will the "new world order" that is said to offer development NGOs "access to ever greater resources and influence" (Edwards and Hulme 1994) last much longer and be any more beneficial than the one announced after the fall of the Berlin Wall? The "new world order" that U.S. President George Bush proclaimed was mostly a creation of optimism and rhetoric. The one that suggests a new role for NGOs could prove to be constructed of the same materials and not much longer lasting. New relationships between public and private sectors around the world are resulting from a range of political, economic, and social transitions and forces (Uphoff 1993, 1994). Governmental bodies are experiencing a decline in both fiscal support and public credibility. Market institutions are gaining greater latitude and confidence with both ideological support and resource advantages. In this situation, NGOs are being described as a "third sector."

But this characterization, I argue, is misleading. The real third sector, located somewhere *between* the public and the private sectors in institutional space, belongs not to NGOs but rather to people's associations and membership organizations. These differ from institutions in the public and private sectors in that they undertake voluntary collective action and self-help. Such a distinction assigns NGOs to the private sector rather than to the middle sector. Which sector NGOs are considered to belong to is important with regard to this book's focus on *accountability*, an increasingly prominent concern in development circles.

My sectoral analysis grows out of an insightful discussion by Guy Hunter (1969) of administration, economics, and politics as means of promoting rural development. His classification was elaborated analytically in Esman and Uphoff (1984) by contrasting three alternative approaches to rural development, as shown in Table 1.1. These three models represent modes of decision making and activity that are alternative but complementary. They are based on different role relations, contrasting objectives, and divergent motivations. These three arenas for

23

Table 1.1   Alternative Approaches to Rural Development

Characteristic	Administrative Approach	Economic Approach	Political Approach
Key process	Exercise of authority	Market interaction	Voluntary association
Institutions	Bureaucratic structures	Private enterprises	Membership organizations
Decision makers	Legislators executives, administrators, experts	Producers, consumers, investors	Leaders and members or constituents
Guides for behavior	Laws, regulations	Price signals, profit and loss	Agreement and consensus
Criteria for decisions	Policy, and the best means to implement it	Efficiency, best ways to maximize profit and/or utility	Interests of members, precedents, purposes
Sanctions	State authority	Financial loss	Social pressure, group sanctions
Modes of operation	Top-down	Individualistic	Bottom-up

Source: Adapted from Hunter (1969, 12).

decision making and action correspond to the public sector (administrative), the private sector (economic), and a very different sector (political). This third sector, which can be referred to as the membership sector, the voluntary sector, or the collective action sector, is a "middle" sector that operates best *between* the public and private sectors, as shown above.

By definition, organizations in the membership and private sectors are nongovernmental. But an examination of the *roles* in which people find themselves vis-à-vis these different kinds of institutions—and of their mechanisms for accountability—suggests that NGOs are best considered a *subsector* of the private sector. This is implied by the synonym used for NGOs—private voluntary organizations (PVOs).[1]

Ten years ago at Cornell, we undertook a large-scale study of local institutions and their contributions to development (Uphoff 1986). Based on an extensive review of the literature, we concluded that there are at least two important subcategories of local institutions for each of the three sectors delineated above. The most significant differentiating factor was the way in which the different kinds of local institutions relate (that is, are accountable) to the people they are supposed to serve or benefit.

Although any institution not in the public sector can be called a nongovernmental organization,[2] such a classification lumps together diverse sets of institutions. It is true that business enterprises, for example, differ from typical NGOs in that the former operate for profit whereas the latter do not. But their relationships with the persons they serve—clients and customers—exhibit essential similarities that set them apart from the other categories of institutions depicted in Table 1.2.

Membership organizations and cooperatives have much in common because both are oriented toward self-help and are responsible to members, a role that is not central or often even salient for NGOs and business enterprises. Service organizations, the category that I think most NGOs belong in, deal with clients or beneficiaries. These people did not create the organization they are dealing with and cannot hold it accountable for its actions in the same direct way that members can. Clients and beneficiaries of NGOs are in a "take it or leave it" relationship, quite similar to that of customers and employees of private firms. The relationship is different from that of individuals who belong to and are served by a membership organization or cooperative.

These differences can be made concrete by considering the provision of services by hospitals, which can be operated in any of the following modes:

- In a public-sector hospital, run by local administration (Ministry of Health) or a local government body (town council), patients enter as citizens and constituents with whatever rights and opportunities for redress this gives them through the courts or through elected representatives.

- A hospital that is privately owned and operated, although regulated by public laws, is basically in business to earn a profit from the provision of services. Its patients are essentially customers or consumers. If they are dissatisfied, they have the option of going to some other hospital, as they would go to a different store if they were unhappy with its products or service.

- A charitable hospital operated on a not-for-profit basis is not much different from a private hospital, except that its managers give free care or are less insistent on being paid for services. The fact that managers make decisions on behalf of trustees instead of owners is not a big difference operationally.

- A cooperative hospital is set up at least in part with members' capital, and it exists to serve them. As members, they help set the rules and the fees, and if they have any complaints about service, they are much more empowered to initiate corrective action than with public, private, or charitable hospitals. Organizations that serve members are in a different situation regarding operation and accountability than are those that fit the more conventional private- or public-sector models serving patients as citizens or customers.

Table 1.2 Complementary Local Institutions, by Sector

Characteristic	Public Sector		Membership Sector		Private Sector	
	Local Administration	Local Government	Membership Organizations	Cooperatives	Service Organizations	Private Enterprises
Orientation	Bureaucratic: agents look upward	Political: agents look downward	Self-help: common interests	Self-help: pooled resources	Charitable: nonprofit	Business: for profit
Role of individuals	Citizens or subjects	Constituents or voters	Members	Members	Clients or beneficiaries	Customers and employees*

* Although all six kinds of institutions can have employees, a hired workforce is most obviously essential for private businesses. Service organizations usually have some employees, as do offices of local administrative and local governmental bodies. Membership organizations and cooperatives are likely to have fewer employees compared with other kinds of local institutions.

Source: Adapted from Uphoff (1986, 5).

Most organizations referred to as NGOs thus belong, analytically, to the private sector, but to its service (not-for-profit) subsector. Although some NGOs have been created by and operate on behalf of members, most NGOs serve persons who are *not* members of the organization. This makes them essentially service organizations, with employees who produce and distribute benefits. Only if most of an NGO's beneficiaries or clients are also its members is it appropriately considered part of the third sector.

It is helpful to make a distinction between NGOs and grassroots organizations (GROs), though the two are actually overlapping sets. The first category is defined according to *sector*, whereas the second is specified in terms of *level* (Uphoff 1993).[3] This means that although some NGOs are GROs, and vice versa, most NGOs are not GROs. Unfortunately, contemporary rhetoric tends to equate the two categories (NGOs and GROs) without much analytical or evaluative thought. An appropriate way to view the relation between them is to see NGOs as being in a position to help promote and sustain GROs.[4] This raises important questions of accountability: are NGOs accountable, or can they be held accountable, to GROs and to the members they serve? Fashioning such links of responsibility could represent a real new world order. But this is not easy and, indeed, may not be feasible or desirable.

Some Skeptical and Affirmative Thoughts on Accountability

As a student of political science, I am surprised that people concerned with NGOs and accountability issues have paid so little attention to the writing of Robert Michels ([1915] 1959), a Swiss social scientist who received much more attention earlier in this century. His admonition "who says organization says oligarchy" thundered off the pages of his book *Political Parties*, predicting that it was the fate of organizations generally to become dominated by a self-perpetuating and self-serving leadership. This has become known as "the iron law of oligarchy."

Service organizations in the private sector are entitled to function as oligarchies. This is their legal right and privilege, so long as they operate within the law. This is best seen in the way that foundations and trusts can use their resources with few restrictions, because the resources they dispose of are "private." Nobody expects foundations or trusts to be internally democratic or to let the recipients of their generosity make decisions about amounts or conditions of benefits. NGOs as service organizations operate much like private businesses.[5] There are structural and philosophical reasons why NGOs that are private-sector service organizations should not be expected to function as agencies responsible to their clientele. In particular, the staff and trustees of such organizations have the burden of mobilizing and managing funds to keep their operations solvent. If beneficiaries could decide how much they would receive and when, such organizations would likely be bankrupt within a year. The fiduciary relationship between NGO staff and trustees and those who provide NGOs with their funds is greater than the NGO's obligation to recipients of benefits. If trust and confidence are not maintained with an NGO's contributors, it will collapse.

Thus, proponents of making NGOs accountable to their beneficiaries face a structural constraint that cannot easily be done away with, however commendable this might be according to certain democratic or normative theories. There are good reasons to be skeptical that the more profound form of new world order for NGOs and GROs suggested above can be realized. But there is a further qualification that flows from Michels's analysis. He was not the crypto-fascist or archconservative depicted by political commentators who have read only his conclusion, not his evidence or reasoning. Michels was an active participant in the democratic socialist and labor movements of Europe at the turn of the century. His conclusion that organizations *tend to* oligarchy (his more qualified statement is more scientifically tenable than the stern quotation above) was based on his observations of the socialist parties and trade unions operating in Europe over half a century.

Michels became disillusioned with these organizations' prospects of introducing greater democracy in their respective countries because they had such difficulty maintaining internal democracy. Leaders became autocratic. They controlled the party or trade union press. They dominated meetings. They engrossed their organizations' treasuries. Most alarming, they maneuvered to be succeeded by their sons or favorite supporters. Such behavior by leaders led Michels to despair about the prospects for genuine democracy. Yet interestingly enough, the one exception he cited was the internal democracy displayed by aristocratic parties in Scandinavia. These parties held leaders in check with internal competition and frequent rotation. This paradox—that organizations that did not seek to promote democracy were themselves more democratic—led Michels to observe that such organizations' members had uniformly higher status, more education, and greater economic resources. Sadly, organizations whose members had low status and little education and lived in poverty were more vulnerable to the domination and predation of their leaders.

One implication of this analysis was that greater organizational democracy could be expected as social conditions (education, health, security, and so on) improved. Perhaps progressive parties and unions could contribute to such advancement even if they were not paragons of the democratic virtues they advocated. Interestingly, Michels's view is supported by one of the classic studies of the American trade union movement.[6]

This digression on social history is relevant to our current concern: how to increase the accountability as well as improve the performance of development NGOs. We are interested in having NGOs assist and benefit the poorer sectors in poor countries—a difficult task in any case if these persons, households, and communities are to become more secure and productive on a sustainable and self-managing basis. Michels's "iron law of oligarchy," taken in its subtler form, predicts that one is least likely to find internal democracy in GROs whose members are least well educated, poorest, and of the lowest social status. Anyone who becomes a leader under such circumstances is, first, likely to rank higher on these characteristics. But second, anyone who becomes a leader is likely to enjoy the benefits of greater status, knowledge, and income and be reluctant to give these up. The longer someone remains in a leadership position, the greater will be the gap between leaders and members (now transformed into followers) in terms of economic, social, and informational resources.

There is evidence for and against Michels's propositions from the literature on NGOs and GROs (Fox 1992; Fisher 1994), but unless we can refute or invalidate his "iron law," the GROs that advocates of greater accountability want NGOs to be responsible to are themselves *least likely* to be internally accountable to their own members. The more power outside agencies give to such organizations, the more benefits may be skimmed off for people in leadership positions or those they favor.

This observation is not meant to justify NGOs' operating paternalistically or autonomously vis-à-vis GROs, invoking Michels to justify their oligarchical mode of operation. Rather, it is intended to sound a note of caution for those who seek accountability in an absolute manner, not considering whether or to what extent the representatives and spokespeople of intended beneficiaries are themselves accountable and truly representative.

I have seen a GRO take root under adverse conditions and establish internal mechanisms of accountability. From 1981 to 1985, with colleagues at the Agrarian Research and Training Institute in Sri Lanka, Cornell faculty and students helped establish farmer organizations to improve irrigation management in a participatory way in what was considered the most run-down and debilitated irrigation system in that country (Uphoff 1992). Farmers in the Gal Oya scheme had been resettled there twenty to thirty years earlier, often under less than voluntary circumstances. They had a reputation for being difficult and quarrelsome as well as poorer and less well educated than most other Sri Lankans. Although members were not the very poorest of the poor, they were smallholders or tenants averaging less than two acres apiece, and many had half an acre or less.[7]

Within a few weeks, farmers were taking impressive initiatives to improve their system's performance, equity, and efficiency. They instituted the rotation of officers at the district level to ensure that there would be a broad pool of experienced leadership for dealing with officials. They trained "understudies" so that responsibilities of leadership could be shared. Farmers gladly accepted our suggestion that they have farmer-*representatives* rather than farmer-*leaders*—the terminology that the United Nations Food and Agriculture Organization (FAO) and the government were using at the time our program started—because they appreciated that representatives could be held accountable more readily than leaders.

The structure of the organization started from the bottom, which helped ensure accountability. Field channel groups managed and shared the water they received from the distributary (or D) canal, doing channel maintenance and water sharing on an as-needed basis. These groups, usually with between twelve and fifteen members, operated informally, with each group choosing a representative by consensus.[8] Field channel representatives constituted a formally recognized committee for the area served by each D canal. They met periodically in an area assembly to have direct two-way communication with officials, and these assemblies chose representatives to sit on system-level and district-level committees.

The project management system that eventually emerged in Gal Oya became the model for a national system of participatory management for all major irrigation schemes in Sri Lanka. A majority of farmer-representatives served on the project committee, which usually had a farmer chairperson. Although it might be thought that this system of indirect representation would be less democratic (and less accountable) than electing project committee representatives through direct elections involving all the members, in our experience, the system minimized the number of rich farmers or nonfarmers (merchants, schoolteachers) who could become farmer-leaders. All the representatives in the system were initially chosen by fellow farmers at the base and remained responsible for the smooth running of their field channels, involving much face-to-face contact with peers and an effective service or problem-solving orientation.[9]

The system of organization established in Gal Oya, which took four years to put in place, continues to operate well almost ten years since outside assistance was withdrawn.[10] As noted above, this system has become national in scope, though with less investment in the establishment of farmer organizations elsewhere and probably somewhat less effective performance. The organizational effort in Gal Oya was catalyzed by a cadre of dedicated young organizers, and farmers insisted that they could not have established this new system of organization by themselves. But with some encouragement and appropriate support, they made the new organization their own and have maintained it with at least as much internal democracy as found in most local governments in the United States or United Kingdom. The role of "institutional organizer" has been accepted by the government and most donors, though not necessarily with the social science foundations and normative orientations that underpinned the effort in Gal Oya.

I mention this case to support a counterargument to Michels's proposition, to suggest that poorer segments of society, with appropriate outside support, can create effective institutions to which outside agencies—governmental and nongovernmental—can and should be accountable. The first requirement is that the local institutions themselves be accountable to their members or constituents. This was an essential feature of the organizations in Gal Oya, and it has been maintained with varying degrees of fidelity in the subsequent organizations established under the sponsorship of the Irrigation Management Division in Sri Lanka. The Mahaweli Economic Agency is presently introducing farmer organizations with the same principles of operation and accountability.

The debate with and within Northern NGOs about accountability should, in my view, be especially concerned with issues of *intra*organizational accountability for the GROs they work with. This is possible but not easily achieved or sustained, as Michels's trenchant analysis and language warn us. This prediction should not be seen as a reason to avoid creating processes of *inter*organizational accountability between NGOs and GROs, however.[11] It would be inconsistent, and send the wrong signals, if NGOs were to insist on GRO leadership accountability if they were unable or unwilling to set a good example themselves in this regard.

As with so many things, the relationships to be institutionalized need to be established iteratively and progressively, with NGOs nurturing accountability at local levels while they create internal mechanisms for resource allocation, planning, and evaluation that give local communities and representatives an effective voice in these processes. But such a voice creates only a *degree* of accountability. Responsibility will remain something that is *shared* between NGOs and those persons and communities that are expected to benefit from NGO activity. The amount and balance of control over programs may change over time, moving more in favor of people at local levels. But accountability will remain a different matter for NGO programs than for those that are authorized and funded from public sources. Thus, accountability for NGOs will remain something broader than just accountability to those who are involved in NGOs' programs.[12] NGOs are accountable certainly to their contributors, and also to any donor agencies that provide them with funds, but also to some extent to public officials and, of course, to their employees (though this is not often stated explicitly). If this sounds complicated, just imagine a business executive telling an NGO counterpart, "Welcome to the private sector!"

Evaluation as a Possible Deterrent to Sustainability: The Importance of Externalities

A separate concern is the possibility that efforts to promote "evaluation" as a means of ensuring accountability—whether to the sources of funding or to the persons served by programs—can conflict with the objective of sustainability, which is a preeminent concern and criterion in many development programs these days. Evaluation is recommended or required to see that scarce resources are put to their best use, often in the name of sustainability. Yet the way that evaluation tends to be conceived and carried out can be inimical to sustainable development. There are great difficulties in knowing what is or is not sustainable. The "proof of this pudding" cannot be known until well after we are no longer around to "do the tasting." But that does not prevent us from making sustainability our current "holy grail." There are good reasons for seeking to ensure that the benefits gained from development programs entailing considerable expense will not be short-lived.

Readers will be relieved that I do not plan to offer yet another definition of sustainability. Sustainability is not a matter to be dealt with by definitions, since words themselves will not change what sustainability is or is not—or what is or is not sustainable. Sustainability is probably not a single thing anyway. I have tried to consider some theoretically grounded criteria that could help us know when we are heading in the direction of sustainable development—or at least when we are heading away from it.

One of the dynamics that makes for sustainable development (and hence a criterion thereof) is the achievement of *multiple benefits* from any particular cost. This means not only that the benefit-cost ratio is likely to be more positive in the short run but also that more stakeholders will be created for the perpetuation of the activity or relationship in the long run. This can be discussed in the language of game theory, comparing *positive-sum* outcomes (where everyone wins or there are clearly more winners than losers) with *zero-sum* outcomes (where anyone's gain comes at someone else's expense, and where winners' gains equal others' losses, as in a game of cards or chess). The least desirable situation is *negative-sum*, where everyone loses, or aggregate losses outweigh total gains.

In a world of zero-sum transactions, there are only transfers, no gains of value or productivity. With negative-sum dynamics, the system runs down to disorder and dissolution over time, because more is being extracted from it than is being put in. Only in a world of positive-sum relationships is there a continuous accretion of productivity and value, making system sustainability possible. Speaking generally, positive-sum dynamics and relationships (situations referred to as win-win) appear to be the essence or crux of sustainability. In situations that are win-lose (where someone's gain is someone else's loss), the relationship between individuals, groups, communities, sectors, nations, or humans and their environment is at best an equilibrium. In the long run, it is likely not to persist because no net margin of value is created and the people committed to maintaining it are balanced (offset?) by those with no stake in its perpetuation.

What will succeed in the long run are relationships that produce multiple net benefits that are broadly dispersed, not narrowly calculated and distributed. These can be described in technical terms as *positive externalities*, which are benefits (greater than costs) that extend beyond the project, community, or enterprise at hand. Unfortunately, these days, projects, communities, and enterprises are treated as closed systems for the sake of analysis, so that costs and benefits can be identified and compared.

Narrow constructions or calculations of benefits, restricted in scope and distribution, tend toward zero-sum thinking and practice. If people take the view that their benefits or advantages should, do, or must come at someone else's expense, this is a zero-sum way of looking at the world. This is a closed-system, static perspective, but it finds much favor among policymakers and analysts because it is thought to be more rigorous.

When evaluating the amount and distribution of benefits deriving from any particular project, program, technology, subsidy, training, infrastructure, or investment, people will minimize and even exclude externalities (positive and negative) in order to make rigorous (replicable) comparisons of benefits and costs, reckoning that these benefits and costs lie beyond the boundaries of the project, program, or whatever else is being considered.

As suggested already, to be sustainable, development must go beyond zero-sum processes in which gains and losses are essentially equal. Rather, it must promote and support positive-sum dynamics that achieve multiple benefits that outweigh costs. The problems that arise when trying to evaluate benefits and costs are that (1) many are remote in time and space, so they are hard to identify rigorously with any particular investment or initiative, and (2) many of the things that add most to our quality of life are not readily quantifiable. Things that are not measurable get ignored, just as those that fall "outside" the system under consideration get excluded.

The demand for evaluation has pushed NGOs—as well as everyone else trying to quantify results—to close up the systems under consideration; analytically and artificially, they count some things as inside and other things as outside, dealing only with the former and making excuses as to why the latter are left out. In particular, positive externalities—benefits that accrue to persons or sectors outside the scope of the immediate organization or program—will be overlooked. Yet these are essential for sustainable development—many people getting benefits from the same investment or expenditure, and many things being accomplished that elude rigorous measurement and comparison.[13]

Sustainable development requires both the attainment of second- and third-order effects (what Robert Chambers calls "wider effects") and the existence of many people who have a stake in some institution, technology, practice, or legislation so that it retains support. Although there is no simple correspondence between the number of stakeholders and a program's prospects for longevity, having more actors who regard it as valuable and desirable certainly enhances its chances. But what we see so often these days is pressure to *restrict* the scope of objectives, to assess only tangible things, to count only direct and not indirect benefits and costs (though this does not mean that there is no fudging of results). The process of evaluation tends to isolate and insulate activities, giving incentives to program managers to maximize internal net benefits and to not invest in those that would be external. This is an oxymoronic, shortsighted strategy for sustainability.[14] We need to be careful about downplaying and even discouraging positive externalities for the sake of achieving greater accountability, because such externalities represent the essence of sustainable development.

Accountability is commonly taken to require much advance specification of objectives and means, so that evaluation can be done in terms of the achievement of those objectives and the timely utilization of predetermined means for achieving those ends. Yet we know from "learning process" theory as proposed by Korten (1980) that this is not what is most essential to development. What is needed is an adaptive, creative, flexible process of matching available and expanding means to emerging and evolving ends, of fitting technology and organization together in beneficial and sustainable ways, of mobilizing additional resources because people's most keenly felt needs are not being met. This, however, is an open-system view of the universe, one at odds with the kinds of cramped, closed-system assumptions that are required and promoted by an effort to do rigorous evaluation.

It is ironic and even tragic that, in today's world, which supposedly desires sustainability, so much effort goes into thinking in closed-system terms to be able to achieve "efficiency," such as in economic benefit-cost calculations. Externalities get neglected and even disparaged as distracting analysts from the optimization of returns from the investment of scarce resources. This view considers only fixed amounts of resources, regarding them as a stock more than as a flow. This view itself is inconsistent with a concern for sustainability, where rates and balances of flows are more important than stocks. I do not want to disparage efficiency, because in a world where sustainability is an increasingly important concern, we need to consider how best to use our limited resources to achieve the greatest and most lasting benefits. But in the name of efficiency, we have set up mental barriers that prevent us from looking for, and at, second- and third-order effects, unmeasurable but admittedly important consequences, and cogenerated benefits that cannot be readily attributed to any one source.

It is surely provocative to suggest that the "evaluation movement" that has gathered pace within the development community over the last fifteen years is a deterrent to efforts to promote sustainability. I do not want to speak against evaluation per se, since wishful thinking that is not tested by observation of results can lead to the wasting of scarce resources. I believe that we need to have more rather than less evaluation; indeed, we need what Trochim (1992) calls an "evaluation culture." But how we do evaluations, and how much we sacrifice inclusive and imaginative evaluation for the sake of narrow and rigorous measurement, should be of concern to anyone who wants to promote the sustainability of beneficial programs and activities. To the extent that we stress a complete prespecification of objectives and restrict our evaluations to quantified costs and benefits, we will exclude many important factors, especially externalities, from consideration. We will treat projects, programs, communities, and institutions as closed systems and will isolate them in our thinking—and in our interventions—from the economic, social, cultural, physical, and other contexts in which they function (one hopes productively and indefinitely).

The Importance of Concepts and Ways of Thinking

This conclusion suggests the need to be more self-conscious and self-critical of our ways of thinking about things, getting away from naive experimentalist or empiricist notions of a world "out there" that exists entirely independent of our own thoughts and perceptions. I am concerned that our concepts and thinking in this present era—when we need to think and act more expansively, more generously, more interdependently—are still based too much on narrow, self-centered, autonomy-seeking thinking and motives. The latter orientations are very much at odds with the much-emphasized themes of accountability, sustainability, and evaluation.

My own involvement with participatory development has led me to question the patterns and premises of thought that underlay my own graduate education in the social sciences, which I suspect was not very different from the training others received. Some analyses by Albert Hirschman helped me appreciate that our preoccupation with equilibrium (zero-sum) concepts in the social sciences stems from seventeenth- and eighteenth-century models of the physical universe. The development of thermodynamic theory in the nineteenth century popularized an entropic (negative-sum) view of possibilities for both the present and the future. Fortunately for the prospects of participatory and sustainable development, the physical sciences in the twentieth century have found new conceptions of reality that are more positive-sum in substance and more useful for dealing with a broad range of phenomena, from the macrocosmic to the subatomic. Relativity theory, quantum mechanics, chaos theory, and now complexity theory have opened up new vistas on the natural universe that I find useful for the social universe as well.[15]

Although this chapter opened with several classificatory schemes that are useful for comprehending and acting within the social universe, ultimately we need to combine such an analytical approach with a more integrative, synthesizing one, transcending and utilizing "either-or" constructions with a "both-and" frame of mind (Uphoff 1992). This can draw on the productive possibilities of apparently contradictory phenomena. As it turns out, accountability, sustainability, and evaluation, like many other important but complex concepts, are fraught with paradoxes and do not lend themselves easily to linear or reductionist thinking. Elaborating on this assertion would require another chapter—indeed, a whole book or more—but I do not want to leave this subject without expressing my growing conviction that however limiting physical resources may be, our minds are more constricting. Thus, that is where we should start looking for solutions to our various resource scarcities and constraints.

Notes

1. The second adjective, "voluntary," is quite ambiguous as a description for PVOs, since most depend heavily on employees and rely at most only partially on voluntary contributions of time or money for their existence.
2. For the sake of brevity, I am not making a systematic distinction between "institutions" and "organizations." In fact, a clear and important distinction should be made, even though the two terms overlap, as seen in the discussion of institutions versus organizations in Uphoff (1986, 8–10).
3. In Uphoff (1986), an inclusive set of ten levels for decision making and action were identified, ranging from the international level to the individual. In between are the national level, the provincial or regional level, the district level, the subdistrict level, the locality level (a set of interacting communities having some market, marriage, or other connections), the community level, the group level, and the household level. The three levels that are commonly understood as being "local"—the locality, the community, and the group—are what is usually meant by the designation "grassroots." For elaboration on this, see Uphoff (1993).
4. Carroll (1992) analyzes the relation between grassroots support organizations (GSOs), which generally correspond to the category of NGOs, and what he calls primary grassroots organizations, classified as local membership organizations and cooperatives here. His category of membership support organizations (MSOs) is a hybrid between nongovernmental and grassroots organizations, in that these are the second or third tier of organizations that are accountable to local memberships.
5. It is true that not all NGOs operate as service organizations. But those that function as advocacy organizations are not accountable in a structural sense to those on whose behalf they speak unless they are *membership* organizations, composed of, by, and for the persons who created the organization and contribute the resources needed for it to operate.
6. See Lipset's study of the International Typographical Union (1956). He documents a lively internal democracy within the ITU over many decades,

with regular changes of officers by election, a de facto two-party system, and an open union newspaper. Typographers, however, had a relatively high educational level among manual workers and one of the higher statuses because they worked with words. Also in terms of higher status and job security, printers contrasted greatly with, say, teamsters or coal miners, whose unions in America have been notoriously undemocratic (at least until recently).

7. We were told by the deputy director of irrigation for water management that if we could make progress in Gal Oya, we could make progress anywhere in Sri Lanka. The senior civil servant in the district told the young organizers that if they could get even ten to fifteen farmers to work together, this would be a great accomplishment. We and they were expected to organize 10,000 to 15,000 farmers (nobody knew for certain how many there were in the area).

8. Since the base-level groups operated informally, tenants could be included along with settlers who had formal rights to their land. That these field channel groups attempted to serve needs equitably is seen from the fact that most of the rotations they set up to share water when it was scarce started by supplying the tail end first. On the process of selection, which was structured to get truly representative farmers into responsible positions, see Uphoff (1992, 334–36).

9. The Chhattis Mauja irrigation scheme in Nepal, established by water users some 150 years ago to irrigate about 3,000 hectares in the Terai region adjoining India, has about 4,000 members who elect a chairman and a secretary at an annual mass meeting. They have been able to keep leaders accountable through direct elections. But their executive committee is made up of nine representatives who come from below through an indirect selection process (Pradhan 1983).

10. The International Irrigation Management Institute started, but did not complete, an evaluation of the Gal Oya program in the fall of 1993. Although a thorough study remains to be done, the main test of success is that farmers there consider the operation of their irrigation system much improved and believe that they can handle problems satisfactorily through the established channels (D. H. Murray-Rust, personal communication, November 1993).

11. Here, NGOs refers to both Northern and Southern NGOs.

12. Note that I have successfully avoided using the term "beneficiaries," even with its mollifying adjective "intended." This paternalistic term is less objectionable than "target groups," but not much.

13. It could be argued that neglecting both positive and negative externalities is acceptable because they more or less offset each other. But in practice, things that are negative are more acutely felt and more easily identified, so positive externalities are more likely to be minimized or discounted in rigorous evaluation, for the sake of not "biasing" the conclusion.

14. When we talk about sustainable development, there is no necessary implication of "sustainable growth," which Herman Daly and others have castigated as oxymoronic. Sustainable development need not mean that gross amounts of outputs are always increasing, only that the total *satisfaction* produced by any given level and distribution of outputs is

greater. Redistribution of goods and services could increase the total volume of satisfaction if distribution had been unequal, for example. The concept of sustainability suggested here, focusing on satisfaction rather than on outputs and based on positive-sum outcomes and valuations, takes a different tack than that which has attracted the critique of Daly and others.

15. This line of thinking is developed in Uphoff (1992). Books that I found useful for trying to rethink the way we understand the social universe and that present new ways of thinking about the natural universe include Bohm and Peat (1987), Briggs and Peat (1984), Gell-Mann (1994), Gleick (1987), Jantsch (1980), Lewin (1992), Penrose (1989), Prigogine and Stengers (1984), Waldrop (1992), Wolf (1981), and Zukav (1979).

References

Bohm, David, and F. David Peat. 1987. *Science, order and creativity.* New York: Bantam Books.

Briggs, John P., and F. David Peat. 1984. *Looking glass universe: The emerging science of wholeness.* New York: Simon and Schuster.

Carroll, Thomas F. 1992. *Intermediary NGOs: The supporting link in grassroots development.* West Hartford, Conn.: Kumarian Press.

Edwards, Michael, and David Hulme. 1994. NGOs and development: Performance and accountability in the "new world order." Background paper for the SCF/IDPM Workshop on NGOs and Development, Manchester, June 27–29.

Esman, Milton J., and Norman Uphoff. 1984. *Local organizations: Intermediaries in rural development.* Ithaca, N.Y.: Cornell University Press.

Fisher, Julie. 1994. Is the iron law of oligarchy rusting away in the third world? *World Development* 22(2):129–43.

Fox, Jonathan. 1992. Democratic rural development: Leadership accountability in regional peasant organizations. *Development and Change* 23(2):1–36.

Gell-Mann, Murray. 1994. *The quark and the jaguar: Adventures in the simple and the complex.* New York: W. H. Freeman.

Gleick, James. 1987. *Chaos: Making a new science.* New York: Viking Books.

Hunter, Guy. 1969. *Modernizing peasant societies.* London: Oxford University Press.

Jantsch, Erich. 1980. *The self-organizing universe: Scientific and human implications of the emerging paradigm of evolution.* New York: Pergamon.

Korten, David C. 1980. Community organization and rural development: A learning process approach. *Public Administration Review* 40(5):480–511.

Lewin, Roger. 1992. *Complexity: Life at the edge of chaos.* New York: Macmillan.

Lipset, Seymour M. 1956. *Union democracy: The internal politics of the International Typographical Union.* Glencoe, Ill.: Free Press.

Michels, Robert. [1915] 1959. *Political parties.* Reprint, Glencoe, Ill.: Free Press.

Penrose, Roger. 1989. *The emperor's new mind: Concerning computers, minds, and the laws of physics.* New York: Oxford University Press.

Pradhan, Prachanda P. 1983. Chhattis Mauja. In *Water management in Nepal: Proceedings of a seminar on water management issues.* Kathmandu: Agricultural Projects Service Centre.

Prigogine, Ilya, and Isabelle Stengers. 1984. *Order out of chaos: Man's new dialogue with nature*. New York: Bantam Books.

Trochim, William. 1992. Developing an evaluation culture for international agricultural research. In *Assessing the impact of international agricultural research for sustainable development*. Ithaca, N.Y.: Cornell International Institute for Food, Agriculture and Development.

Uphoff, Norman. 1986. *Local institutional development: An analytical source-book with cases*. West Hartford, Conn: Kumarian Press.

————. 1992. *Learning from Gal Oya: Possibilities for participatory development and post-Newtonian social science*. Ithaca, N.Y.: Cornell University Press.

————. 1993. Grassroots organizations and NGOs in rural development: Opportunities with diminishing states and expanding markets. *World Development* 21(4):607–22.

————. 1994. Introduction to *Puzzles of productivity in public organizations: Reinventing development administration*, edited by N. Uphoff. San Francisco: Institute of Contemporary Studies Press.

Waldrop, M. Mitchell. 1992. *Complexity: The emerging science at the edge of order and chaos*. New York: Simon and Schuster.

Wolf, Fred A. 1981. *Taking the quantum leap: The new physics for non-scientists*. San Francisco: Harper and Row.

Zukav, Gary. 1979. *The dancing Wu Li masters: An overview of the new physics*. New York: Bantam Books.

2

Negotiating Room to Maneuver

Reflections Concerning NGO Autonomy and Accountability within the New Policy Agenda

Stephen D. Biggs and Arthur D. Neame

This chapter argues that NGOs run the risk of being co-opted by the new orthodoxy being promoted within the agenda of the "new world order." On the surface, this appears to be the result of increased funding to NGOs from official donor agencies: "he who pays the piper chooses the tune." Although at one level this is true, we argue that the formal, linear, mainstream approach to development planning (which is part and parcel of donor funding) is more of a threat to the development aspirations of some NGOs, and the individuals within them, than is a growing dependence on donor funds per se. Funding has been and always will be a problematic issue for NGOs and other agencies. The important considerations are how these funds are negotiated and who is accountable to whom, for what, at what time, and by what process.

That process of negotiation, and particularly the terms under which it is conducted and the parameters by which it is defined, is itself a reflection of power relations in international development. We suggest that a key task in the debate over accountability must be how to open up the negotiation process to greater popular scrutiny in a way that challenges the perceptions of funders, governments, NGOs, people's organizations, and the public at large.

Linear Approaches to Development, and Room to Maneuver

By the linear or mainstream approach, we mean an approach that treats development as a set of predictable outcomes to be achieved by the ordering of project inputs and outputs through the "logical framework" or its derivatives (see Chapter 13 of this volume; Porter, Allen, and Thompson 1991). Although some official aid agencies are attempting to modify and soften this approach (for example, the introduction of "process projects" in the case of the British Overseas Development Administration [ODA]), it remains characteristic of most bilateral and multilateral donors (ODA 1992).

Underpinning the mainstream approach to development is the implicit assumption that we know what is meant by "development" and what interventions are required to achieve it. The logic starts with the assertion that there is a need for development in a particular place. So we talk of specific villages, regions, or countries as though they can be defined in isolation. The logic also assumes that development can be measured and that spatial, administrative, ecological, or technical boundaries can be defined and are unambiguous in relation to the task at hand. Plans, inputs, and outputs are placed within a detailed time frame, the end result being a set of desired and predictable outcomes. The process involves identifying "constraints" to development that need removing or "gaps" between existing and desired conditions that need filling. Filling these gaps forms a major part of the rationale for NGO activities. The apparent common sense of the management techniques used in the mainstream development dialogue has a tremendous ability to co-opt people into thinking that the world did, does, or should behave like the model says it should. A sociopolitical perspective puts such management methods, theories, frameworks, and techniques back into the toolbox and treats them like tools (see Senaratne 1990; Clay and Schaffer 1984; Long and Van der Ploeg 1989).

In the mainstream approach, NGOs are viewed as cost-effective instruments for the delivery of inputs and the achievement of outputs. Little attention is paid to factors and influences outside the NGO and the project. We argue that by adopting this approach to development planning, NGOs run the risk of ignoring the wider social and political context of development intervention and funding. But no institution can be divorced from the wider context in which it operates and from the links that develop over time between actors and organizations in the same area.[1] Indeed, as we show below, it is these linkages and networks that underlie the effectiveness of both NGOs and development interventions. In such networks, it is important that NGOs retain and expand their room to maneuver so that they can adapt to changing circumstances, maintain their accountabilities to different constituencies, and, if necessary, subvert or maneuver around vested interests. It is precisely this room to maneuver that it is curtailed by the adoption of linear approaches to planning (Clay and Schaffer 1984).

The Case for a Greater Role for NGOs:
Questioning Current Orthodoxies

Underlying much of the current dialogue on NGOs is the idea that they form a "third" sector distinct from the "first" (government) and "second" (commercial private) sectors. Like Uphoff (1993), we view this as misleading.[2] NGOs are often put forward as appropriate vehicles to increase participation, protect human rights, or strengthen local-level planning or as agents of democratization. Such assertions are not always supported by the evidence and diminish the importance of the historical and institutional context, which affects the ability of coalitions of social groups to find room to maneuver in reaching their goals.

The experience of Samakhya described by Korten (1990, 5) illustrates these points. Samakhya and its associated people's organization, the Multicoops' Association (MCA), fought against the government of Andhra Pradesh and its ruling political party to restore democracy and member control to cooperatives. The division between the NGO (Samakhya) and the grassroots cooperative organization (MCA) was blurred, and the actors involved in promoting democracy switched from using one organization to the other, depending on strategic and tactical criteria. Importantly, we are told that:

> Samakhya had its own independent board of trustees consisting of prestigious and well connected individuals from Andhra Pradesh who were known for their outspoken commitment to an independent cooperative movement. Some were former government officials. . . . These and other Samakhya trustees had excellent political and administrative connections, and could speak with a powerful voice in support of independent cooperatives with little fear of being accused of seeking personal advantage. Samakhya's secretary, M. Rama Reddy himself had become an established political figure in Andhra Pradesh long before MCA and Samakhya were formed. From his earliest career he knew many of the key politicians and administrators in AP. (Korten 1990, 4–5)

This case is held up as a great success for NGOs. Although we are not disputing that the NGO was clearly a major actor in bringing about significant institutional change, the wider context must be noted. From Korten's detailed narrative, it is clear that some government officials were highly involved in working with the NGO in an unofficial as well as an official capacity. They brought to bear their past and present knowledge of working at senior levels of government in order to help the NGO achieve its goals.

A clear lesson to be drawn from this case is that although Samakhya was legally constituted as an NGO, the actors within and around it found room to maneuver by working in a far broader arena than that offered by the NGO itself. The individuals involved did not succeed by working within strictly defined, specific notions of NGOs, civil society, autonomy, or accountability but by using their deep understanding of the roles that they, as individuals working in alliance with one another, could play within a specific context. The work of another effective NGO, the Grameen Bank in Bangladesh, is also characterized by "continuous concern with mobilizing support and legitimization from a broad range of interest groups" (Von Pischke 1991).

The experience of many other organizations confirms that NGO staff and trustees come from a broad range of public- and private-sector interest groups (Edwards and Hulme 1992). What characterizes these cases is a history of negotiation, coalition, and change in NGO structure and behavior in response to the interaction between the agency and its changing social and political context. One of the most significant observations concerning NGO effectiveness is that networking and coalitions with other NGOs and with other public and private actors are often the key to results (Harding 1994; Long and Van der Ploeg 1989). If one views development as the articulation of a series of local struggles and processes, it is obviously vital to understand the means by which networking succeeds. If NGOs are to tap into local processes in diverse arenas more effectively, it is also important that they recognize the diversity that exists within professions and bureaucracies and acknowledge and network with the relevant experience wherever they can find it. Despite these lessons, the "independence" of individual NGOs is still frequently used to advocate a growing role for NGOs in development.

NGOs' Comparative Advantage

It is often claimed that NGOs have a comparative advantage over the government sector in doing certain types of work. Fowler (1990, 12) writes, "NGOs and their supporters share the view that, in comparison with governments, they are better able to . . ." and then lists sixteen such advantages.[3] Advocates of this position believe that these comparative advantages derive from features such as the way NGOs design their organizations; their strong moral commitment to helping the poor; their professionalism; a close and participatory working relationship with poor people; and an ability to innovate.

There are at least three problems with this analysis. First, one cannot have an NGO unless there is government. The nature of the government and what it does with its power and resources determine whether an NGO might "do development better." By the same token, one has to look at specific NGOs in particular contexts to see whether they do better in these circumstances. There is no *general* case to be made.

The second criticism comes from economic theory. Neoclassical welfare economics argues that, to achieve "Pareto optimality," it is more efficient for society if each actor concentrates on what it is best able to do—the origins of the theory of "comparative advantage." Problems arise, however, when markets are imperfect. Under these (real world) conditions, overall economic welfare is not increased by a particular actor following the logic of comparative advantage; to the contrary, both that actor and society at large might be worse off. Neoclassical theory has little to say about the distribution of wealth and income. Since equity and empowerment are often the declared objectives of NGOs, it is strange that the language and arguments of neoclassical theory are so significant in making the NGO case.

Third, Fowler (1990) states that the roots of NGO comparative advantage lie, first, in the quality of relationships that NGOs can foster with clients and, second, in the way they create and design their organizations. Government-citizen relationships are said to be based on control and authority, whereas NGOs are able to form unambivalent relationships with their clients and "design their organisations in ways which are optimal for the situations and development tasks they themselves select." In contrast, "demands on governments lead to hierarchical and bureaucratic structures which rely on uniformity, standardisation and rigidity" (Fowler 1990, 12). Our experience suggests that this is a romanticized view of NGOs set against a "straw-man" representation of governments. The notion that NGOs select their development tasks hints at mythical autonomy and is highly questionable if NGOs are supposed to be acting in response to local needs and as agents of empowerment.

"Third-Generation" NGOs

In 1987, David Korten wrote a paper that has been important to the growth in official support for NGOs. The paper suggests that NGOs move through a linear evolution to a "third-generation stage." From a focus on relief and welfare (first generation), they move to address the structural context of local self-help action through organization and the mobilization of local resources (second generation). Then comes the time to seek changes in institutions and policies at national and subnational levels that inhibit effective self-help action (third generation). Although we have no quarrel with some of the details reviewed by Korten, we are concerned about the stages he suggests and the linear progression they supposedly represent.

NGOs have sought to change institutions for at least a century. The suffrage movement for the emancipation of women and the Anti-Slavery Society in the United Kingdom are cases in point. In addition, many NGOs in the Philippines with a long-standing commitment to fundamental change have moved from political mobilization to the provision of relief and welfare, as a response to militarization in 1987. This was not a backward move on their part (as Korten's typology suggests) but simply a humane one that suited the needs of the context. By the same token, the creation of Samakhya in Andhra Pradesh in India in the 1980s represented a specific response by NGOs and other actors who joined a flexible coalition to achieve their goals.

NGOs and Civil Society

Currently, in the Philippines and elsewhere, there is much talk of a new role for NGOs as leading actors in a vibrant civil society. But within the evolving economic and political context, there is little questioning of whether NGOs are appropriate vehicles for the process called "democratization." Furthermore, the achievement of democracy tends to be seen as a smooth, linear, time-based progression from one pre-defined set of outcomes to another. The Forum for Philippine Alterna-tives describes civil society in the following terms:

> Civil society is an arena of social and political life autonomous from state domination where progressive values and political practices can be articulated, counter-hegemonic institutions can be created, which can nurture and nourish the creations of autonomous political actors who are able to articulate and defend their interests, propose alterna-tive projects for structuring the state and society, and transform the relations of state and society. (Gershman and Bello 1993)

Such a position views civil society and the state as entirely distinct entities, and although it acknowledges the influence of civil society on the state, it does not appear to acknowledge the link between state and society. The state is represented as the instrument of one particular group in society rather than as an arena for negotiation. Simplistic definitions of civil society and democracy trivialize philosophy and political science; the danger lies in the possibility that NGOs and donors may think that NGOs alone can ensure the "delivery" of democracy and civil society—that these are goals to be achieved rather than processes and are-nas that continually evolve. Such views, reinforced by donors and NGOs alike, portray Southern governments as passive bystanders (see Fowler 1992) and set up NGOs and people's organizations as the victims and pawns of a triumphant world capitalism. They fail to acknowledge that resistance to all hegemonies takes place in many different forms on many different fronts, and that NGOs may be just one small front on which praxis evolves.

NGOs as Innovators

Some authors argue that NGOs have particular skills in developing new methods and approaches for research and development plan-ning that government agencies and other development actors can adopt (Chambers 1992). However, a critical historical account of the growth of farmer participatory research methods shows that many of the new developments came from highly trained professional staff in government research institutions, universities, and international institutes (such as the International Potato Research Institute [CIP] and the Institute of Development Studies [IDS] Sussex), as well as from practitioners in the field with few (or no) government or NGO affiliations. As regards research capabilities (the ability to collect, analyze, and reflect upon data), the

Bangladesh Rural Advancement Committee (BRAC), the largest NGO in Bangladesh, would be the first to admit that the development of a high-quality reflective research capacity is a difficult process, which it has struggled with for a long time (Biggs and Senaratne 1986). Oxfam-U.K. has taken years to develop the capability of producing documents that provide research guidance for its staff and for others (Pratt and Loizos 1992; Marsden and Oakley 1990). Although action research is used by NGOs such as Proshika (Wood and Palmer-Jones 1990), it is a very demanding research methodology that requires considerable professional resources on the part of the people and organizations involved.

At the level of technology development, where NGOs are sometimes seen as performing more effectively than other actors, there is also a need for caution. In a worldwide review of research projects on animal-drawn agricultural equipment, Starkey (1987) illustrates that NGOs appear to be no better or worse than other (private and public) organizations in developing new technology for poorer farmers.

One has to look at the particular context to see whether NGOs are any better at developing methodological or other innovations. When successful developments do occur, they are often the result of the combined efforts of a large number of government, NGO, private, and "beneficiary" actors.

A Duty to Scale Up?

By any measure, the level of developed country (donor) funding of NGO activities has increased over the last ten years (Fowler 1992; Edwards and Hulme 1994). Fueled in part by the availability of donor funds, many NGOs see growth as a "duty." It appears that some NGOs view an increase in their activity as synonymous with greater impact. Evidence of this growth-oriented mentality is especially common with regard to NGO entry into Eastern Europe. This is not to say that there is no role for NGOs there, but the haste with which NGOs have entered that arena—with, by many accounts (admittedly often anecdotal), mixed results—leads to a question: are NGOs the reflective organizations they claim to be, or are they, like their commercial counterparts in the private sector, simply responding to market opportunities—the widespread availability of official aid for NGO activities in Eastern and Central Europe after the fall of the Berlin Wall? Of course, there are NGOs that are not fixated on growth and are keen to maintain their identities. The danger lies in a tendency to conflate growth with impact and effectiveness in all circumstances.

In summary, NGOs must always be seen in a broad social and political perspective. When this is done, it is clear that NGOs have much in common with formal and informal coalitions, which have been exploring and developing room to maneuver under difficult social and political circumstances for many years. Generalized rhetoric about NGOs and their effectiveness does not square with the reality of local contexts and variations. More serious for us is the fact that the growing role for NGOs that this rhetoric engenders may make NGOs willing adjuncts of the mainstream planning approach. Uncritical support for NGOs plays to the formalizing tendencies sought by large donors. In the guise of protecting flexibility and diversity, the current discourse actually limits the room that NGOs have to maneuver and confines them to the role of service agents within a "modernizing" model of development.

Acceptance of this dominant discourse may be logical to those who subscribe to the New Policy Agenda. Use of the language of the New Policy Agenda may also be acceptable to those who do not accept its practical implications but wish to enter into tactical negotiations with donors and governments. However, there is a risk that the techniques and language will become so embedded in NGOs that any sense of critical perspective will be lost; reliance on the linear, mainstream model— with its emphasis on developmental input-output indicators—will become the essence of NGOs' existence. Such a lack of critical perspective detaches NGOs from the real-world politics in which they are situated, limiting them to ready-made policy options that stifle creativity and fail to challenge the dominant economic and political forces at global and local levels. This is not to subscribe to a simple conspiracy theory or to write off Northern donors or Southern governments as monoliths, but to make the point that all development discourses have a habit of becoming new hegemonies—be it participation, dependency theory, liberalization, civil society, sustainability, process projects, or a host of others.

Ways Forward

We have no recipe or set of instructions for making a better way forward. However, there are some signposts that might be useful to those who want to retain and further develop the room to maneuver that NGOs have frequently offered in the past.

Questioning the Withdrawal of Government

It is argued by some that the retrenchment of government under structural adjustment policies implies an even greater role for NGOs in development. To accept this argument uncritically is to accept one of the first premises of the New Policy Agenda, but doing so allows the state to opt out of many of the difficult and complex dilemmas that should be discussed in the open, public arena. Rather than taking on some of the former roles of the state, there may be cases in which NGOs (if they are serious about their commitment to challenging poverty and injustice) should support and facilitate the empowerment of the state or progressive elements within it. Such an approach would mean strengthening the will not just to find common cause with individuals and institutions within all social and political arenas but to build common cause, based on an individual's own judgment of what is feasible, desirable, and within his or her own capacity.

In a discussion of social security in developing countries, Dreze and Sen (1991, 28) argue that "public action includes not merely what is done *for* the public by the state, but also what is done *by* the public for itself" (emphasis added). In this context, they see a particularly important political role for NGOs in pressuring governments to recognize deprivation and take action to reduce poverty. Uphoff (see Chapter 1) argues that more emphasis should be given to the support of membership organizations rather than intermediary NGOs. However, one is left with the basic political question of which types of people's associations and membership organizations the state is going to help, respond to, ignore, or discourage. The role of NGOs in acting to influence public policy still remains. Clearly, there are major differences between a powerful membership organization representing the interests of large commercial farmers and a membership organization representing landless laborers. To suggest that all membership organizations will lobby for (or that the state will introduce) general legislation that is evenhanded is naive. Thus, although we agree with Uphoff concerning the general modes of behavior of NGOs and membership organizations, we see a clear need to be aware of the interests and contexts in which all such organizations are acting. NGOs, government agencies, and the private sector are made up of a great variety of people. NGOs need to move away from rhetoric that suggests that their staffs are more committed to reducing poverty than those in the public sector, toward an understanding that some public-sector staff are as committed and effective in poverty alleviation as any self-proclaimed activist. If NGOs become more reflective, they will see in their own behavior some of the actions of those in governments and the private sector that they often condemn (self-promotion, a failure to learn, and so on).

The Intractable Nature of Autonomy and Accountability

If the New Policy Agenda drives some NGOs into the linear approach to development intervention, then clearly this raises issues of autonomy and accountability. A return to a mythical autonomy is neither possible nor desirable for NGOs; rather, the question is how to broaden accountability. It might seem that the more accountable NGOs are, the less autonomy they have. Pure autonomy and multiple accountability are clearly incompatible. However, by increasing the number and types of arenas in which NGOs are accountable, they may create greater room to maneuver as they gain spheres in which to negotiate.

If NGOs are to avoid entrapment by the agendas of others and are to pursue creative relationships with their proclaimed multiple constituencies, then both formal mechanisms of accountability (such as legal regulations) and informal mechanisms (such as affective ties and patronage) warrant more transparent and serious consideration. Many NGOs are willing to devote time and effort to developing broad critiques of the framework and context in which accountability is constructed but are less willing to undertake a thorough examination of the concrete mechanisms that both affect and are affected by those frameworks and contexts. In seeking room to maneuver, NGO personnel (just like other individuals) need to acknowledge and understand these mechanisms and their effects.

For example, the use of patronage is condemned by some NGOs without reflection on the fact that NGOs are, or can be, purveyors of patronage themselves (White 1991; Neame 1993). Patronage is constructed over time through the acquisition and dispersal of resources, with decisions being made at both conscious and unconscious levels. Little time is devoted to such informal decision-making processes within NGOs themselves, although all who work for NGOs are well aware of their existence. Informal decision making is part of the control and dissemination of information and occurs just as often in the "listening NGO" as it does elsewhere. The choices NGOs make regarding the information they give to their public subscribers, "beneficiaries," or even trustees are clearly open to control and manipulation. Acceptance of this fact is of paramount importance if greater transparency and accountability are to be achieved. It is at this point that the responsibility of the individual, as a member of an institution and as a person who is willing to question what is important and why, comes to the fore (Schaffer 1984; Chapter 18 of this volume).

This chapter has argued that the issues raised for NGOs by the New Policy Agenda are not new. What is new is the form that the discourse is taking. The effect of the New Policy Agenda is to formalize, label, and use NGOs as service contractors, agents of democratization, or sources of innovation. NGOs become instruments for the delivery of services, democracy, or innovation on the basis of clearly defined inputs, outputs, and NGO interventions. Such a view, we argue, brings about a return to the "project mentality" of old; it ignores the complex historical, political, economic, and cultural processes and power structures at work in the real world. Similarly, it fails to acknowledge the heterogeneity that exists among individuals and interest groups in all institutions, including NGOs. By adopting such a formalized approach, NGOs are encouraged to look only at their individual performance. This contrasts with much evidence that major achievements of NGOs come through operating as partners in formal and informal networks and coalitions involving other NGOs, government agencies, and the private sector.

A further concern to emerge from the New Policy Agenda is the predilection of bilateral and multilateral funders to see NGOs as a panacea for many of the intractable problems of development. NGO concerns, and those of other practitioners and academics, center on the supposed loss of autonomy that this might entail. This chapter has argued that the real concern should not be with loss of autonomy as such but with the erosion, rather than the necessary strengthening, of multiple accountabilities. NGOs, like other actors in the development process, have never been wholly autonomous of other actors or the contexts in which they operate. Since autonomy is always relative and shifting, the major issue facing NGOs is how to increase their capacity to negotiate with their multiple constituencies and thus enhance their room to maneuver. Such negotiations are always at the center of NGO activities. They cannot be avoided. In the final analysis, negotiation requires that individuals inside and outside NGOs be aware of, and responsible for, the terms in which the current debate is being conducted.

Notes

We would like to thank Davine Thaw and Jenni Wishart, coeditors of the Olive Information Service, Durban, South Africa, for editing and improving an earlier version of this chapter that was brought out in their *Avocado Series* as report no. 07/94. We also appreciate the support and helpful comments from David Hulme and Michael Edwards. The *Avocado* paper covers the same ground as this chapter, but in much greater detail.

1. In a revealing paper on the work of a large NGO in Pakistan, Marsden (1990) identifies the normative development imperative in the work of the Aga Khan Foundation. The size of the NGO involvement; the funds coming from such agencies as the World Bank, the Ford Foundation, and Oxfam; and the full support of the government of Pakistan would make a nonpolitical and asocial analysis of the development project naive, to say the least.

2. Uphoff (see Chapter 1) argues that more attention and support need to be given to seeing people's associations and membership organizations as the important "third" sector rather than placing nonmembership NGOs in this role. Uphoff prefers to view NGOs as service organizations set within the private sector. Our point is that all organizations exist within and function by virtue of their particular configurations of power relations. These frequently defy any notions of strict or indeed meaningful categorization.

3. The list that Fowler (1990, 11) gives is (1) reach the poor (that is, target assistance to chosen groups); (2) obtain true, meaningful participation of intended beneficiaries; (3) achieve the correct relationship between processes and outcomes; (4) choose the proper mix of assistance—educational, technical, material; (5) be flexible and responsive; (6) strengthen local-level

institutions; (7) achieve outcomes at less cost; (8) tailor interventions to the needs of specific situations; (9) experiment with alternative ideas and practices; (10) employ long-term, strategic perspectives and time scales; (11) undertake people-centered problem identification and research; (12) utilize indigenous knowledge and other local resources; (13) learn from and (re)apply experience; (14) analyze and identify with the reality of the poor; (15) motivate and retain personnel; and (16) promote development that is sustainable.

References

Biggs, S. D., and S. P. F. Senaratne. 1986. *Who does what research and why: The role and organization of research in BRAC.* Dhaka: Bangladesh Rural Advancement Committee.

Chambers, R. 1992. Spreading and self-improving: A strategy for scaling-up. In *Making a difference: NGOs and development in a changing world*, edited by M. Edwards and D. Hulme. London: Earthscan.

Clay, E. J., and B. Schaffer, eds. 1984. *Room for manoeuvre: An exploration of public policy in agricultural and rural development.* London: Heinemann.

Dreze, J., and A. Sen. 1991. Public action for social security: Foundations and strategy. In *Social security in developing countries*, edited by E. Ahmad, J. Dreze, J. Hills, and A. Sen. Oxford: Clarendon Press.

Edwards, M., and D. Hulme, eds. 1992. *Making a difference: NGOs and development in a changing world.* London: Earthscan.

———. 1994. *NGOs and development: Performance and accountability in the "new world order."* Background paper for the SCF/IDPM Workshop on NGOs and Development, Manchester, June 27–29.

Fowler, A. 1990. Doing better? Where and how NGOs have a comparative advantage in facilitating development. *Bulletin* 28:11–20. University of Reading Agricultural Extension and Rural Development Department (U.K.).

———. 1992. Distant obligations: Speculations on NGO funding and the global market. *Review of African Political Economy* 55:9–29.

Gershman J., and W. Bello, eds. 1993. Struggles for democracy and democratic struggle. In *Re-examining and renewing the Philippine progressive vision.* Quezon City: Forum for Philippine Alternatives (FOPA).

Harding, D. 1994. *From global to local: Issues and challenges facing NGOs.* Avocado Series 02/94. Durban, South Africa: Olive Information Service.

Korten, D. C. 1987. Third generation NGO strategies: A key to people-centred development. *World Development* 15(suppl):145–59.

———. 1990. *People versus government: Restoring cooperative democracy through voluntary action in Andhra Pradesh, India.* Boston: Institute for Development Research.

Long, N., and J. Douwe Van der Ploeg. 1989. Demythologizing planned intervention: An actor perspective. *Sociologica Ruralis* 24(3/4):226–49.

Marsden, D. 1990. *Definitions of development and the development of definitions: Building models in the Hindu Kush* (mimeo). Swansea, Wales: Centre for Development Studies, University College of Swansea.

Marsden, D., and P. Oakley, eds. 1990. *Evaluating social development projects.* Oxford: Oxfam.

Neame, A. D. 1993. The search for empowerment in the Philippines: Practitioners or prophets. Master's dissertation, School of Development Studies, University of East Anglia (U.K.).

ODA. 1992. The process approach to projects. *Technical Note no. 4.* London: ODA.

Porter, D., B. Allen, and G. Thompson, eds. 1991. *Development in practice: Paved with good intentions.* London: Routledge.

Pratt, B., and P. Loizos. 1992. *Choosing research methods: Data collection for development workers.* Oxford: Oxfam.

Schaffer B. 1984. Towards responsibility: Public policy in concept and practice. In *Room for manoeuvre: An exploration of public policy in agricultural and rural development,* edited by E. J. Clay and B. Schaffer. London: Heinemann.

Senaratne, S. P. F. 1990. The transformation of the rural economy: A societal perspective. *Upanathi* (spring).

Starkey, P. 1987. *Animal-drawn wheeled tool carriers: Perfected yet rejected.* Berlin: GTZ.

Uphoff, N. 1993. Grassroots organizations and NGOs in rural development: Opportunities with diminishing states and expanding markets. *World Development* 21(4):607–22.

Von Pischke, J. 1991. *Finance at the frontier.* Washington, D.C.: World Bank.

White, S. 1991. *Evaluating the impact of NGOs in rural poverty alleviation: Bangladesh case study.* Working Paper 50. London: Overseas Development Institute.

Wood, G., and Richard Palmer-Jones. 1990. *The water sellers: A collective venture by the rural poor.* London: IT Publications.

3

Board Games

Governance and Accountability in NGOs

Rajesh Tandon

There has been considerable recent debate among donors and NGOs on the issue of accountability (Edwards and Hulme 1994). However, there is as yet no agreed-on definition of NGO accountability. Although all parties aspire to a comprehensive view of the subject, in most practical situations, NGO accountability boils down to the domain of finance. This narrow operational definition is partly a consequence of the ease of establishing specific and quantifiable criteria for measuring financial accountability. It is also partly due to the fact that donors (and other resource providers) have been the most vocal commentators on the issue. The regulatory dimension of accountability has also been emphasized in many contexts (including India), being narrowly defined in relation to finance (submitting regular financial reports that are externally certified to ensure legitimacy). The regulatory context in which an NGO operates defines the laws, rules, and procedures that prescribe parameters and behaviors relevant to NGO accountability. For a detailed analysis of these regulatory aspects in India, see Tandon (1989).

Therefore, it is not surprising to find elaborate mechanisms and regulations being proposed and imposed to improve NGO accountability. This has been a recent trend in India, where several European NGO donors (most notably EZE of Germany) have started to create formal, local, and professional mechanisms for close monitoring and reporting of the financial aspects of the NGOs they support. However, the need to examine this issue from a wider conceptual perspective continues. As actors within civil society, NGOs are autonomous institutions inspired by a particular vision of the society they wish to see develop, pursuing their defined mission in that regard (Tandon 1991). Thus NGOs find themselves in a web of complex interactions in a particular context.

The concept of multiple stakeholders furthers our understanding of NGO accountability. The constituency that is the focus of NGO interventions could be seen as one such stakeholder. When this constituency comprises a local community where NGO programs are carried

53

out, further differentiation arises, creating multiple interests or stakes within the broad category of community stakeholders. Donors and other resource providers have a stake in the outcomes of NGO performance too. There is often a chain of donors, each being accountable to the next level in their hierarchies, thereby further expanding this aspect of stakeholdership.

In this complex web of stakeholders, one aspect of NGO account-ability that is often neglected is that which relates to the NGO's own governance. There has been considerable discussion, training, and codi-fication of practice with respect to NGO governance in many countries in the North (as can be seen from the vast literature produced by insti-tutions such as the National Center for Non-Profit Boards [1992] in the United States). But this area has been neglected in most countries of the South (particularly in South Asia). Therefore, this chapter elabo-rates the different forms of NGO governance that exist in South Asia, examines the linkages between them and NGO accountability, and raises a number of questions in relation to the need to strengthen NGO governance from the perspective of performance, accountability, and institutional development.

NGO Governance

The governance of NGOs implies the totality of functions that are required to be carried out in relation to the internal functioning and external relations of organizations. It is not the same as NGO manage-ment. The governance of NGOs focuses on issues of policy and identity rather than on the issues of day-to-day implementation of programs. Thus, governance implies addressing the issues of NGO vision, mission, and strategy; it focuses on future directions and long-term strategic consid-erations; it addresses the issues of policy in relation to internal program-ming, staffing, and resources; it defines norms and values that are the basis of institutional functioning; it includes obligations entailed in ful-filling statutory requirements applicable to NGOs; and it focuses on defining the external positions that are consistent with the overall thrust of NGOs as institutions in civil society. Most importantly, the governance of an NGO is concerned with its effective functioning and performance in society. This is both a legal and a moral obligation. Therefore, gover-nance requires the creation of structures and processes that enable an NGO to monitor performance and remain accountable to its stakehold-ers. In the for-profit sector, most criteria for performance are monetary. In the case of NGOs, however, they are based on vision, mission, and values. To that extent, creating and sustaining appropriate structures and processes of governance in an NGO are much more complex and chal-lenging tasks.

Forms of Governance

In the case of most voluntary development organizations and NGOs in South Asia, certain patterns of governance reoccur regularly. For those NGOs that are legally incorporated, statutory forms of governance provide the basic framework. The two most common statutory forms are the society and the trust (Tandon 1987), which prescribe mechanisms for purposes of governance in legal terms. This mechanism is variously called the executive council or committee, the governing board, and so on. Also included are statutorily identified positions such as chief executive officer (CEO), variously labeled as secretary, president, convener, coordinator, director, or executive director. The legal basis of these structures dates back to the colonial period in the Indian subcontinent, and many of the details of these statutes date back to the nineteenth century. The present reality of such forms of governance poses serious questions in relation to the efficacy and effectiveness of governing mechanisms. Current practice displays a range of behavior of what could be called "board games," described below and illustrated with case studies from South Asian experience.

Family Boards. One of the common characteristics of many NGO boards is their family character. In both composition and style of functioning, these boards operate like a family, with all the necessary informality, affection, and trust that a small family-held business demonstrates. At the formative stage, such boards provide support (emotional, physical, and material) for the launching and stabilization of the NGO. However, they do have limitations in situations of growth and expansion; they also demonstrate behavior that is characteristic of a patriarch in a family-run business facing the assertion of his offspring. When new staff or volunteers begin to feel like part of such an organization, family boards are unable to provide a competent governing mechanism.

Grameen Vikas Samiti in North Bihar was set up as a voluntary organization in 1978 by Sudhanshu Misra. Misra was very active in the student movement inspired by Jayaprakash Narayan. When the Janata government in Delhi failed to deliver, Misra (and many others like him) felt disillusioned by party politics. His commitment to organize and empower the landless rural poor led to the rapid acceptance and growth of Grameen Vikas Samiti. When the Samiti was incorporated, Misra asked some of his family (wife, brother, and father) to be cosignatories. Later, his wife's brother and his brother's wife also joined the managing committee. When the Samiti undertook an adult education program in 1979, it recruited a full-time staff of 35 and 300 part-time teachers. The Samiti grew rapidly, but due to a sudden change in government policy, all adult education projects had to be wound up. This created a difficult situation for Misra, as he could no longer pay his staff. When he announced the decision that most staff had to leave the Samiti, Misra was abused and demonstrations were mounted against him.

Invisible Boards. Many NGOs have largely invisible boards comprising small coteries of friends and family, assembled by the founder or founders for the purposes of meeting statutory requirements on paper. The actual functions of governance are carried out by the founders, with or without the help of other staff in the NGO, and the board acts only as a "rubber stamp." It is not uncommon to come across examples of boards that have not met for many years; the founders merely obtain the thumbprints of board members on the minute book from time to time. Such a situation clearly provides the founders with the ease of pursuing their visions with speed and energy, unencumbered by the usual hurdles related to paperwork and bureaucracy. However, when the founders need advice or support, the invisible boards remain both invisible and inaudible. In addition, the absence of a clear separation between governance and management in such organizations reduces the avenues available for internal accountability.

Abhay Singh was a student activist in Osmania University, Hyderabad, who decided to work with tribal groups to strengthen tribal knowledge, culture, and art. He set up the Institute for Socio-Cultural Development in Hyderabad to support this work. Since he spent most of his time in the villages, he requested three of his college friends (now teachers in Hyderabad) to join the governing council of the institute. The positive impact of Singh's work resulted in a grant to develop a large three-year project focusing on tribal culture. This grant helped Singh set up a small residence-cum-office in the tribal area, recruit ten outside students, and train nearly thirty tribal youths as part-time animators. Nearly two years after the project began, Singh and two of his colleagues were abducted by a militant Naxalite group that was active in the area. The media coverage of the incident resulted in a number of government inquiries about the institute. When the commissioner of police in Hyderabad asked the three teachers on the governing council to bring the institute's files, documents, and minute books to help the police in their search for clues to trace Singh's abductors, they pleaded complete ignorance of any of the organization's paperwork.

Staff Boards. It is quite common for NGOs in South Asia to have boards largely composed of current staff. When an NGO has been set up by a group of people in pursuit of a shared vision, they often decide to become the board themselves. In other cases, senior staff members are brought onto the board subsequently, similar to the concept of representation by trade union or worker representatives on the boards of for-profit corporations. Such boards are very effective in ensuring a shared vision of and a common perspective on the direction of the NGO, and there is a collective commitment by the board to the well-being of the organization. These boards also help in the process of building and strengthening staff members' stakes in the future of the NGO. However, one of the major problems that arises is the confusion over, and blurring of, the distinction between the requirements of governance and the needs of day-to-day management. It is not uncommon to find situations in which staff confuse programmatic accountability to the CEO with shared responsibility for governance. In many such cases, the board gets bogged down in issues related to the interests of the staff, sometimes at the expense of larger institutional concerns (a situation not too different from that found in corporations in which workers' representatives are nominated to the board). Also, when serious ideological, programmatic, or perceptual disagreements emerge among senior staff in the organization (a situation that is widespread in the functioning of most NGOs), the governing mechanism is unable to deal with disagreements rationally, since the conflict is brought forward and replayed in the board itself.

Such boards are also unable to provide a fresh, objective, and balanced perspective on the strategies, programs, and functioning of the organization. Staff members develop perceptual blocks and vested interests in pursuing particular strategies and programs, and these remain unquestioned by such a board because it is composed mostly of such staff.

Akriti Sansthan in Gujarat was set up by five social workers who had worked together previously in a large rural development agency. They decided to create a new organization in another district where they worked with women agricultural laborers. The executive committee of the Sansthan was made up of the five founding members. After five years of intensive work, the state government offered the Sansthan a large grant for integrated rural development in 250 villages in the area. Within the agency, debates among this "gang of five" over whether to accept the offer became polarized around two personalities. An embryonic leadership struggle surfaced and divided the entire staff. Over the next two months, the Sansthan's fieldwork came to a standstill while the debate and conflict intensified. One of the five founders was acting as secretary of the Sansthan and signed a contract with the government to accept its offer. A week later, two of the original founders and thirteen other staff left the Sansthan and created another voluntary organization a few blocks away.

Professional Boards. The composition of professional boards is based largely on the shared vision of a group of like-minded people, but it also includes consideration of the professional and strategic requirements of the institution. In such situations, the composition and functioning of the board exhibit a more formal character: board appointments are made with careful consideration of the requirements and future direction of the institution; the board has a formal system of meetings, discussions, decision making, and recording (agenda papers, minutes, and so on); members take individual and collective responsibility for different aspects of governance (such as subcommittees and the roles of chair, treasurer, and secretary); the performance audit and review of the institution as well as that of the CEO and other senior staff are undertaken by the board on a regular and formal basis; and the institution is represented in external forums by different members of the board.

Such boards tend to provide ongoing professional direction to the institution and help shape its policies and strategies in a rational and coherent manner. In situations of stability, they ensure the periodic assessment of mission and strategy and its translation into programs and internal mechanisms. In situations of crisis, such boards are able to take on the true function of governance, rising above day-to-day management. However, in many cases, it has proved difficult to generate and sustain a shared vision in such a board, particularly when the board functions merely as a collection of well-meaning and concerned individuals (and not as a coherent, unified, and effective group acting together). It is also difficult to generate and sustain the commitment of the board as a stakeholder, particularly when individual board members do not serve for long periods of time. Other studies tend to confirm these observations for NGOs elsewhere in the world (Billis and Mackeith 1993).

Sita graduated with a master's degree in social work from the Tata Institute of Social Studies in 1970. She worked in a voluntary organization outside Bombay among rural women, helping to organize a dairy cooperative. Later, she moved back to Bombay to set up an NGO called Creative Development to assist women's groups in undertaking livelihood projects. Sita decided to seek the advice of a few colleagues and, in the process, insisted that they join the governing board of Creative Development. These board members were a professor from the National Institute of Bank Management, a scientist from the Indian Council of Agricultural Research, a graduate from the Indian Institute of Management currently working with Lever Brothers in Bombay, the directors of two other rural development NGOs from Maharashtra, and her favorite professor from the Tata Institute. During the first year, the board met three times to elaborate a set of policies that enabled Sita to carry forward the program.

Even from this brief typology, it is clear that the form and functioning of governance mechanisms in many South Asian NGOs are inadequate from the perspective of accountability. When the board is "sleeping" or invisible, the full spectrum of governance functions cannot be performed properly. In many other situations, the style of functioning of the board results in the curtailment of governance. Weaknesses in governance limit the possibilities of continual, objective, and appropriate feedback on the implementation and management functions of the NGO.

Other Governance Issues

A key issue in the arena of governance arises in situations in which the founder is the leader of the NGO for a substantial period of time. Inevitably, the NGO begins to reflect the vision and perspective of its founder; its culture and programs imbibe the style and background of the founder too. Over time, the NGO's identity becomes closely linked to the person of the founder-leader. In such situations, the board is initially assembled by the founder, and most board members are individually known to and associated with the founder-leader. This has the potential to limit the autonomous identity of the board (even in the case of a professional board) and creates a particular set of dynamics. On the one hand, the founder-leader provides the bulk of the energy and ideas for the NGO, thereby building up "sweat equity"; on the other hand, the long-term sustainability of the NGO requires the institutionalization of energy and ideas beyond one person. The conduct of the totality of the functions of governance in such circumstances poses a range of interesting and practical challenges.

The second issue of relevance to this discussion is the fact that priorities in governance change over time. In the early formative stages, defining the vision and mission and building a program take precedence; once established, the NGO turns its attention to issues of growth in size, coverage, and resources. The life cycle of an NGO thus determines the priority of issues. The composition and functioning of the board tend to be more informal and spontaneous at the formative stage; this helps provide support and space for the founder. During the phase of growth and consolidation, the board needs to acquire greater formality and professionalism in its structure and processes. This temporal dimension of governance requires understanding and attention if effectiveness and accountability are to be maintained.

Another issue in NGO governance that is gaining increasing currency (particularly with donor agencies) is the active role of different stakeholders. It is being repeatedly argued by some donors that beneficiary participation and representation on boards is crucial to ensure NGO accountability to their "clientele." Some donors even ask for evidence of this at the time of approving a grant. In response, some NGOs provide for a token beneficiary representation on their boards. A similar argument is often made for including donor representatives in the governing structure. Even governmental funding and regulatory agencies sometimes ask for this as a matter of right. For example, some states in

India have attempted to incorporate such a requirement in their modified society registration acts. Rather than simply acceding to these demands from donors and regulators, some NGOs have experimented with creative solutions.

In the case of the (legitimate) need for beneficiary participation in the planning and implementation of NGO programs, this can be, and is being, carried out through systematic consultation and participation mechanisms on the ground. In the case of (legitimate) donor concerns about having an input into the direction and programs of the NGOs it supports, regular joint review and planning forums are common practice. However, the demands of regulatory agencies are clearly aimed at strengthening controls over NGOs and should not be seen as legitimate merely for the purposes of regulation.

It is important to distinguish here between the concept of stakeholders and the concept of governance. A stakeholder, by definition, is any party that has a stake in the outcomes of an NGO. In this sense, beneficiaries, donors, and regulators are all stakeholders, as are other NGOs and NGO staff. However, their stakes relate to the performance of the institution, not to its governance. Hence, their demands for access to the institutional governance of the NGO relate to the requirement that the NGO perform effectively. Here, critical and regular performance monitoring by stakeholders is the key to ensuring the NGO's accountability to them. This situation is somewhat akin to that in a for-profit corporation, where consumers of its products or services have a stake in and therefore a right to corporate accountability, without needing to be part of the formal governance mechanism of the company. Donors to NGOs are supporters of desirable processes and outcomes, and their interests and concerns must be matched by the performance of the NGO in order for resources to continue to flow. A major cause of ambiguity at present, however, is that undue importance is given to the existence of a shared vision and perspective between NGO and donor, and less emphasis is placed on the performance and the results obtained. Accountability to donors needs to be more clearly related to output indicators than is the case in current practice, and not to NGO governance. Innovative practices and ongoing documentation of best practice are needed to promote better performance accountability. Social audits provide one such approach (see Chapter 17).

Linkages to Accountability

In light of this discussion, it is important to understand the linkages that exist between NGO governance and accountability. NGO accountability is related to three dimensions:

1. *Accountability vis-à-vis its mission.* As an institution oriented to social change within the framework of civil society, an NGO needs to define, refine, and pursue a clear mission.

2. *Accountability vis-à-vis its performance in relation to that mission.* Demonstrable performance, both in process and in outcome terms, is essential to generate feedback to the programs and approaches implemented in a given time frame.

3. *Accountability vis-à-vis its role as an actor in the civil society.* Norms, rules, and styles of functioning should match the standards of a good civic institution.

In all three respects, the governance of an NGO is a critical element. An effective system of governance enables an NGO to formulate, review, and reformulate its mission in a changing context. Good governance ensures that programs follow the requirements of the NGO's mission; promotes a performance orientation and accountability in the institution; and requires that the values (integrity, participation, professionalism, quality, commitment), statutes (reporting and legal standards and procedures), and norms of socially concerned civic institutions are articulated, practiced, and promoted. An effective structure and process of governance in an NGO are absolutely critical for ensuring accountability in this wider sense.

Even in its narrow sense, financial and statutory accountability requires an active, alert, and functioning board that feels both a legal and a moral obligation in this regard. Such a board provides a set of measures to ensure the necessary checks and balances for proper recording and reporting according to agreed-on targets and rules.

The governing board of the Society for Participatory Research in Asia (PRIA) has been conscious of developing standards and procedures of good governance over the years. Program monitoring and review are carried out at least annually by a group of partners and concerned professionals. The board conducts annual organizational and staff reviews. A separate annual performance review of the executive director is carried out by the board. Over the past fourteen years, PRIA has had three external evaluations. The board coordinates and facilitates these evaluations. A system of monthly internal audits by an external professional is used to generate feedback on financial management. The treasurer also reviews these reports with the executive director. Over the years, PRIA's governing board has established high-quality formal policies of human resource management. Many of these policies, systems, and procedures have become models of good practice for other NGOs in the region. The norms and procedures for the functioning of the governing board are continually evolved, upgraded, and established.

In recent years, donors and regulators (such as government agencies) have demanded better performance with respect to NGO goals and programs. In the post–Cold War world, there are going to be even greater demands for demonstrable performance. This will require better documentation of existing performance as well as the enhanced, transparent, and critical functioning of mechanisms for NGO governance. In this sense, performance, accountability, and governance are likely to become linked with one another more and more closely. Particular attention needs to be given to improving this linkage in operational terms so that NGOs can face these emerging challenges proactively.

Future Challenges

Inadequate attention is being paid to the issue of effective governance in NGOs in many countries of South Asia. It is crucial that NGOs, their supporters, and their donors begin to understand the meaning and significance of effective governance and its contribution to NGO accountability. There is also a need to document, analyze, and promote good practice in relation to NGO governance and accountability. Such interventions must be viewed as part of the fabric of institutional development efforts needed to strengthen NGOs. Strategic planning and capacity building need to include interventions directed at making NGO structures and processes of governance more effective. A number of such efforts, studies, and manuals have been developed and used in countries in the North and can help clarify and support this challenge in the South (Conrad and Glenn 1976).

Although a basic understanding of NGO governance already exists in most countries, considerable ambiguity remains with respect to the situation of NGO networks and associations. The considerations discussed in this chapter become even more complex when applied to a body that brings together a set of independent and autonomous institutions. Much of the practical experience with governance in such associations has been unproductive and frustrating. There is much useful experience in other countries from which our current understanding and practices could benefit. There is also a need to develop educational programs and learning materials on the theme of NGO governance, so as to strengthen NGO practice. The growing emphasis on NGO performance and accountability *must* include the challenge of making NGO governance more effective.

References

Billis, David, and Joy Mackeith. 1993. *Organising NGOs*. London: Centre for Voluntary Organisation, London School of Economics.

Conrad, William R., and William E. Glenn. 1976. *The effective voluntary board of directors*. Athens: Ohio University Press.

Edwards, Michael, and David Hulme. 1994. *NGOs and development: Performance and accountability in the "new world order."* Background paper for the SCF/IDPM Workshop on NGOs and Development, Manchester, June 27–29.

National Center for Non-Profit Boards. 1992. *Annual report.* Washington, D.C.: National Center for Non-Profit Boards.

Tandon, Rajesh. 1987. *Forms of organisations: Square pegs in round holes.* New Delhi: PRIA.

———. 1989. *Management of voluntary organisations.* New Delhi: PRIA.

———. 1991. *NGOs, the state and the civil society.* IDR Occasional Paper Series. Boston: Institute for Research Development.

Part II
Case Studies

4

Scaling Up, Mainstreaming, and Accountability

The Challenge for NGOs

Frits Wils

In many fields—including poverty alleviation, women's emancipation, and sustainable development—NGOs are ascribed a range of virtues, based partly on presumed advantages such as efficiency, effectiveness, flexibility, participatory approach, and proximity to vulnerable people. However, such virtues are rarely proved: they are brought out in an invidious comparison with the "vices" of the state. Another motive for emphasizing the role of NGOs is ideological: those of a social democratic persuasion attach great importance to bottom-up participation, especially of less privileged groups; those with neoliberal values prefer a reduced role for the state and a strengthening of private initiative. On the basis of such arguments, expectations of NGOs run high, especially if they can overcome weaknesses such as their localism and limited outreach, lack of technical or professional expertise, and constraints in working at both micro and macro levels.

"Scaling up" and "mainstreaming" represent two separate but interrelated approaches to overcoming these weaknesses and improving NGOs' capacity to utilize more systematically their experience in developing effective and efficient models and in dealing with the problems of poverty and powerlessness. Scaling up relates to the challenge NGOs face in applying small-scale solutions on a large scale; mainstreaming involves the conversion of such solutions from alternative, NGO-implemented, or parallel programs into the generally and officially accepted policy framework. "Access strategies" are defined as those that empower poor people to gain access to the resources and programs of third parties; "parallel strategies" are those in which NGOs develop their own programs and institutions. This chapter explores how NGOs respond to these challenges on the basis of research into the growth and dynamics of three big NGOs (BINGOs) in South Asia and six in Latin America (Wils, Neggers, and Beets 1988; Wils et al. 1998–90; Wils, Madduri, and Sohoni 1993; Wils, Remmerswaal, and Neggers 1993).

The capacity of NGOs to respond to these challenges is also related to issues of accountability. NGOs want to benefit as many people as possible, effectively and efficiently. This is an essential part of their mission, and both beneficiaries and donors hold them accountable in this respect. However, as NGOs scale up or mainstream, they face the question of how to preserve their accountability to beneficiaries and donors without losing autonomy and identity (Edwards and Hulme 1994). Accountability to the grassroots may conflict with accountability to donors, including governments. Much depends on what NGOs provide and how they scale up and mainstream: the cases reviewed below show considerable variation in this respect, ranging from the delivery of services without empowerment, through parallel programs, to the promotion of self-reliant and autonomous popular movements that demand the redistribution of resources and power. The five strategies used by NGOs in the study to scale up their impact are reviewed in sequence, before turning to the linkages that exist between scaling up and accountability.[1]

NGO Strategies

The BINGO Option

The BINGO strategy (increasing the number of staff, size of budget, and direct outreach) is particularly visible in South Asia, especially in Bangladesh, India, and Sri Lanka. In this region, our research defined a BINGO (in 1987) as having at least 500 staff members, having an annual budget of at least US$1 million, and working directly in 1,000 or more rural communities. In Latin America, by contrast, such large NGOs are rare. In Peru and Bolivia, for example, the criteria for BINGOs (in 1991) were a minimum of 125 staff members, an annual budget of US$1.2 million, and a direct outreach covering 25,000 families.

What induces such growth in an NGO? Our research found the following factors at work: the extent of real and perceived poverty in a country, and the failure of government agencies to provide an effective response; the original vision of the founder or founders; the occurrence of disasters that demand a sudden, sharp increase in staff, funding, and outreach; and an ability to overcome the fear of and problems related to growth inside the NGO during its expansion. In addition, it appears that sectoral programs favor large-scale activity,[2] especially when the emphasis is placed on standardized and easily replicable packages to meet basic needs (in health, education, credit, and nutrition) rather than on productive activities.[3] Finally, the willingness (and sometimes even the stimulus) of donor agencies to underwrite the cost of expansion is an important factor.[4] Social compensation funds intended to cushion the impact of structural adjustment policies on the most vulnerable groups nearly always rely on NGOs as the principal channel of assistance, yet we found that such funds promote the growth of NGOs only when the

NGO's overhead costs are covered, thus enabling the NGO to increase its staff and not just its operational expenditures (Wils, Remmerswaal, and Neggers 1993).

The BINGO option certainly produces complexities at the level of management and internal organization. The transition from group to institution is not an easy one. The original founder or founders often have great difficulty in relinquishing centralized control; the need for an "external shield" and separate identity (vis-à-vis the state, donors, and other NGOs) is often used by NGO managers as an excuse for retaining power in their own hands. Such management problems are often associated with changes in the internal organization of BINGOs: the gradual emergence of (and struggles over) a clear organizational structure (a division of labor along sectoral lines and geographical decentralization in decision making to lower-level units); the evolution of a bottom-up planning system combined with a process of consolidation at higher levels; the formalization of management, labor relations, and working conditions of staff; the "flattening" of the hierarchy by reducing the number of layers between senior management and field teams to no more than two or three; the gradual development of an intervention cycle that permits the programmed shift of staff from one region to another, promoting the autonomy of beneficiaries and enabling the NGO to increase its outreach over time without having to continue growing; and the elaboration of a programming, monitoring, and evaluation system (PMES) to balance a high level of decentralization with the maintenance of a sufficient degree of centralized control. The latter is especially important in relation to information, financing, and the provision of high-level but costly technical expertise to field teams and grassroots units. The Bangladesh Rural Advancement Committee (BRAC), for example, employed brick-making experts whose costs, though high, could be distributed over a large number of producers.

These problems and solutions are well known to all who are familiar with modern organizations, whether private or public. But in the case of NGOs, they are embedded in a structure that is systemically "flatter" and more decentralized than that of private enterprises or government agencies. It is this kind of structure that permits a BINGO to remain an NGO and retain the "virtues" thereof: flexibility, a participatory approach, and bottom-up planning. Nevertheless, the growth of a small NGO into a BINGO is rarely smooth. Some staff and donors fear and resist growth, adhering to the gospel that "small is beautiful." Others consider vocation to be incompatible with professionalism or specialization and consider withdrawal from a region on completion of an intervention cycle as tantamount to abandoning or betraying the NGO's target groups. Such problems must be dealt with constructively if the process of growth is to continue effectively.[5] For example, CEDEP in Peru and INEDER in Bolivia decided not to expand further. INEDER also opted to strengthen the autonomy of regions so that they could graduate from the program, though in this case, disputes over financing and authority reduced the effectiveness of this strategy.

Hence, BINGOs differ significantly from one another despite having organizational similarities. Such differences reflect not just variations in context but also the outcomes of ongoing debates and choices. AWARE (in India) had the most "political" approach of the NGOs in our research, supporting tribal people and Harijans to articulate a stronger identity, claim their rightful share of public resources, and organize themselves into a movement. In contrast, the Sarvodaya movement in Sri Lanka applied traditional community development and service delivery approaches. BRAC in Bangladesh was somewhere between the two (in 1987): it focused on large-scale parallel service delivery and development while adopting a more careful approach to empowerment and organization among beneficiaries. Our study accounted for these differences in terms of national policies with regard to the poor, the political space available to NGOs for engaging in "political" activities (including nonparty politics), the identity of poor people in socioeconomic and ethnic terms, the extent to which a parallel or access strategy was viable, the religious background of the countries, and the BINGO's philosophy (Wils, Neggers, and Beets 1988).

Multipliers

Multiplying the scale of an NGO's outreach by working with and through other organizations is obviously easier in countries like the Philippines and India and in Latin America, where the political space for popular movements is greater. Our research found that opportunities for working with existing popular organizations were most evident in Bolivia (including trade unions) and Brazil, making it possible for bigger NGOs in these countries (though still of only middle range from a South Asian perspective) to reach tens of thousands of families effectively. In Brazil, NGOs have also had success in supporting the establishment and rapid expansion of new grassroots organizations. In extreme cases, small NGOs can reach tens of thousands and sometimes hundreds of thousands of beneficiaries. For example, CESE in Salvador (Brazil) finances a small group of economists and accountants to work with federations of unions of sugarcane workers; their work helps the unions formulate an annual package of claims when bargaining with the plantation owners, directly affecting hundreds of thousands of families. In such cases, powerful multipliers are at work.

Another example is AWARE, which seeks to empower newly established organizations of tribal people and Harijans to make and defend their claims vis-à-vis the state programs that are targeted at them. Sooner or later, these new apex organizations begin to act as multipliers of

alternative models (such as different types of farming), a more asser-
tive identity, and new gender relations. Popular organizations may
demand direct access to the NGO's donors and raise doubts regarding
the NGO's role (as happened, for example, in Bolivia). Moreover, where
such organizations exist,[6] they are often linked to political parties; this
may or may not be an obstacle (depending on the NGO's own political
ties) and may lead to cliental connections. But such connections may
also evolve when the organization owes its emergence, and many of
the benefits it receives, to an NGO. There are few NGOs that know how
to handle such risks by promoting the autonomy of grassroots organizations from the very start.

Opting for other kinds of organizations as multipliers (universities,
church-related organizations, associations of professionals) works
well only if they possess their own implementation capacity and have
their own linkages with vulnerable groups. Such conditions rarely
exist, though they are more common in the field of human rights work.
For example, under repressive military regimes, churches often set
up their own programs to support the victims of human rights abuses,
and NGOs have attempted to increase their outreach by working with
and through such church-related programs. An interesting example is
AGRARIA in Chile. Although consisting of only four or five professional
staff, it had a considerable impact in the 1980s by working with and
through diocesan programs targeted at small farmers and via its influence over academics and students in the universities in Santiago.

From our research, NGO networks do not emerge as strong vehicles for
scaling up: the mere aggregation of the capacities and corresponding outreach of NGOs affiliated with a network produces no incremental net
effect. Only when the network decides to add resources and activities to
those already undertaken are net gains achieved, but such additional out-
lays are often not supported by donors.[7] Gains in outreach may also be
made when NGOs succeed in increasing their efficiency and productivity as a result of an exchange of experiences in the network and the adoption of similar methods of programming, monitoring, and evaluation. As
a result, the existing program can be implemented in less time, and
resources are freed up for new tasks; the NGOs can take on more work
with the same staff or provide a more diversified package of services to
the same target group.

Planned Diffusion of NGO Alternatives
through Seminars and Publications

With this strategy, NGOs design an explicit plan to influence key targets on the basis of alternative models (policies, projects, methods) that
they have tried out in pilot projects and whose adoption and diffusion
they seek to promote within and outside government. For example,

DESCO in Lima and BRAC in Dhaka organize seminars on policy issues, inviting politicians, policymakers, and professional associations to discuss subjects such as alternative industrialization strategies, the development of peasant agriculture, and rural education.

Multiactor Programming: Widening the Horizon

When NGOs begin to think and act bigger, they can move to approaches that cover a whole city, province, department, or state instead of a small number of communities. Even medium-sized NGOs can apply this strategy, relying on both their own staff and links with carefully identified multiplier organizations. Such strategies exist in Bolivia, where bigger NGOs are beginning to consider whole provinces as their working areas, and in Peru, where they covered a large part of metropolitan Lima-Callao or (in the case of IDESI) practically all departments in Peru (Wils, Remmerswaal, and Neggers 1993).

Opportunities to follow such strategies increase under structural adjustment and the associated reduction in the role of the state, decentralization, and strengthening of civil society. In these cases, NGOs dropped most of their traditional antagonism towards the state, though they still sought to maintain their autonomy and identity when applying models on a larger scale. What they *do* reject is *total substitution* for the state. In some examples, the NGO, together with committees related to a popular organization, implemented large-scale health programs under contract to the health ministry in areas where such programs never existed; elsewhere, NGOs (again with grassroots committees) undertook basic health and other activities complementary to those of the state. Such collaborative efforts entail official recognition and state subsidies for the cheaper and more effective models of the NGO, so long as they meet certain basic standards. NGOs may also start to work with regional planning corporations, chambers of commerce, parishes, colleges, and professional associations in the development of a regional plan, carving out their own (subregional or thematic) niche.

Through such a multiactor approach, and by bringing popular organizations into wider platforms or councils, NGOs can help defend and articulate the interests of poor people at a macro level and as an integral part of a broader plan. Thus, NGOs can help secure multiple entries for themselves and for organizations of the poor into the process of designing and carrying out plans and projects for the region. This demands from the NGO a shift and flexibility in thinking so that it is more prepared to work with government and the private business sector, accept funding from them, and enter into the sort of commitments that entail accountability to local actors other than grassroots organizations. The NGO loses its isolated and very private position, becomes a "public" actor, and enters into a more open and transparent world of action.

Mainstreaming

Mainstreaming means the incorporation of NGO models into the official policy framework, involving the recognition of the model (for example, a new institution, method of work, special program) and in many cases a (partial) subsidy for its implementation. Such models can be found in housing, primary health care, education, agricultural extension and technology transfer, associative enterprises, credit programs, technical assistance for informal producers, and support programs for women. Even more than multiactor planning, mainstreaming requires the NGO to widen its universe of thinking and action. Especially for NGOs born under authoritarian regimes, such a shift is a major step and takes courage. It also raises difficult questions concerning the NGO's mandate and accountability: On what basis and with what mandate does it advocate alternative models—to the poor, to members, or to donors? What criteria should such alternatives meet in order to qualify for public recognition and support?[8]

These questions thrust the role and identity of NGOs onto center stage. The public recognition they enjoy from multi- and bilateral agencies, followed (with notable reservations) by their own national governments, pushes NGOs into the foreground as important actors in the field of poverty alleviation (and in issues related to gender, ethnic minorities, human rights, and ecology). But such public recognition rarely extends to the popular organizations with which the NGOs are working. Should NGOs therefore speak on behalf of these organizations, or speak out only via or together with them? NGOs respond to this question in different ways: some act as professionals committed to the cause of the poor but speak out with a voice of their own; others attempt to keep popular organizations involved as much as possible. Some NGOs situate themselves between popular organizations and government agencies and attempt to bring the two together and facilitate a consensus on particular proposals and policies. As the work of Bratton (1989) and Fowler (1991) on African NGOs suggests, the weight of an NGO's voice at the macro level depends on the technical quality of its proposals, the level of perceived popular support for them, and the capacity of the NGO to maintain good and workable relations with government. A real or perceived connection with grassroots organizations is therefore an important asset. These observations are even more valid for Asia and Latin America.

NGO alternatives are characterized by small-scale, low-cost, and participatory design; by the use of people's own traditional technologies; by being paced in their application in accordance with the target groups' own possibilities in terms of time, savings, and inputs; by some contribution of these groups to the costs of operation and maintenance; and by effective comanagement. These features (and especially grassroots participation, control, and contribution) render such alternatives viable, sustainable, and responsive to grassroots needs and possibilities. If such proposals were accepted as mainstream methods of organizing the provision of basic needs, adjustments would clearly be required in the public sector and in the roles and responsibilities of state and civil society. Community participation and shared management would be incompatible with vertical, standardized, and centralized government control. Hence, mainstreaming NGO models requires sufficient political, economic, social, and institutional space to make room for them.[9]

Scaling up does not necessarily imply major changes in the relationship between NGOs and the state, especially when NGOs continue to expand their own parallel programs through foreign funding. Mainstreaming, however, implies an important qualitative shift in the relationship between civil society and the state—between organized groups of the poor and access to policymakers and resources. Mainstreaming the adoption and implementation of NGO alternatives often demands reforms in the relationship between society and the state—for example, in rethinking traditional, centralized policies and programs; decentralizing decision making and resource allocation from central to local levels; increasing the claim-making and participatory capacities of organized groups of the poor; moving the state from a dominant to an enabling role; and introducing new public-private funding for social programs.

In this process, informal grassroots and NGO solutions can be linked to formal systems and granted a more formal status, but without losing their roots in the community. Cofinancing of the sort already visible in municipalities in Chile and Colombia supports such systems, though reforms in the state are hard to achieve, even in the limited forms related to structural adjustment policies. Difficult questions are raised by mainstreaming in this way. For example, does it not lead to formalized systems targeted exclusively (as in a parallel strategy) to the poor? Would such a "parallel" system for poor communities not be seen as discriminatory, smacking of "dual citizenship"? How would universal requirements (say, in the field of primary and adult education) be combined with the special needs of groups such as poor women and ethnic minorities? How could economies of scale be preserved when buying medicine, teaching materials, and inputs for microenterprises while simultaneously maintaining effective local participation and control in the design and implementation of programs? How would the costs of such programs be divided among state, grassroots, and NGO? These and other questions will inevitably emerge as different actors learn to steer a course that is viable and sustainable. In the "politics of mainstreaming," obstacles and opportunities have to be confronted continually as popular organizations and NGOs come to play more dynamic and "public" roles.

Scaling up, Mainstreaming, and Accountability

From the narrow viewpoint of cost-effectiveness as well as from the broader perspective of NGO responses to the endemic problems of poverty and powerlessness, NGOs simply cannot avoid the challenge of trying to scale up the effective outreach of their work. NGOs are accountable for their performance in relation to this challenge, to their own mission and potential, and not simply to third parties such as donors and governments. Of course, scaling up must not be achieved at the expense of quality and depth, and our research shows that there is not necessarily a trade-off between scale and effectiveness. This applies both to the social and political effects of large-scale programs and organizations, especially big NGOs that combine multiplier and access strategies with empowerment (as in AWARE in India and IPTK in Bolivia), and to the social and economic effects of BINGOs such as BRAC, IDESI, and FOVIDA (in Peru) and AWARE's access strategy in rural Andhra Pradesh (Wils, Neggers, and Beets 1988: Wils, Madduri, and Sohoni 1993).

The three criteria related to scale identified in our research (number of staff, total yearly budget [institutional and operational costs], and number of families or communities reached directly or indirectly) are interrelated but not necessarily strongly correlated. In any analysis of scaling up, attention should be paid to each of the three criteria separately and to the ways in which the NGO tries to find an optimal combination of them. Yet among NGOs and donor agencies (including most of those in the Netherlands), there is still a strong current of opinion that continues to argue that small is beautiful and big is ugly. From our perspective, any NGO should, in principle, consider using one or more of the strategies discussed above to scale up its impact (see also Edwards and Hulme 1992).

Current levels of interest in results and impact (rather than in activism and good intentions) reflect a shift in the external basis of legitimacy of NGOs and the source of their funding, in both Northern and Southern countries. Whether or not the current neo-liberal near-hegemony persists, strengthening civil society and the role and position of the poor in it remains a basic mission of NGOs and is often spelled out in their constitutions. The fulfillment of this mission demands that poverty and powerlessness be tackled on a relevant scale. Whether NGOs do this alone or together with other NGOs, making a difference is, to a large extent, a function of mass. Hence, there is also an internal basis of legitimacy for NGOs to scale up effectively. The NGO itself may remain small or medium-sized, but it faces a real challenge to maximize the outreach of its work.

The problems of NGO accountability referred to by Edwards and Hulme in the introduction of this book especially affect those NGOs that possess considerable absorptive capacity (the big NGOs), which renders them attractive to domestic government as well as to multi- and bilateral donors. To assume that these NGOs passively accept the conditions applied by donors is erroneous; our research shows that bigger NGOs have a significant degree of bargaining power, precisely because of their absorptive capacity and because they have succeeded in developing viable alternatives in service provision or economic support to the poor. They took the initiative and sought and obtained public financing for their own programs. As in India and Bolivia, even when big NGOs agree to help implement government programs, they succeed in reformulating and improving such programs to a significant extent. For example, while helping to implement the government's health program in its region under contract, IPTK managed to include the work of grassroots health services and committees and link these informal systems to the formal system of the government.

Other variables that affect the relationship between scaling up and the accountability of NGOs "upward" to the state are the type of program and the approach adopted for implementation. As Tendler (1987) noted, and as our studies of big NGOs confirm, social service programs often generate less social conflict locally than economic programs and are more readily supported by public agencies. In addition, an "empowerment approach" that promotes autonomous apex organizations and the claim-making power and assertiveness of the poor in competing for access and control of (especially public) resources is prone to upset the status quo and appears less palatable to local government agencies and the groups closely linked to them. In contrast, central governments and official donor agencies vary in the degree to which they accept and are willing to actively support such an approach. A more equitable redistribution of power and resources and considerations of sustainability and grassroots participation and support are not the sole prerogatives of NGO discourse; they figure in public agencies too.

Hence, problems of NGO accountability (especially of big NGOs) should not be oversimplified nor be seen only in connection with their growing dependency on public funding. Such public sources (both domestic and external) are far from monolithic and vary considerably in interests and ideology: NGOs are not powerless either, especially if they are large. Our research shows that accountability to domestic and external donors is mediated by the nature and strength of NGO connections with the grassroots; the scope and depth of this connection help NGOs legitimize themselves vis-à-vis domestic and foreign donors. Any move to distance NGOs from their grassroots connections must be resisted. A central theme in this debate is how to strengthen *downward* accountability among NGOs. Our studies suggest that NGOs that use an empowerment approach with autonomous apex organizations of beneficiaries (or with popular movements) are more accountable downward than NGOs that focus primarily on the delivery of services (such as Sarvodaya in Sri Lanka, CIPCA in Bolivia, and CEDEP in Peru). AWARE in India, IPTK in Bolivia, and FOVIDA in Peru are good examples of the former.

Thus far, downward accountability is poorly instrumentalized in most NGOs. Participatory PMESs are one of the best and most promising instruments, especially when linked to contractual agreements between NGOs and their target groups. Examples include AWARE and CYSD in India, SUNGI in Pakistan, ENLACE in Mexico, SERGUS in Guatemala, and TIN-TUA in Burkina Faso. These agreements need to specify the gradual and systematic transfer (where possible) of projects and resources to organized groups at the grassroots level over the course of an inter-vention cycle. Participatory monitoring can maintain accountability in this way as the work evolves (Neggers and Wils 1987). Such agreements also help prevent (or at least weaken) NGO paternalism and help make NGO links with the grassroots more transparent and balanced than is usually the case. Current decentralization policies may also help improve the local (rather than the external) accountability of NGOs, in relation to both grassroots organizations and other sectors and groups in local society, private and public. This is particularly important when their respective resources are being pooled, articulated, and programmed in the context of joint (micro) regional planning. These and other issues render the challenge of NGO accountability more serious, complex, and important than it has ever been before.

Notes

I gratefully acknowledge the important contributions of Jan Neggers (NOVIB), with whom I share many of the ideas and insights set out in this chapter. I also thank Jacques Remmerswaal of the Dutch Ministry of Devel-opment Cooperation, who participated in the Latin American studies, and the participants who actively contributed to my course at the Institute of Social Studies on NGDOs and development.

1. These strategies are similar to those presented by Edwards and Hulme (1992), who distinguish "additive" strategies (implying organizational and program growth), "multiplicative" strategies (networking, policy and legal reform through advocacy, working with government, and training), and "diffusive" strategies (spontaneous and informal).
2. The importance of a clear sectoral focus confirms Tendler's (1987) conclu-sions. It should be recognized, however, that sectoralization does not exclude and often facilitates the articulation of intersectoral connections at an operational level.
3. More specifically, we found that in productive programs, larger-scale operations usually referred to inputs, marketing, the processing of outputs, and the provision of support in areas such as credit and training, rather than to productive activities proper. The latter tend to remain small scale,

require the assembly *in loco* of various kinds of inputs, and are themselves rarely amenable to large-scale operations.

4. The donor consortia for BRAC and other BINGOs in South Asia are good examples, something that still seems hard to achieve in Latin America.

5. It is possible that large NGOs generate a "critical mass" that helps overcome personalized tensions and conflicts. It would also be interesting to examine in detail what happens to staff turnover in such NGOs; a high degree of staff commitment may not be the best basis for sustained action, since staff may be more vulnerable to frustration. In addition, salary levels and working conditions, including opportunities for upward mobility and training, are important. Such conditions are often better in large NGOs than in small ones.

6. Autonomous popular organizations are more frequent in Latin America than in Asia and Africa.

7. What is needed is not just more human and material resources. Also necessary (and here donors often hesitate) are special organizational measures (reflected in additional overhead costs) to design, monitor, and evaluate the extra programs.

8. The accountability of NGOs to the poor is often more of a self-professed obligation among NGOs than a real and effective practice, supported by participatory systems, consultative or participatory bodies in the NGO for policymaking and review, and so on.

9. In a sense, this means going back to the historical sequence of Western patterns of development, in which what later became public and universal programs and provisions were originally developed through a bottom-up process from local to higher levels, sharing methods, modules, training, and resources. Many Southern countries have attempted to reverse this sequence by starting with the end product: a state made responsible for welfare, but without the resource base to make this possible.

References

Bratton, M. 1989. The politics of NGO-government relations in Africa. *World Development* 17(4):569–87.

Edwards, M., and D. Hulme, eds. 1992. *Making a difference: NGOs and development in a changing world.* London: Earthscan.

———. 1994. *NGOs and development: Performance and accountability in the "new world order."* Background paper for the SCF/IDPM Workshop on NGOs and Development, Manchester, June 27–29.

Fowler, A. 1991. The role of NGOs in changing state-society relations: Perspectives from east and southern Africa. *Development Policy Review* 9(1):53–84.

Neggers, J., and F. Wils. 1987. Self evaluation among NGDOs and local organisations in third world countries. Paper presented at the Consultation on the Promotion of Autonomous Development, CEBEMO, Oegstgeest, the Netherlands.

Tendler, J. 1987. *Whatever happened to poverty alleviation?* New York: Ford Foundation.

Wils, F., J. Laforce, P. Renaud, and L. Zivetz. 1988–90. *The view from the field: An analysis and evaluation.* New York: United Nations Development Program, NGO Division.

Wils, F., K. Madduri, and N. Sohoni. 1993. *Aware and its work with tribals and Harijans in Andhra Pradesh: An impact study.* The Hague: Institute of Social Studies.

Wils, F., J. Neggers, and N. Beets. 1988. *Big and still beautiful: Enquiry in the efficiency and effectiveness of three big NGOs (BINGOs) in South Asia.* Programme Evaluation Report no. 32. The Hague: NOVIB/Ministry of Development Cooperation.

Wils, F., J. Remmerswaal, and J. Neggers. 1993. *Big NGOs in Latin America: Case studies in Peru and Bolivia.* Programme Evaluation Report no. 47. The Hague: NOVIB/Ministry of Development Cooperation.

———— 5 ————

European NGOs and Democratization in Central America

Assessing Performance in Light of Changing Priorities

Kees Biekart

After visiting twenty European NGOs in 1993 to survey their policies on Central America, I was left with the impression that Northern NGOs (NNGOs) are experiencing an often productive crisis of identity. Mission statements are being reviewed, policies and priorities redefined, management reorganized, and legitimacy questioned. Although some NNGOs have been temporarily paralyzed by this internal reassessment, it is a positive sign that profound rethinking is going on, which may give a new impulse to the debate on reshaping nongovernmental development cooperation at the dawn of a new millennium.[1]

This new sense of urgency has coincided with the ideological changes of the post–Cold War period but has also been influenced by tighter requirements for management and organization and by increased dependence among NNGOs on official aid. One of the questions arising from this reassessment concerns the impact of development projects implemented by NNGO partners in the South. Although many individual development projects have been successful, their combined impact on macro structures has been disappointing (Edwards and Hulme 1992). The performance of NGOs has been seriously questioned in recent years by journalists, academics, and former NNGO workers.[2] As private contributors have become more critical and conscious of development issues, these public doubts have had to be countered, for example, by commissioning independent impact studies.[3]

A common conclusion of these studies is that it is difficult to assess the impact of NGO development programs as a result of poor data, diffuse objectives, rapidly changing circumstances, and poor-quality evaluation; performance cannot be quantified and has to be judged by anecdotal and circumstantial evidence. Issues of efficiency, internal organization, and financial management are easier to assess and have led to changes in policies and a number of useful recommendations. At the same time, evidence from Central America shows that the policies of European NGOs toward their local partners have changed significantly over the last fifteen years, with important implications for the ways in which performance and impact are measured. The central question of this chapter is: what lies behind these changes if performance *is* so difficult to assess?[4] Are Northern agendas more important than impact defined in local terms?

The following analysis is based on the results of a research program initiated by the Transnational Institute (TNI) in which Central American and European researchers carried out an assessment of the impact of European NGO–financed programs on democratization in El Salvador, Guatemala, and Honduras (Biekart 1994). The findings show some inconsistencies between performance assessment and decisions over programming, which shed new light on the changing relationships between NGOs in the South and the North. In particular, the changing political context for aid since 1980 has led to important shifts in policy and performance measurement that have not been discussed or negotiated openly between Northern donors and their Central American partners.

European NGOs and Central America

Two issues need to be examined in order to understand the special position of Central America in current NNGO policy debates: the priority given to the region by European and Canadian NGOs and official agencies during the 1980s, and their widespread disillusionment following the defeat of the Sandinistas in the 1990 Nicaraguan elections.

Political Priority during the 1980s

Aside from two earthquakes in the 1970s that attracted international humanitarian assistance, Central America rarely appeared on the maps of Northern development agencies before 1980. However, in 1980, aid began to increase rapidly, tripling to US$1.7 billion a year by 1987 (Visser and Wattel 1991). Some 15 percent of this total was provided by European and Canadian NGOs and by solidarity groups, which started to operate programs first in Nicaragua and then, from the mid-1980s, in other Central American countries. Over 30 percent of the total aid budget of some NNGOs was dedicated to Central America during this period.[5]

These large amounts of nongovernmental aid (in comparison to the small size of the region) were a reaction to the political crisis that followed the victory of the Sandinista revolutionaries in Nicaragua in 1979. Under newly elected President Reagan, the U.S. government made the rollback of revolution in Central America one of the top priorities for U.S. foreign policy. Starting in 1981, U.S. intervention marked the beginning of a regionwide eruption of civil war that transformed Central America into a major battleground of the Cold War. One reason that so much assistance was channeled to the region by some European agencies during this period was their explicit rejection of U.S. foreign policy. NGOs in Europe also saw the Sandinista revolution as a genuine, alternative development path worthy of strong support. In a context of widespread war and repression in Central America, social organizations that had emerged in the 1970s suffered a serious setback. New intermediary NGOs were established by the political opposition, and they became the partners of European and progressive North American NGOs in counterbalancing the activities of U.S.-financed NGOs acting under the umbrella of "counterinsurgency." As one observer put it, "only two institutions have consistently flourished in the Central American crisis: the military and the NGOs" (Lewis 1990, 1).

For this reason, all development aid to the region had a strong political dimension. NNGOs were used by European governments to channel aid to Southern NGOs (SNGOs) and grassroots organizations (GROs) in Central America, thereby avoiding direct contact with U.S.-backed authoritarian regimes. Local opposition groups constantly referred to European NGOs as agencies of "international solidarity," although many tried to maintain a more neutral profile. While Nicaragua was converted into a "playground" for experimental development strategies, aid to NGOs in El Salvador and Guatemala served mainly to give more room to maneuver to a clandestine opposition struggling to preserve its physical survival, protect human rights, provide relief for refugees and displaced people, and channel resources to urban and rural social movements. The development discourse in Europe prioritized empowerment and poverty eradication, but this masked the reality of political survival for local partners. European NGO field representatives were aware that these realities affected the quality and sustainability of SNGO projects, especially in areas of conflict. As a Danish NGO manager put it, "when local project staff were contracted, political criteria were more important than the technical or administrative experience of the candidates."[6] It was a public secret that funds for development projects were often diverted to political and military struggles. Long-term planning and strategy were absent from the Central America desks of most European NGOs at this time. Only a quarter of the NNGOs in our survey produced written policy documents on Central America, leaving policy decisions to the political judgment of local representatives. This pattern was to change substantially in the 1990s.

After 1990: The Postrevolutionary Era

The end of the Cold War coincided with the end of the Sandinista government and its loss of credibility in the aftermath of the Nicaraguan elections.[7] This, combined with the desperate military offensive of November 1989 in El Salvador and the reopening of peace talks, provoked profound reflection among NGOs in Europe on development policies toward Central America. With the gradual return to peace, the region lost its status as a top-priority area for emergency assistance and international attention, although official and private foreign aid to Central America was not reduced.[8] However, the sudden political changes in the region generated unrest among the SNGO community, along with fears that foreign aid would be cut. For example, the transition to peace in El Salvador caused NGOs to redefine their ties with political parties and grassroots organizations and to take up a more cooperative relationship with state institutions in charge of the National Reconstruction Plan. The NGOs of the 1980s found this transition exceptionally difficult, especially since many were also criticized by their former beneficiaries for being paternalistic and corrupt.[9] The breakdown of the revolutionary perspective obviously generated disillusionment, with NGOs having to rethink their work in relation to democracy, development, and the role of the state.

On top of the confusion created by changing political conditions in the region in the late 1980s, Central American NGOs were faced with a new aid discourse emanating largely from bilateral and multilateral agencies in the North after the end of the Cold War. Market-oriented strategies and "good governance," combined with a more prominent and professional role for NGOs, appear to be crucial elements in this new agenda. Calls from the Northern donor community for greater efficiency and more professionalism increased, and it became clear that the era of unconditional funding born of political solidarity was at an end. The Central American NGO community is now taking a defensive attitude toward the demands emerging from Northern agencies as a result of these changes.

Democratization and the Limits to Performance Assessment

One of the goals of TNI's research is to find out whether European NGO assistance has contributed to higher levels of participation and to the strengthening of GROs. However, reviewing the experience of Central America in the 1980s from the new and still confusing perspective of the 1990s is a difficult task. As other chapters in this book show, NGO performance assessment is always a complicated affair; in Central America, the changing context for aid and development brings further difficulties. For example, the application of performance criteria concerning internal democracy to NGOs in Central America is now considered essential by donors, but these criteria were not in use ten years ago. This makes retrospective evaluation of NGO impact on democratization misleading.

Measuring the impact of NGO activities directed at enhancing participation and organizational capacities is a complex enterprise not only because of the wide range of influences at work but also because crucial data are not available. Reliable data from the initial stages of projects, and information concerning the political context at the project level, are scarce. Initial objectives and success criteria are rarely documented. As noted above, even European NGOs did not have written policy documents dating back to the 1980s. Obviously, this makes performance assessment virtually impossible.

In the 1980s, European NGOs rarely included impact assessments in their project evaluations and were therefore obliged to judge the results of their assistance from personal impressions. Their judgments are generally positive, especially in terms of grassroots-level empowerment and political survival. As an Oxfam-U.K. respondent commented, "the final balance of our work in Central America is positive if we use the indicator that many people managed to survive thanks to foreign NNGO aid." Some NNGO staff members complained about the weak impact of SNGOs on government policies, but macro-level change was not the goal of NGOs in Central America at this time because of the scale of political repression that existed and its impact on the political space available for GROs and NGOs. Again, NGOs in Europe were applying criteria retrospectively that had not been used at the time grants were made.

Our research also included participatory evaluation to find out what the beneficiaries of SNGO work felt about the results of empowerment-oriented projects. From these evaluations it became clear that donors and beneficiaries were using different definitions of impact and performance. Donor NGOs tended to overemphasize financial management and short-term material outputs; beneficiaries tended to look for modest changes in organizations over longer periods of time. For example, the impact of a training center for union leaders in Honduras was praised by trainees; for them, it had clearly contributed to closer collaboration between unions that had not wanted to work together before.[10] Union leaders measured performance in terms of high and regular attendance at classes and the fact that some had managed to secure more responsible positions in the union as a result of their training. In other words, they valued modest changes with a nonquantifiable impact in the long run. However, the main NNGO donor to the project announced that it would cut its funding, arguing that the training center was using "old-fashioned" methodologies and that the organization was too closely related to a particular political faction.

The fear of exposing confidential linkages between local NGOs and clandestine political parties makes research on NGOs in Central America highly sensitive. Even independent local researchers on the team confessed that they were unable to touch on this topic for reasons of security and because SNGOs feared that aid would be cut if (even previous) linkages with politico-military parties were exposed. Even in El Salvador, where connections between SNGOs and the five political tendencies within the FMLN[11] are being discussed publicly, both SNGOs and researchers avoided an issue that is crucial to any understanding of the political survival mechanisms of the 1980s in that country.

The New Policy Agenda of European NGOs in Central America

TNI's research focused on European NGOs because they were the most committed to supporting the political opposition in Central America during the 1980s. Current changes in European NGO priorities can be analyzed in three areas: financial commitments, thematic priorities, and organizational demands.

Funding Levels

After the collapse of the Nicaraguan revolution and the signing of the peace agreement in El Salvador, NGOs in Central America feared that aid to them would be cut drastically and that any new aid would be channeled directly to the newly elected governments. However, the evidence (up to 1993) does not confirm these fears.[12] On average, European NGOs' allocations to Central America between 1990 and 1993 remained the same as 1980s' amounts; and in some cases, they even increased their allocations, though the figures vary from one country to another.[13]

NNGO assistance to the rest of Latin America has certainly declined, however. For example, Hivos (a Dutch NGO) allocated 65 percent of its overseas budget to Latin America in 1987 but only 48 percent in 1992; the figure will continue to fall in the years ahead, as NGO programs in Chile, Brazil, and other industralizing countries in Latin America are closed down in the face of social, economic, and political improvements. Will the same trend also affect Central America? The evidence shows that *official* aid to Central America from the United States, Italy, Spain, and France has already been reduced (Hansen 1994), and pressure on official aid budgets will have repercussions for those European NGOs that are highly dependent on funding from their own governments.[14] It is therefore to be expected that funding levels from European NGOs to NGOs and GROs in Central America will eventually decline. Consequently, they will have to look for new sources of funds from multilateral agencies such as the United Nations Development Program and the Inter-American Development Bank, which have introduced significant new programs in Central America since 1990.

New Priorities

Given the great variety of priority areas for European NGO investment in Central America and the fact that many European NGOs only recently produced policy documents for the region, care must be taken in generalizing about trends. However, two new (post-1990) themes emerged from TNI's research: production-oriented projects and advocacy. It is not surprising that the emphasis at the project level has moved from political to economic survival. For example, the number of "political education" projects has fallen in favor of projects that aim to strengthen market capacities.[15] In addition, European NGOs are pressuring their partners to redefine their role in democratization and to clarify their responsibilities in relation to other actors in civil society. One of the frequent criticisms made of NGOs in Central America is that they have been taking on the role of social organizations and political parties and should start to play a more technical or professional role in the new political climate.[16] These new roles could include advocacy and technical assistance to newly emerging networks of social organizations in the region, although some NNGOs doubt the legitimacy of these regional networks.[17] Performance in both these areas is more easily assessable in the short term than were previous strategies devoted to empowerment or methodologies of political education. This is, perhaps, no accident.

New Organizational Requirements

The most fundamental policy changes revealed by the research are found in European NGOs' attitudes about how development projects ought to be organized and managed.[18] Tighter requirements for efficiency, cost-effectiveness, and professionalism are now applied to NGOs in Central America. Internal reorganization and market-oriented strategies are supposed to lead to economically sustainable organizations, and partner agencies are being pressured to diversify their funding sources and develop a greater level of self-sufficiency. Other requirements deal with improving accountability via systematic monitoring and evaluation.

None of these new requirements will seem unusual to anyone in the donor community, but they have had a major impact in Central America. Although SNGOs admit that they should operate more professionally and efficiently, this was impossible during the crisis years of the 1980s. Central American NGOs consider it unfair to impose new criteria in response to perceived poor performance during previous years when they faced very different conditions.

Consulting or Imposing?

This brings me to my central argument. Changes in the policies of European NGOs toward Central America seem to have been generated by changes in values and criteria that were, in turn, the result of developments taking place outside the region. They have little to do with the transition from war to peace in Central America, and this makes them hard to accept for SNGOs locally. Although efforts were made by donors to consult their partners on these new policy priorities, TNI's research encountered a widespread feeling that changes had been imposed. This reflects a one-sided transparency in relations between donors and partners: many SNGOs and GROs complained that they understand neither the reasons for European NGO policy changes nor the relationship between these policy changes and the origins of NNGO funding. These feelings are directly related to weaknesses in the partnership between European and Central American NGOs and the generally low level of accountability of NNGOs toward their partners.

Faced by the revision and restructuring of aid policies by NNGOs, NGOs and GROs in Central America have taken up a defensive position. Mutual competition for new aid resources (extremely intense in the cases of El Salvador and Nicaragua) is weakening efforts to improve coordination and threatens to relegate issues of quality to the bottom of the list of priorities. This is alarming, but understandable. Many SNGOs are still in the middle of a transition from wartime (when autonomy vis-à-vis donors was higher) to a postwar period where they find themselves more vulnerable to external pressures. This transition becomes more difficult the longer they lag behind in debates that are taking place within the Northern aid community.

Are the claims of inconsistency in European NGO policies reasonable? Certainly, old and new policies are sometimes applied simultaneously, which causes a good deal of confusion. An example is Guatemala, which, since 1991, has been a priority for European NGOs in Central America following the successful end of the war in El Salvador. Key priorities in Guatemala (where civil war continues) are the return of refugees from Mexico and the protection of human rights. These are implicit political issues, as they were in El Salvador during the war. However, the new enthusiasm of NNGOs for improved management and performance makes Guatemalan NGOs feel that they are being treated differently from their Salvadoran counterparts during the latter's civil war in the 1980s. At the opposite extreme, Nicaraguan and Honduran NGOs argue that it is inconsistent of European NGOs to diminish their activities in these countries and increase aid to Guatemala, when Guatemala has lower poverty figures than they do. Herein lies the dilemma of delinking policy from performance in a rapidly changing environment.

It is also inconsistent to apply performance criteria developed in the 1990s to the much more difficult period of the 1980s, when aid to SNGOs and GROs was not used for development (except in Nicaragua) but rather to ensure the survival of the political opposition. The impact of European NGOs on democratization in the region is difficult to assess, since the data do not exist. However, the political opposition did survive in many countries (as in El Salvador), thanks in part to foreign aid. Current criticisms being made by NNGOs about the poor performance of SNGOs in the 1980s are unfair and cannot be used to justify policy changes in more recent years.

In light of these problems, what can be said about the capacity of SNGOs to pursue their mission of social transformation in spite of the constraints put forward by the New Policy Agenda of Northern donors? In the particular case of Central America, it is possible to foresee a combined role for NNGOs committed to supporting the process of social transformation and the community of local NGOs and GROs, under the following conditions: European NGOs need to make an effort to increase mutual coordination of their projects and policies in Central America, to prevent unnecessary competition and improve joint advocacy toward their home governments and publics. More transparency and accountability toward their partners on internal policy discussions are vital; active involvement of SNGOs in policy and decision making will pay off in the long run. Policy making should be based much more consistently on mutually agreed-on performance standards in order to prevent confusion and indifference from setting in. It might even be better to drop the term "partnership" in favor of more systematic attempts to reduce the financial dependence of NGOs in the South.

Although Central American NGOs and GROs are not enthusiastic about the new requirements for better management and more professionalism that are an inescapable part of the New Policy Agenda, they accept that performance will benefit in the long run. However, their reactions to this debate go much further than negotiations over performance criteria; there are at least three much more fundamental changes.

First, there is a need to increase SNGO capacity to undertake policy-oriented research, produce viable policy alternatives, and develop mechanisms for coordination and joint advocacy at the national and international levels, together with Northern partners. This is especially important for networks of GROs such as ASOCODE (the network of peasant organizations in Central America).

Second, it is important to develop local (Southern) standards for performance assessment. This presupposes, however, a self-confidence within the SNGO community that is often lacking and the absence of feelings of insecurity that are caused by widespread fears of aid cuts.

Therefore, and third, there is a crucial need to move to longer-term self-sufficiency and the exploitation of local financial resources. Moves in this direction could strengthen the legitimacy of SNGOs and make them less vulnerable to the policy shifts of NNGOs and official donor agencies in the North. This would make the development of an indigenous cultural and political identity much more probable and improve the likelihood that NGOs and GROs in Central America will be able to pursue a mission for social transformation both effectively and efficiently in the late 1990s and beyond.

Notes

1. A good example is Riddell (1993).
2. Many examples could be mentioned, especially from Northern Europe, such as public reaction to the Dutch NGO impact study and the controversy in Belgium surrounding the publication of *Het Orkest van de Titanic* (1993), in which a former NGO worker criticized the Belgian NGO community.
3. See Danida (1989), Riddell (1990), the impact study of four Dutch NGOs (Betekenis van het medefinancieringsprogramma 1991), and Finnida (1994).
4. Chapter 13 in this volume lists some of the difficulties involved in measuring the performance and impact of NGOs.
5. For example, the Swedish NGO Diakonia allocated 38 percent of its overseas budget to Central America in 1987; OXFAM Belgium increased its expenditure for Central America from 27 percent of its total aid budget in 1987 to 38 percent in 1992.
6. Central America coordinator of IBIS, a Danish NGO, in a speech to the Third International Consultation on Development Cooperation, Managua, 1991.
7. After the elections, it became known that Sandinista government officials had taken advantage of their positions to confiscate former state properties, which became known as the *piñata* (a traditional Nicaraguan birthday game for children).
8. Official aid from European governments grew between 1987 and 1993 but declined thereafter (Hansen 1994).
9. See *Pensamiento Propio* 87 (January–February 1992) and 91 (June 1992), in which the regional coordinator of ASOCODE (the network of peasant organizations) openly criticized the NGOs they were working with. This generated a public debate in Nicaragua and Costa Rica on the role of NGOs and their relations with GROs.
10. The case study looked at the Honduran NGO IDEPH and the Dutch NGO Hivos.
11. The Farabundo Marti National Liberation Front was the principal political and military opposition force in El Salvador during the decade of civil war.
12. We calculated that combined European NGO aid to Central America increased from US$120 million in 1987 to nearly US$200 million in 1992. The European NGOs we surveyed in 1993 had already made their commitments for the coming year and did not foresee drastic cuts before 1995.
13. Nicaragua was the highest priority throughout the 1980s in terms of aid allocations from European NGOs. In 1990, El Salvador became the main recipient, and since 1992, Guatemala has been given the highest priority. This variation explains why complaints about aid cuts are made especially by the well-organized NGO communities in Nicaragua and El Salvador.
14. Three major Dutch NGOs (Cebemo, ICCO, and Hivos) and three German NGOs (EZE, Friedrich Ebert Foundation, and the Konrad Adenauer Foundation) are 100 percent dependent on government funding. This makes them very vulnerable to official policy changes.
15. This change of emphasis from "political relevance" to "economic relevance" (as it is called by many NNGOs) was, in the case of the Honduran NGO IDEPH, perceived as a rejection of popular education. However,

the donor agency (Hivos) explained that popular education could never be an end in itself and had to be treated in the future as an integral element of development projects.

16. This was the central message of the Dutch NGO Cebemo to its key partners in the region when discussing new forms of cooperation. See Cebemo (1993).

17. The Danish NGO Danchurchaid commented that it is not always clear who these regional networks of farmers' and workers' organizations represent, nor who controls them. The non-church-based NGOs in Europe (such as Oxfam-U.K., Ibis, Hivos, and NOVIB) have been the most supportive of regional advocacy efforts.

18. All the NNGOs surveyed mentioned the improvement of organizational capacities among partners as the major challenge in Central America, with variations in emphasis: the Swedish NGO Radda Barnen considered internal democratization of partner organizations as the major priority, whereas the Danish NGO IBIS mentioned management training and institution building of SNGOs as its main challenge in Central America.

References

Betekenis van het medefinancieringsprogramma, een verkenning. 1991. Oegstgeest: GOM.

Biekart, K. 1994. *Las agencias Europeas de cooperacion no-gubernmental y la democratizacion en Centroamerica: Lecciones de la decada del ochenta y politicas para las noventa.* Amsterdam and San Salvador: TNI/PRISMA.

Cebemo. 1993. *Documento basico Montevideo.* The Hague: Cebemo.

Danida. 1989. *Danish NGO report.* Copenhagen: Ministry of Foreign Affairs.

Edwards, Michael, and David Hulme, eds. 1992. *Making a difference: NGOs and development in a changing world.* London: Earthscan.

Finnida. 1994. *Strengthening the partnership: Evaluation of the Finnish NGO support programme.* Helsinki: Finnida.

Hansen, Finn. 1994. *Coherencia o contradicción? Las políticas de la Unión Europea, el caso de Centroamérica.* Documento de Trabajo CRIES no. 94/4.

Het Orkest van de Titanic. 1993. Leuven: VUBPRESS/Student Aid.

Lewis, David. 1990. *NGOs and international aid in Central America: The development dialogue between North and South.* Paper presented at the CCIC consultation NGOs and the North-South Dialogue in the 1990s, Quebec, May 8–12.

Riddell, R. 1990. *Judging success: Evaluating NGO approaches to poverty-alleviation in developing countries.* London: Overseas Development Institute.

———. 1993. *Discerning the way together.* Report for Christian Aid, ICCO, EZE, and Brot für die Welt.

Visser, E., and C. Wattel. 1991. Las relaciones de cooperacion entre la Comunidad Europea y America Central. In *Mas alla del ajuste: La contribucion Europea al desarrollo democratico y duradero de las economias Centroaméricanas,* edited by R. Ruben et al. San Jose: DEI.

6

From Accountability
to Shared Responsibility

NGO Evaluation in Latin America

Héctor Béjar and Peter Oakley

In Latin America today, NGOs are the subject of much critical comment and debate, most of which is coming from European governments and NGO financing partners in Europe and Canada. At the same time, multilateral organizations such as the World Bank, the Inter-American Development Bank, the United Nations Development Program (UNDP), and others are "discovering" NGO virtues and skills. What are these qualities? In Latin America, it could be argued that the close relationship NGOs have with grassroots organizations (GROs) is their greatest strength. NGOs show a real commitment to change in their societies and generally work with lower overheads than governmental and multilateral organizations; the levels of salaries, office space, and facilities of most NGOs in Latin America are evidence that they function on very tight budgets. At the same time, the number of NGOs is proliferating in line with global trends (UNDP 1993): in several countries—Brazil, Colombia, and Peru, for example—this growth has been spectacular. In Peru, there were an estimated 218 registered NGOs working on development issues in 1980; that number had grown to 897 by 1993 (Noriega and Saravia 1994).[1]

But as expectations of NGOs have grown, the nongovernmental community has become more concerned about impact, assessment, evaluation, cost-benefit analysis, and sustainability. In this dialogue, Latin American NGOs are becoming the targets of more critical observation. In this debate, it is important to recognize the influence that macro-level policies have had on NGO work in Latin America. Recent years have registered important changes that are reshaping the macro context in which Latin American NGOs work. In poststructural adjustment economies, there is emerging evidence that some of the vitality of GROs has been swept away by the free market. For example, the major trade unions of state employees have either lost influence or been dissolved as massive layoffs have greatly reduced their membership. Similarly, many industrial workers' unions have been weakened through loss of membership due to the prolonged recession. In rural areas in Latin America, violence and the rolling back of enthusiasm for land reform have debilitated a range of social movements and organizations. In this situation, the relationship between NGOs and GROs in Latin America has inevitably been weakened (El Taller 1993).

In this context, new social actors have emerged who are beginning to replace the more traditional forms of popular organizations. Some, such as women's groups and organizations of small businesses, are already beginning to link up with existing NGOs through training and credit programs. Other actors, such as the swelling ranks of the unemployed, working children, and casual workers, are visible and numerous, but they still lack organizations or spokespeople to represent them. In this situation, new issues and problems have arisen; for example, in countries affected by violence, human rights are an increasingly important area of work. New groups are becoming the target population for NGO work: microenterprises, children, women, and victims of violence. In fact, there is a new agenda, and with this new agenda comes the need for new methodologies of NGO work. NGOs are assuming a more direct dialogue with their societies and governments, and frequently, they play a protagonistic role in defending human rights and protecting environmental resources. At the same time, they continue to provide welfare services to those hardest hit by economic and social change. NGOs are obliged to attend to a population in extreme poverty and, as a result, their expectations of structural change in society have had to be postponed.

Recently, many of the resources of Northern NGOs have begun to be provided by Northern governments (Hulme and Edwards forthcoming). The amount of public funds managed by Northern NGOs has been increasing for some years. Increasing dependence on government funding strengthens the chain of influence that derives from government policies, continues through Northern donor agencies and then through Southern NGOs, and ends with GROs or directly with target groups in the South. In this process, the presence and weight of Northern governments are becoming more and more important. However, having compared the costs and benefits of this approach, some policymakers in the North now think that this process is too expensive. They argue that it is necessary to diminish or even eliminate the role of one of these intermediaries: the Northern NGOs (Bebbington and Riddell forthcoming). If these recommendations become a reality, Southern NGOs will depend increasingly on the direct support of Northern governments and multilateral organizations. And if this trend continues, over the long term, civil society's role will tend to decrease, and accountability to governments will tend to increase. The impact of international cooperation and private development initiatives should not be exaggerated, however. They form only a small proportion of the financial and trading links that operate in a world where barriers erected by the richest countries are maintained at the expense of the economically weak. Often, the benefits provided by international organizations are erased by the costs of commercial and other financial forces.

Therefore, it is difficult to measure "results" and to evaluate the work of NGOs in Latin America without taking a global approach to international cooperation. Of course, it is not our intention to say that actors in the South are not accountable at all in this difficult situation. Rather, we suggest two key propositions: first, responsibilities must be shared by NGOs in the North and in the South; and second, NGOs must work together to secure changes in global macro policies. In theory, the concept of shared responsibility also refers to governments, multinational enterprises, multilateral organizations, and financial institutions. However, in the South, the reality is that policies are often dictated or imposed on governments by international financial institutions. In this situation, the key task is to abandon unequal relationships between donors and recipients in favor of an effective South-North dialogue around common and practical tasks. This also means that it is necessary to have a common commitment toward (and understanding of) the strengthening of civil society throughout the developing world.

Evaluation and Accountability

In the past decade or so, Latin American NGOs, like development agencies in other parts of the world, have had to come to terms with the question, how effective are we? How far can we argue, in general terms, that NGOs are able to achieve their stated goals? This is not, of course, an exact science; nor is it possible to produce authoritative statements that represent an accurate description of the whole universe of NGOs in the region. The NGOs from whose work these conclusions are drawn are intermediary NGOs that concentrate on information work, strategies to multiply their impact, advocacy, and institution building (Carroll 1992). They are not service providers. For such NGOs, accountability is currently seen largely in terms of satisfying the donors who support them; trends toward "downward" accountability (to the people they supposedly serve) are much less strong. These NGOs argue that they make a reality of the current "popular" view of NGOs as development agencies: participatory, flexible, and innovative. They also agonize over the whole process of program and project evaluation; they question its relevance, and they often have widely conflicting views of how to go about doing it. "Evaluation" is an emotive word to most Latin American NGOs, and its mere introduction into a debate can spark off an intense exchange of views.

In trying to make some general statements and suggest some conclusions concerning NGO evaluation and accountability in Latin

America today, we drew heavily from the practical experiences we have been involved in over the past few years, particularly from the following:

- An evaluation of the work of ADAR, a Peruvian NGO working in the health field among rural communities along the banks of the Peruvian Amazon. The evaluation was undertaken by a joint team of ADAR staff and external consultants and focused on both an assessment of the impact of ADAR's work in the health field and the institutional development of the agency itself.

- An evaluation of the work of KAUSAY, a Peruvian NGO that runs an integrated rural development program in the altiplano region of southern Peru. The evaluation focused on assessing the changing role and impact of an NGO with limited resources in a very difficult environment.

- A one-week workshop in 1994 with twelve Peruvian NGOs, facilitated by one of the authors. The theme of the workshop was project monitoring and evaluation, and it focused heavily on NGO evaluation methodology.

- A one-week seminar in Colombia organized by Misereor, which brought together NGOs from all over Latin America to focus on qualitative evaluation.

- A substantial evaluation undertaken by two external consultants of a twelve-year integrated rural development program in the district of Santa Barbara, Honduras. The program had been run by Save the Children–U.K. during this whole period, and a principal purpose of the evaluation was to try to assess what had been achieved.

- Internal reviews undertaken by two Brazilian NGOs in the northeast (Retome Su Vida and GAPA-Bahia). Both exercises took place about eighteen months after the beginning of the projects and concentrated on trying to assess whether, in broad terms, the projects were on the right track. An important aspect of these exercises was the involvement of a *companhero critico* (critical friend), an outside resource person whose key role is helping the project formulate its ideas and evaluate its work.

- An evaluation of the Integrated Rural Development Programme (PRONORTE) in Nicaragua, which was largely quantitative.

- An evaluation of the Caranavi Health Programme in Bolivia, in which the emphasis was placed on community involvement.

From these experiences, the following general observations can be made about the current state of evaluation among NGOs in Latin America.

The Context of Evaluation

The first question is, what aspects of NGO work in Latin America are being evaluated? In many instances, the evaluation process is concerned with small-scale, isolated projects without any linkages among them. Evaluation may also refer to the overall work of an NGO in a wider context and its capacity to establish a synergistic force in a local or national space—that is, its ability to mobilize and energize other social actors and to capitalize on this ability and broaden the impact of its activities. When an NGO manages to establish an institutional presence within society, the wider context is especially important.

In the case of small projects, evaluation is a relatively simple issue, a question of measuring the achievement of objectives and goals independent of the wider context. But when considering the effects of NGO work on the living conditions of the population, impact is much more difficult to measure. The issue of impact is currently one of the most widely debated among Latin American NGOs, but we have not yet found a way to measure the impact of an NGO on the life of a local group or on the national context more generally. Discussions of impact are often confused by a failure to specify whether it is being measured in terms of the NGO as an actor in development issues at a national or international level or in terms of the broader effect of the NGO's work on the livelihoods of the people with whom it works. Too often there is a feeling that the NGO itself is being evaluated rather than the work it undertakes. If the donor is content that the NGO as an institution is on the right track, then the assumption is that its project work must be equally sound.

The Approach to Evaluation

The harsh winds of cost-effectiveness, logical framework analysis, and "strategic thinking" have clearly buffeted Latin American NGOs over the past five years. In evaluation terms, the 1970s and 1980s were years of relative indulgence; the 1990s have brought new demands from a changing world of development assistance. There is no doubt that in earlier decades the dominant approach of Latin American NGOs to evaluation was interpretative—an emphasis on description, explaining change in a historical sense, and generally seeing evaluation as a people-centered, qualitative exercise. Increasingly fashionable (in fact, obligatory) these days is a more technocratic approach to evaluation based on clear objectives, measurement, targets, quantitative outcomes, and so on. The change in emphasis is perceptible, as are the agonies it has caused.

The meaning of the word "results" has been renegotiated, and Latin American NGOs are having to be more specific, tangible, and measurable in what they say they are going to achieve. Northern NGOs have led the way in all this, and, in the current order of things, the Latin American NGOs have had to "swim with the tide." But one senses national NGO's discomfort with this change; it is not an easy transition, and any reversal in thinking would probably be welcome.

Diagnosis and Systematization

The current evaluation vocabulary of Latin American NGOs is dominated by two words: *diagnostico* (diagnosis) and *sistematización* (systematization). It is almost impossible to avoid the substantial use of these two terms in any project evaluation process. The *diagnostico* (or situation analysis) is the bedrock of the whole exercise, the meticulous and detailed description and interpretation of the context in which the project is taking place. It is the key element in the evaluation litany, an exercise that must be undertaken before one can take a step forward. To suggest that there is no *diagnostico*, or at least an inadequate one, would stop an evaluation exercise dead in its tracks. Clearly the diagnostico is a critical element in any evaluation exercise. The issue is how much do we need to know before we move forward? Latin American NGOs tend to lean toward exhaustive situation analyses and eschew attempts at a "quick and dirty" approach.

Sistematización is undoubtedly the current favorite term of Latin American NGOs, and it is not easy to nail it down to any particular interpretation. *Sistematización* reflects an internal ordering and sequential interpretation of actions and activities. Supposedly, *sistematización* produces an effortless flow of information and analysis, allowing one to understand what is happening at any given moment. At present, *sistematización* in evaluation among Latin American NGOs lacks a common language and has a range of meanings. In terms of ordering and providing a focus, *sistematización* can give an evaluation exercise a clearer perspective and can help structure what is often a diffuse process. Yet *sistematización* sometimes appears to have no apparent direction or outcome; it can lead to continual invention and reinvention, and it is almost always difficult for an outsider to grasp its real character. But few evaluations in Latin America are currently launched without a commitment to systematize the whole activity.

Outdated Vocabulary

The development vocabulary of the 1960s and 1970s maintains an overwhelming presence in the theory and practice of Latin American intermediary NGOs. A conceptual veneer colors the way most NGOs see the world; it inevitably spills over into their work in evaluation, and NGOs are still struggling to come to grips with it. Awareness creation, human promotion, participation, and critical analysis, for example, are still fashionable concepts and form the bedrock of the conceptual perspective of many NGOs. Yet after over twenty-five years of promoting such concepts, Latin American NGOs still struggle to explain what these concepts mean in practice and how it is possible to understand their effects. There have been major leaps forward in terms of wrestling with qualitative notions of evaluation, but to date, the conceptual still dominates, and practical tools are lacking. There is little evidence, for example, of any substantial evaluation of the widespread use of *conscientización*. Curiously, Howard Richards's seminal text *The Evaluation of Cultural Action* (1985), based on such work in Chile, is perhaps more widely known and consulted outside of Latin America than within the region. It is important to recognize the major contribution that Latin American NGOs have made to the work of organizations in the region, but the pressure is mounting on NGOs to break through the conceptual barrier and begin to develop the practical tools at the project level that would explain the advances made in this critically important work.

The Evaluation Package

In terms of practical evaluation methodology, one tool that is common among Latin American NGOs is the "evaluation package." This package has no fixed content or single meaning, but the term is used to describe a fairly common approach to project evaluation among NGOs in the region. The variable elements in this package are as follows: it is an internal exercise; it can last up to four months; it is often "accompanied" in the sense that an external agent plays a facilitating role (see below); it is based largely on the analysis of verbal descriptions of work to date; and it takes place through a series of internal meetings in which the whole exercise is played out. It is an exhaustive and detailed approach that often becomes lost in a wealth of description and comment; it eschews the "quick and dirty" and seeks to leave no stone unturned. Eventually the process produces a report that is the base from which future actions move forward. The whole process reinforces the internal strengths of the project team and helps develop a common vision of where things are going. On the downside, as a single approach to project evaluation, it allows for little variation and often appears to be an exaggerated response to a stage in project evaluation that demands a faster and less complicated approach.

Accompanied Evaluation

Who evaluates and who is evaluated? Some NGOs in Latin America and their European partners are developing an evaluation system whose objective is to support the institutional development of the NGO. This system is called *evaluación acompañada* (accompanied evaluation). Within it, donor agencies analyze the institutional development of the NGO that is being evaluated, together with staff from the NGO itself. Equal importance is given to both sets of actors. Such a system requires a permanent dialogue and the examination of the common problems that arise between the partners, reinforced with specialized technical inputs when necessary. Rather than evaluating a project after it has finished, the "accompaniment" approach puts the most important questions on the table from the start. When the dialogue between donor and NGO, or between NGO and GRO, starts with an open discussion of their respective interests, the inevitable tensions that arise in the evaluation process can be managed more effectively. The Save the Children Fund– U.K. has employed this approach in Brazil, with the "critical friend," being a neutral outsider whose fundamental role is to support the project team and to serve as an independent point of contact between the team and SCF (Save the Children Fund 1994).

The issues raised and the comments made in this chapter do not come from an authoritative empirical study of NGOs in Latin America; they have been made after personal reflection on NGO evaluation activities in several countries over the past few years. It could be argued that most Latin American NGOs still find themselves in the conceptual circles of the 1960s and 1970s. As terms such as "accountability" and "evaluation" become common, this circle is not renegotiated, but strenuous efforts are made to incorporate the new terms within it. For some Latin American NGOs, accountability is framed in terms of society as a whole, not in terms of particular social organizations or sectors. Inevitably, however, the pressure is mounting to improve accountability at the program or project level.

Furthermore, given the explosion in the number of NGOs in the region in the 1980s, and the apparently tenuous relationship they appear to have with their supposed constituents, it is necessary to raise the question of NGO "legitimacy" (Pearce forthcoming). NGOs have concentrated on raising their profiles, building and playing a greater role in civil society, and developing contacts at the international level. But in the process, the interests that this "movement" is supposed to represent, its accountability to those it claims to speak for, and the real outcomes of its work are all too often relegated to a secondary position on the NGO agenda.

In summary (and though the evidence is not conclusive), Latin American NGOs have not evolved very significantly as a "species" since the 1960s and 1970s. The passion, the commitment, the macroanalysis, and the broad involvement in society are all there, and these elements continue to maintain their primacy despite the harder-edged and more critical world of accountability that lurks on the horizon. Perhaps this is not such a bad state of affairs; as actors in the broader social movements of Latin America, NGOs can point to substantial impact, at times, in countries such as Chile, Brazil, Nicaragua, and Bolivia (Lehmann 1990). But they still suffer from a genetic fault in terms of a propensity to exaggerate and a tendency to mount time-consuming and circular exercises when more discrete action would be more appropriate. In addition, the centers of power still tend to dominate: urban, middle class, and professional, speaking on behalf of the less powerful in the region.

But with all their faults, inconsistencies, and contradictions, and in comparison with the supposedly democratic governments of the region, we are convinced that legitimacy and accountability are being given more serious consideration on the agendas of Latin American NGOs today. The legitimacy of NGOs is being severely tested as their links with popular movements are weakened and have yet to be firmly established with new and emerging social groups. Furthermore, NGOs in Latin America, like their counterparts in other parts of the world, struggle in their own particular fashion to explain the effect and impact of their work. It is not difficult to pick holes in their practice, and it is important not to be complacent, but for all their inadequacies, NGOs in Latin America are the only real and viable agents of the social changes that are necessary to provide a better livelihood for the increasing millions who live in poverty in the region.

Note

1. NGOs are defined in this chapter as local intermediary organizations, not Northern NGOs or grassroots organizations. In most Latin American countries, the concept of an NGO refers to an institution formed by professional people (not always volunteers) who work on development, environmental, or human rights issues, frequently in support of GROs.

References

Bebbington, A., and R. Riddell. Forthcoming. New agendas, old problems: Governments, NGOs and myths about direct funding and civil society. In *Too close for comfort? NGOs, states and donors*, edited by D. Hulme and M. Edwards. London: Macmillan.

Carroll, T. 1992. *Intermediary NGOs: The supporting link in grassroots development*. West Hartford, Conn.: Kumarian Press.

El Taller. 1993. *Las ONGs Latinoamericanas frente a la situación actual*. Tunis: El Taller.

Hulme, D., and M. Edwards, eds. Forthcoming. *Too close for comfort? NGOs, states and donors*. London: Macmillan.

Lehmann, D. 1990. *Democracy and development in Latin America: Economics, politics and religion in the post-war period*. Philadelphia: Temple University Press.

Noriega, J., and M. Saravia. 1994. *Peru: Las organizaciones no gubernamentales*. Lima: Desco.

Pearce, J. Forthcoming. NGOs in Latin America: Accountability and legitimacy. In *Too close for comfort? NGOs, states and donors*, edited by D. Hulme and M. Edwards. London: Macmillan.

Richards, H. 1985. *The evaluation of cultural action*. London: Macmillan.

Save the Children Fund. 1994. *Relatorio de aviliacao do projeto Retome Su Vida*. Recife: Save the Children Fund–U.K.

UNDP. 1993. *Human development report*. New York: UNDP.

7

Accountability and Participation

A Case Study from Bombay

Vandana Desai and Mick Howes

This chapter reviews the experience of Apnalaya—an organization working in the slums of Bombay—as a means of testing a number of general propositions about the nature and determinants of NGO accountability under the New Policy Agenda. The first section summarizes the broad themes to be explored. The second provides a brief overview of the organization and its work. This is followed by a more detailed exploration of the activities undertaken and the forms of accountability associated with each one. In a concluding section, we return to the propositions outlined at the beginning of the chapter to ask how relevant they are in light of Apnalaya's experience, and what implications they might hold for the future. The main thrust of our argument is that the New Policy Agenda has begun to impinge upon what Apnalaya does, and that some of its implications are indeed negative. At the same time, we aim to show how pressure for greater accountability can, if responded to in particular ways, be converted into a force for positive change.

The Problem of Accountability

In the introduction and in Chapter 13, it is suggested that the ways in which NGOs presently account for what they do have a number of inadequacies. Reporting of performance tends to focus on the achievement of immediate outputs and only rarely delves into the longer-term and more fundamental effects and impacts with which NGOs are supposed to be especially concerned.[1] Attention is restricted mainly to "functional" accountability to the exclusion of the "strategic"—that is, to what is happening at the level of individual projects as opposed to the achievement of wider programmatic goals (Avina 1993). As Edwards and Hulme stated in the introduction, accountability is generally interpreted as "the means by which . . . organizations report [upward] to a recognized authority . . . and are held responsible for their actions," with insufficient attention directed "downward" to the views of intended beneficiaries.

These difficulties stem, at least in part, from the fact that, unlike governments (which must submit themselves for periodic reelection) or businesses (which must make profits in order to survive), NGOs have no readily acknowledged "bottom line" against which performance can be measured. This is made worse by the tendency for the broad social goals that NGOs set for themselves to be influenced by a wide range of factors beyond their control, making it hard to attribute causation or apportion credit or blame for any changes that may occur. Furthermore, unlike civil servants, who must report to government and be available for cross-examination in committee, NGOs generally have no one particular body to which they are accountable or any single mechanism through which they may be brought to account.

An already difficult situation is complicated further by the increasing support NGOs are now receiving from governments and official aid agencies. The types of activities that these official bodies have conventionally supported, and the hierarchical structures that have arisen to administer them, embody a view of development as an essentially linear and predictable enterprise. This is at variance with the far more contingent and unpredictable "open-system" world perceived and inhabited by NGOs. Imposed systems of accountability deriving from "linear" worldviews, with targets and sanctions to be imposed in the event of nonachievement, reinforce other pressures for NGOs to transform themselves into routine service providers, reducing in the process their capacity to explore new ideas or to tackle the more deep-seated and intractable problems of institutional development. It may therefore be that the economic dimension of the New Policy Agenda now being pursued by the major aid donors conflicts with, and may ultimately supersede, the political objective of promoting wider participation, stronger democratic institutions, and a more vibrant civil society.

Apnalaya: The Organization and Its Work

Apnalaya was founded in 1972 to provide day care to children in one small part of Bombay and has grown into an organization that works with slum dwellers in five different areas. Although building most of its activities around a core competence as an innovator in the development of health and educational services, it has, from the outset, adopted a nondirective or participatory community development approach, based on the principle of working with local organizations to identify and act on people's own priorities. Experience on the ground reveals no one distinctive model but rather a series of initiatives that reflect the expertise of the organization and the distinctive needs of the people with whom it works. Drawing on its direct experience with communities, Apnalaya has sought to build a distinctive role as a provider of training to other NGOs and government organizations and as a source of ideas that it disseminates through networks and other forums. It does not see itself as a provider of services per se and takes on operational involvements only as a means of keeping in touch with realities "on the ground."

Apnalaya (which means "sharing") was founded by an Australian diplomat and has benefited from the active involvement and encouragement of an English social worker who is resident in the city. But from the outset, it has been an Indian-run organization that has only occasionally received foreign financial support and draws its primary inspiration from Indian rather than international sources. A number of formative influences have helped make it what it is today. In the early years, Apnalaya sought out the experiences of innovative health and education programs, and these were to prove highly significant in shaping subsequent developments. The work of the Foundation for Research in Community Health and the educational experiments of Anutai Wagh were of particular importance in this regard. Academic contacts at the Urban and Rural Community Development Department at the Tata Institute of Social Sciences played an important part in identifying models and exploring how they could be adapted to urban conditions. The department has also supplied several of Apnalaya's professional social workers. Apnalaya now employs fifty-five people, including a core of professional social workers and a larger body of paraprofessionals, community-based workers, and other helpers recruited mainly from within the slums themselves. More than 75 percent of the staff, including the director, are women, but the organization has not embraced an overtly feminist agenda.

Money is raised from a variety of sources. Individual donations and contributions from charitable trusts have proved particularly important, helping Apnalaya to build a substantial corpus, which has tided the organization over during its periodic financial crises. Some support is received from the central and municipal government, a portion of which derives ultimately from international donors. Funds may also be channeled from official sources through specialist NGO funding bodies. The underlying trend has been for annual income and expenditures to rise steadily, although often with large annual variations: total expenditures for 1994 were estimated at 1.5 million rupees, or approximately US$45,000.

The diverse influences that have shaped Apnalaya, the different ways in which it is funded, its nondirective approach, and the relative informality that remains possible in a small organization have all combined to produce a rather fluid structure. Of late, this has given rise to a certain amount of internal dissatisfaction, with staff sometimes becoming frustrated by a lack of clarity in their roles. The system that has now evolved approximates a matrix structure. This is built around five geographically defined community development projects and four

cross-cutting activity-based programs covering early childhood education, drug prevention and rehabilitation, training, and AIDS awareness
and prevention. The location and the close association of some of the
programs with individual project offices mean, however, that a clear distinction between the two is sometimes difficult to maintain.

As indicated earlier, Apnalaya now operates in a number of different
locations, but its greatest challenge and largest input have been at Shivaji
Nagar, where it first started work in 1976. Built on low-lying and poorly
drained land in a peripheral area of Bombay, this is a sprawling slum
that is home to approximately 300,000 people relocated from slums in
other parts of the city over the past thirty years. The area suffers from a
range of problems. Infrastructure is rudimentary. Health care provision
is poor, and infant mortality rates are unusually high. With the exception of a small number of households with relatives in the Gulf, living
standards are generally low, with most people depending for their
livelihoods on a range of poorly paid casual or informal-sector jobs,
including pulling rickshaws, operating handcarts, and selling vegetables.
Tensions exist between the Muslim majority, who make up some two-
thirds of the population, and the Hindu and other smaller minorities.
Communal institutions are fragmented and generally weak, and there is
a high level of criminal activity. Together with the sheer size of the slum,
these factors combine to produce a challenge of a quite different magni-
tude from that which Apnalaya confronts elsewhere. Nothing approach-
ing the comprehensive delivery of services to all households—which can
be contemplated at its other, much smaller sites—is feasible.

Activities and Mechanisms for Functional Accountability

How then does Apnalaya account for what it does? In addressing this
question, we focus mainly on what happens at Shivaji Nagar, the project
that encompasses the broadest range of activities, including all the cross-
cutting programs. As the location that poses the most severe challenge,
Shivaji Nagar provides the most demanding test of Apnalaya's capacity
to account for its activities. We look first at the system of accounting for
individual activities, discussing them in the order in which they arose
historically.[2]

Community Development

Work began with broad-based community development initiatives
designed to help young people organize themselves into a youth group.
Then began the process of identifying the form that projects should take.
With support provided by the Tata Institute for Social Sciences, initial
emphasis was given to management and leadership training. A number

of initiatives followed in areas such as drug and alcohol abuse, which in turn laid the foundations for some of the developments described below.

These and subsequent activities centered around a building provided, at a nominal rent, by the Bombay Municipal Corporation (BMC). This building is maintained by community members and was extended in the 1980s using community labor and the support of local contractors. Additional building costs, the salaries of social workers and other staff, and a range of other expenses have, for the last three years, been covered by a grant from the Housing Development Finance Corporation (HDFC), an independent body established to address housing needs in the city. BMC does not require Apnalaya to account for what it does in the building, but the organization is dependent on BMC's continuing goodwill and therefore occasionally sends in written reports of its activities, which are usually not acknowledged. HDFC requires light quarterly reporting and provides limited feedback, indicating whether it is satisfied or not. HDFC staff are also invited to attend events organized under the project, where they have the opportunity to meet beneficiaries and find out for themselves what is going on.

Education

Following from the early community development work, the next major initiative to be undertaken involved the establishment of three preschools run by women teachers recruited from the community and provided with training. The schools cater to about thirty children each. They are also used as teacher training and support centers under the early childhood education program, which services other preschools in the area. Apnalaya's schools use the community development center and therefore do not have to pay rent. Teachers' salaries and materials were previously covered by fees, but parents' incomes have fallen behind general increases in wage inflation and are now sufficient to meet only the cost of materials. Salaries are covered under the HDFC grant, and an NGO funding agency known as Child Relief and You (CRY) funds the training program.

Apnalaya provides a quarterly report covering enrollment and attendance rates on the schools it runs itself, and organizations sending trainees supported by CRY to Apnalaya courses are also obliged to report on their progress. Over and above this, Apnalaya is planning an evaluation study to ascertain the degree of success achieved by its former trainees in other schools. This will go some way toward satisfying a perceived need within the organization to move beyond the rather narrow and exclusively quantitative forms of assessment required by funders.

In addition, parents of preschool children are invited to monthly meetings to hear about what has been going on in the school, to receive the results of medical checks that may have been carried out, and to raise any matters that concern them. These meetings are generally well attended, although parents feel constrained from offering substantive comments by their lack of knowledge of the education system.

Drug Abuse

Most of the drug abuse work in Shivaji Nagar is preventive, and the salary and other expenses that this entails are covered by Apnalaya's general funds.[3] Over and above this, counseling services for addicts and their families are provided in a room that is made available without charge by the BMC in its nearby Urban Health Centre. As is the case with the main building, there is no formal reporting requirement, but Apnalaya sends an annual letter and report. Apnalaya also runs a day-care center at Malad to which addicts from Shivaji Nagar and other locations may be referred. In addition to the salaries of the four staff members, a number of other costs are incurred. For some time, all these costs, together with the costs of counseling services, were covered by a central government grant. However, this was conditional on treating thirty people at a time, a target that had been set without visiting the premises, which had the capacity to deal effectively with only fifteen. Various other conditions were imposed that required Apnalaya to depart from well-tried procedures, and when these were not complied with, the grant was withdrawn, obliging the organization to draw on its corpus fund to keep the center running. This is one of a small but potentially important number of instances in which attempts to tighten accountability have failed. Its wider significance is discussed in the final section of this chapter.

Riot Relief

The riots that engulfed Bombay in 1992 and 1993 confronted Apnalaya with a completely new situation—one that was to exert a powerful influence over its future development.[4] Riots were at their most intense in Shivaji Nagar, where many lives were lost, large numbers of people suffered injuries, housing was destroyed, and livelihoods were seriously affected. Nearly all the victims were Muslims. Apnalaya, supported by the Tata Institute and other voluntary organizations, was able to draw upon its contacts and local knowledge to make a critical contribution to the relief and rehabilitation work.

In the immediate aftermath, hundreds of people were treated at emergency clinics. Cases of missing people were followed up, assistance was provided in identifying the dead, and counseling was offered to victims' families and to others who had been traumatized. Food, fuel, blankets, and other necessities were distributed. As a first step in the process of rehabilitation, Apnalaya coordinated the initial collection of data on loss of life, injury, damage to property, and prospective police cases, which were then processed by the Tata Institute and submitted to the relevant authorities. In the absence of any official provision, a special loan scheme was set up in consultation with local representatives to restart small businesses; a similar channel was established for the replacement of housing and for other forms of economic rehabilitation. Assistance was provided in the preparation of a large number of claims for compensation. Efforts were made to restore relations with the police.

These activities involved Apnalaya in the receipt and channeling of funds from a diversity of government, NGO, and other sources, for which it accounted collectively after the event. Two important effects followed from the riots. The first was a reinvigoration of Apnalaya's community development work, with a number of new initiatives launched to strengthen local groups and promote harmony by bringing people together to work on common problems such as tuberculosis control, drug abuse, and HIV and AIDS awareness.

Health

The second major effect of the riots was to bring the organization into contact with residents of a particularly disadvantaged part of the slum for the first time. This provided the impetus for a new initiative involving the establishment of a clinic offering immunizations, prenatal and more general medical care, and the training of community-level health workers, who have now started to engage in a wider range of preventive activities. Salaries and training costs are covered under a grant administered by SOSVA (another NGO support agency) under a central government program funded by the U.S. Agency for International Development (USAID). Vitamins and vaccines are supplied mainly by the BMC. The bulk of the medicines required are provided by Concern (an international NGO). Other trusts and pharmaceutical companies make smaller contributions. User charges cover the balance, which amounts to some 40 percent of the total cost. The SOSVA grant is tightly regulated, with specific targets being imposed for different areas of work: for example, ten children per 1,000 population have to be immunized each year, and similar goals have been set for family planning work. These objectives have proved difficult to measure, and the data are time-consuming to compile. Performance has to be reported and discussed at quarterly meetings with SOSVA, where the difficulties encountered have been raised: thus far, the government has offered no response.

In return for its support, BMC expects regular indications of the number of people treated, which it then includes in its own reports as if it had supplied the services directly. Apnalaya points out that this is not a meaningful indicator, since the success of a primary health care program should be measured by a reduction, not an increase, in the number of people presenting themselves for treatment. In the mean-time, Apnalaya has been recording its own impressions of the benefits arising from its intervention, a form of monitoring that it finds more meaningful than that required by official bodies. For example, people now come forward voluntarily for immunization where previously they had to be rounded up; they now tend to complete a course rather than dropping out midway; and weaning practices have been improving in response to the advice offered.

Strategic Accountability

Three formal mechanisms are used by Apnalaya to satisfy account-ability "upward." The first is the annual report on expenditures that has to be made to the Indian Charity Commissioners. This is complied with, but no feedback is ever received. The second is the obligation to report every three years to the Income Tax Department in order to obtain the certificate that gives a 50 percent tax exemption to anybody providing the organization with financial support. These are largely regulatory pro-cedures, designed to ensure that the organization engages only in activities that are consistent with its charitable status; they do not require that a *strategic* view be taken of its work. The third mechanism is provided by Apnalaya's own board of trustees. This is a two-tiered body consisting of a group of appointed members that, in turn, elects an executive committee. In the early years, there were as many as thirty members, but the number has now been reduced to fewer than ten, nearly all of whom are active as volunteers in the day-to-day running of the organization. The president, for example, is currently one of the doc-tors working on a health project.

Formally, the committee meets quarterly to review expenditures, fund-ing, new activities, and any problems that have arisen. In practice, and in keeping with the nondirective style of Apnalaya as a whole, most busi-ness is transacted at weekly meetings attended by senior staff and committee members, or even more informally through the day-to-day contacts that take place. In Tandon's terms (see Chapter 3), this is not an "invisible" board, but neither is it a "professional" one. It is a hybrid of Tandon's "family" and "staff" types, with the typical combination of strengths and weaknesses they embody. The practical consequence is that the board does not really require the organization to take a strategic view of its overall portfolio of activities and programs either.

Although there is no strong pressure for strategic accountability com-ing from above, Apnalaya argues that the merits of alternative initiatives and courses of action are actively reviewed "from below." It holds monthly meetings for parents and has a number of more informal channels to communicate with the groups it serves. The willingness of consumers of educational and health services to assume at least part of the cost introduces an element of market discipline. The fact that a high proportion of staff is recruited from the communities served keeps the organization in touch with what people really want. Perhaps most importantly, Apnalaya's determination to strengthen local institutions that can articulate and participate in the satisfaction of needs should in itself ensure that proper account is taken of local views.

All these arguments are valid, but a residual concern remains. Apnalaya's nondirective approach means that the organization must be on its guard to avoid becoming a mirror image of the community it seeks to serve, with all the class, gender, ethnic, and other inequalities this embodies. Apnalaya is alert to this danger and works hard to circumvent existing power structures wherever it can. Inevitably, however, compromises have to be made, and to this extent, the ideal of full downward accountability cannot be attained. It is also true that accountability mechanisms operate only at the level of individual project locations and do not encompass the entire spread of the organization's work.

An Assessment of Apnalaya's Accountability System

Taken as a whole, what are the key features of Apnalaya's accountability system, and to what extent do they conform with the expectations reviewed in the introductory section of this chapter?

Principle and Practice

It is obvious from discussions with staff that the organization is strongly in favor of the principle of greater accountability, and its record appears strong compared with that of other NGOs. There are clearly identifiable mechanisms in place for the majority of the activities in which it engages. Although some of these are externally imposed, there is a clear willingness to go beyond formal requirements and seek alternative indicators when those available fail to reflect the true significance of what is being attempted. A fairly high degree of accountability has been achieved despite the fact that no outside evaluations have ever been carried out and the organization has been under relatively little external pressure. However, this is not to suggest that all the difficulties anticipated in the literature on accountability have been avoided.

Determining Longer-Term Impact

Apnalaya appears to be vulnerable to the criticism that it focuses too heavily on immediate outputs in its reporting, to the exclusion of longer-term effects and impacts. This may not matter much in relation to certain aspects of health and education, where longer-term consequences can be difficult to trace and where (for example) the numbers of children enrolled in schools or receiving immunizations may provide reasonable proxies for desired outcomes. But in other areas, it would certainly be desirable to explore further down the chain of causes and effects than is presently the case. Apnalaya itself recognizes this shortcoming in relation to its teacher training program. A similar course of action may well be appropriate with regard to the strengthening of institutions in Shivaji Nagar and elsewhere, where the demonstrable success of some groups in generating new activities needs to be set against the (currently unknown) number that have fallen by the wayside. Data on inputs to particular activities are also hard to come by and would greatly strengthen Apnalaya's capacity to analyze its work. Given the complexity of what Apnalaya is attempting, the presence of other agencies offering overlapping services, and the volatility of the environment in which it operates, it may be difficult to prove success conclusively, but the easier task of demonstrating that it has not failed in key areas would in itself represent a considerable improvement on the present state of affairs.

Taking a Strategic View and Accounting "Downward"

The earlier discussion of Apnalaya's activities showed how the organization takes on the views of those with whom it works. The small size of the organization and the ease with which senior staff can visit project locations are also important contributory factors here. At the same time, strategic accountability at best operates only at the level of what is happening in individual project locations. Equally important is the capacity to define core operational competence or determine what can be supported most cost-effectively; to decide whether to consolidate in existing locations or expand to new ones; and to determine the optimal balance between operational, training, and wider opinion-forming work. In these areas, Apnalaya is weaker, though this may simply reflect the lack of a clear "bottom line" or ultimate authority to whom it must account.

Negative Implications of the New Policy Agenda

The implications of the New Policy Agenda are more difficult to evaluate, since Apnalaya has been partially insulated by its unusual capacity to raise private funds locally. But to the extent that Apnalaya *has* been exposed to new trends, its experience clearly confirms the negative consequences anticipated in the literature. This is particularly apparent in some of its dealings with government, where demands for information are increasing rapidly. Given the relative shortage of reporting skills within the organization, these demands are now beginning to constitute a serious burden on managers. An already difficult situation is exacerbated by the imposition of unattainable targets without prior consultation, in a fashion that suggests the continuation of traditional bureaucratic high-handedness, with only the most superficial commitment to enhancing the performance of those receiving resources (see the example of the clinics described earlier). This impression is reinforced by the widespread tendency of officialdom to offer no response to the information it receives. The likely long-term result is that reporting will become a mechanical exercise devoid of real meaning or purpose. In the words of one member of the organization, "reporting is like throwing messages in bottles into the sea—you never know if anyone is reading them or not." Put in slightly different terms, there is a danger that the economic dimension of the New Policy Agenda will be subverted by the existing hierarchies and authority structures through which it is filtered, with the end result that energy drains away at the grassroots level rather than being generated and focused in the fashion that was intended. Criticisms that NGOs are insufficiently accountable "downward" pale into insignificance when compared with the performance of official bodies.

The Sustainability Problem

These difficulties are exacerbated by a desire among donors to achieve "sustainability," which translates into an unwillingness to commit resources for anything more than a three- to five-year period. Although Apnalaya also wishes to achieve self-sufficiency, circumstances conspire against this objective and the "linear" view of development on which it rests. This has been apparent in attempts to recover costs in preschool education and health activities, both of which ultimately foundered as a result of an unanticipated deterioration in the wider economic circumstances of intended "customers." The system adopted by CRY in its support for preschool teacher training recognizes these problems of targeting and linearity. Indicators are agreed on, not imposed, and no rigid targets are enforced. This is far more sensible when so much uncertainty surrounds the outcome of any undertaking. The relatively light reporting of the type encouraged by the HDFC and used quite widely in other areas of Apnalaya's work seems similarly appropriate.

New Directions

Our research suggests two broad conclusions. The first is to confirm that the effects of the New Policy Agenda are indeed potentially perverse. The second is that, even if such an agenda did not exist, it would still be in the interests of the organization (and those whom it seeks to serve) to review and improve its accountability mechanisms. The need for repositioning that the New Policy Agenda imposes on NGOs can thus, at least to some extent, be turned into a positive opportunity. But for this to happen, innovations in accountability are required at both functional and strategic levels.

At the functional level, it is important to recognize that Apnalaya is engaged in several types of activities and that different forms of accountability may be required for each one: institutional development work should be distinguished from the development and delivery of services. The former, as embodied in Apnalaya's attempts to strengthen local groups and build effective leadership, can be assessed only partially by itself; to a large extent, it rests on the level and types of other activity generated. With service provision, it is also necessary to separate activities that address known and predictable problems from those provided under unstable conditions (such as riot relief), where only light forms of reporting could reasonably be expected. A further distinction should be made between mature services, where it is legitimate to require that targets be set in advance, and those such as HIV and AIDS services, which are experimental. In the latter, relevant criteria for assessment can be developed only as the process unfolds. Mature services should be further subdivided into those (such as preschools—at least under earlier economic circumstances) in which the capacity to recover costs from users provides an indication of relevance and success, and those (such as primary health care) in which a heavy element of subsidy is likely to be involved. Finally, over and above any attempt to assess what Apnalaya is doing "on the ground," provision needs to be made to review its performance in influencing the behavior of others through its training and opinion-forming work.

Strategic Change

Developing a range of mechanisms tailored to the requirements of these different functions would help create a genuine system of accountability in place of the patchy provision that currently exists. This could then pave the way for a second and more strategic set of initiatives that would support the changes taking place at the functional level. Externally, this might entail the appointment of a more professional and active board for Apnalaya. Internally, it might be desirable to create clearer roles in research, policy, and information. For an organization that has been in existence for twenty-four years and that regards itself as being in the business of disseminating ideas, Apnalaya has committed little to paper. The creation of a specialist position of this kind would make it possible to draw together, and make more accessible, the wealth of ideas presently stored in individual diaries and other forms throughout the organization. While helping Apnalaya to improve its overall effectiveness, such changes would also enable the organization to project an image more in keeping with present orthodoxies. A certain amount might have to be sacrificed in the process, but such an initiative would be likely to gain Apnalaya the space and support it requires to preserve its core values of innovation in response to the expressed needs of those it seeks to serve.

Notes

Apnalaya is one of the case studies from Vandana Desai's research on urban NGO effectiveness and from Mick Howes's project on NGOs and the development of grassroots institutions. Both are funded by the Economic and Social Committee on Research of the U.K. Overseas Development Administration, to which thanks are due. We are also grateful to the staff and associates of Apnalaya for their cooperation, their willingness to talk openly, and their comments on the draft of this chapter. The views expressed and any errors, however, remain entirely our own responsibility.

1. The notion of a sequence leading from inputs, through outputs, to effects and impacts (see Casley and Lury 1982, 2–30) provides a useful starting point for thinking about questions of accountability but is, at the same time, subject to the criticism of "linear" development models discussed a little later.
2. This part of the discussion draws heavily on Apnalaya (1994a, 1994b).
3. This part of the discussion draws on Mehta and Ganega (1992).
4. This account paraphrases Apnalaya (1993).

References

Apnalaya. 1993. *Relief and rehabilitation work undertaken in Shivaji Nagar, Govandi, during December 1992 and January 1993*. Mimeo. Bombay: Apnalaya.

Apnalaya. 1994a. *Background and philosophy* (mimeo). Bombay: Apnalaya.

Apnalaya. 1994b. *Report for the year 1993–94* (mimeo). Bombay: Apnalaya.

Avina, J. 1993. The evolutionary life-cycle of non-governmental development organisations. *Public Administration and Development*, 13(5):453–74.

Casley, D. J., and D. A. Lury. 1982. *Monitoring and evaluation of rural and agricultural development projects*. Baltimore: John Hopkins University Press.

Mehta, A., and S. Ganega. 1992. Apnalaya. In *Drug abuse demand reduction: Focus on community based approaches*, edited by V. Nadkarni. Bombay: Tata Institute of Social Sciences.

Strategies for Monitoring and Accountability

The Working Women's Forum Model

Janaki Ramesh

Empowering women and enabling them to succeed in their daily struggle for survival is a mammoth task way beyond the scope of individuals or organizations, even very large ones. Only through the concerted efforts of mass-based women's movements can the discrimination that women suffer in spite of their hard work and invaluable contributions to national economies the world over be challenged. Today, it is imperative that governmental efforts to promote the well-being of women and uplift their status be supplemented by NGOs. One such movement that has grown into one of the largest NGOs in the developing world is the Working Women's Forum (WWF) of India. This chapter explores the monitoring and evaluation strategies adopted by the WWF to measure its performance and ensure its accountability to its members, donors, the government, and society as a whole.

WWF Activities

The WWF was established in 1978 in Madras as a grassroots union of poor working women. The WWF was never a social service organization providing welfare services to the poor. From its inception, its main strategy has been not to help but to empower poor women and enable them to challenge the existing exploitative and oppressive power structures in society. The first activities of the forum centered on the provision of credit facilities to poor women in urban slums. In 1980, the scope of the WWF's activities was broadened to include the provision of health and family welfare services and training and advocacy programs. What started as a union of about 800 women has grown into an organization of over 200,000 members in the three southern states of Tamil Nadu, Andhra Pradesh, and Karnataka.[1] Efforts are under way to extend its outreach to other states, including Orissa and Bihar.

The WWF is characterized by its grassroots orientation and feminist approach, by the promotion of leadership among poor working women, and by its large-scale outreach. As a movement, its purpose goes beyond material assistance to raising awareness and promoting collective action for social change. As a recent independent evaluation report concludes, "it is a mature organization with credibility and recognition at the community level" (United Nations Fund for Population Activities [UNFPA] 1994). The activities of the forum fall into three main categories: credit, family welfare services, and training. Credit services are provided under the auspices of the Indian Cooperative Network for Women (a national cooperative), but the other two components are implemented directly by the WWF. A dedicated band of health workers, drawn from the grassroots, is specially trained to cater to the health and family welfare needs of the community. The training and research division of the WWF, staffed by target group research investigators (TGRIs) and headed by the director, is engaged in the continual training of members, research on the impact of the forum's development work on the lives of members, and the creation of new strategies and programs for their benefit.

In the credit program of the Indian Cooperative Society for Women, all beneficiaries become shareholders of the society. The disbursement of loans to groups of individuals rather than to individual members brings an element of peer pressure to bear on repayment. The whole group is blacklisted if a single member makes a default in the repayment schedule. Making beneficiaries into shareholders increases their interest in the performance of the credit society, since they have a real stake in its survival.

The organizers employed by the WWF are previous beneficiaries of the credit program, and they are entrusted with the task of identifying and evaluating the repayment capacity of potential beneficiaries. The organizers, who are allotted specific geographical areas, recommend deserving cases to the cooperative society's staff. The society's staff then conducts inspections of the work sites of the potential borrowers, formed into groups by area, to appraise the creditworthiness of the applicants. Only after the staff is satisfied are the loans disbursed. Each group elects one member to be the leader, who is entrusted with the responsibility of ensuring the prompt repayment of loan installments and receives a larger loan as an incentive. This form of decentralized monitoring ensures the continual success of the credit program, despite a phenomenal growth in size (see Table 8.1). Income from loans and deposits fully covers the program's direct operating costs and 69 percent of its total operating and financial costs, a significant achievement in itself (UNFPA 1994, 20).

The element of peer pressure in the group serves to ensure prompt repayment and is also an effective monitoring system. The repayment rate of 98 percent achieved by the cooperative in 1994 is proof of the effectiveness of its monitoring methods. The organizers monitor not only credit repayments but also the use to which each loan is put—whether it is used for productive purposes, to further the business, or for other

Table 8.1 Statistics for WWF Credit Program, 1994

Place	No. of Members in WWF	No. of Loans	Loan Amount Disbursed	Outstanding Loan Amount	Recoverable Loan Outstanding (%)	Bad-Debt Amount (%)	Recovery Percentage
Madras (Tamil Nadu)							
South	64,910	47,589	25,072,898	2,217,398	340,469 (1.36)	272,400 (1.08)	97.56
Rural Tamil Nadu							
Adiramapattinam	27,842	27,582	10,644,800	1,951,560	118,050 (1.11)	148,200 (1.39)	97.50
Dindigul	25,150	25,048	9,894,200	3,286,195	80,700 (0.81)	44,300 (0.75)	98.44
Vellore	22,409	22,154	9,187,600	1,521,181	98,700 (1.07)	200,700 (2.27)	96.66
Kanchipuram	13,641	10,601	11,134,200	4,465,104	86,400 (0.77)	97,300 (0.87)	98.36
Dharmapuri	1,626	1,238	521,200	408,800	—	—	100.00
Karnataka							
Bangalore	30,074	22,636	8,945,800	2,385,600	270,700 (3.02)	115,300 (1.29)	95.69
Chennadaana	7,400	7,177	2,353,535	4,211,410	24,300 (1.03)	22,400 (0.95)	98.02
Bidar	15,520	15,043	4,761,000	488,022	108,200 (2.27)	28,600 (0.60)	97.13
Bellary	1,736	1,371	420,887	74,641	—	—	—
Andhra Pradesh							
West Godavari	44,649	44,144	15,351,400	1,201,600	19,400 (0.13)	9,400 (0.06)	99.81
East Godavari	14,176	14,366	4,924,600	844,320	4,200 (0.08)	4,300 (0.08)	99.84
Bnimavaram	11,761	11,619	4,146,100	803,600	2,500 (0.06)	1,100 (0.03)	99.91
Palakol	8,087	7,905	2,463,300	849,800	6,200 (0.25)	2,800 (0.10)	99.64
Total	288,989	258,173	109,821,520	24,709,231	1,129,819 (1.00)	946,800 (0.79)	98.47

Amounts are given in Indian rupees.

purposes. A WWF survey of 500 members in Kanchipuram indicated that many had increased their incomes by between 100 and 200 rupees per month (the target is 300 rupees). Loans have enabled women to lessen their dependence on moneylenders and gain more control over assets, such as houses in their own names. However, some are still unable to pay off their largest debts (such as freeing their children from bonded labor, which requires a lump sum of 2,000 to 3,000 rupees); the small size of loans poses a real problem in this respect (UNFPA 1994, 15).

Accountability

Using decentralized monitoring, grassroots involvement in planning, and staff who come from the communities in which they work, the WWF has managed to preserve "downward" accountability and retain its effectiveness despite rapid program growth. Administrative costs have been kept below 15 percent of the total budget throughout its history and are covered increasingly by membership fees and interest on loans. The forum made a decision early on to limit its external funding sources and maximize income from its own members, thus reducing the time and energy required to meet the demands of multiple donors and preventing the WWF from being stretched in too many directions at once. It has never allowed foreign funds to compromise the ultimate objective of empowerment (UNFPA 1994).

The organizational structure of the WWF has itself contributed to the success of its monitoring strategies and the maintenance of accountability. The forum adopts a bottom-up approach, wherein planning, implementation, and monitoring emanate from the grassroots. Plans are not formulated at the top of the hierarchy and thrust onto members. Rather, the members are involved at every stage of project formulation from inception onward, so that all programs reflect and fulfill their needs. Except for the president and a few others, the forum's staff are all members of grassroots communities, and all are sensitive to people's needs and expectations. The president retains overall supervisory control only, leaving project implementation to the members themselves.

The research and training division of the forum is engaged in conducting training programs to increase members' awareness of their rights and responsibilities. On becoming members of the WWF, women participate in a one-day training program in which they learn about the goals and programs of the forum, the functioning of the credit society, and a host of other related matters. Training is a precondition for access to credit. Effective accountability requires an honest statement of goals. The training helps apprise members of the intended goals of the forum, which can then be questioned, debated, and monitored more closely. Such training is not a one-time effort but a continual process. Leadership training is also organized for the group leaders. WWF staff undertake research to evaluate the impact of these training programs and (when required) refresher training is provided.

The general body of the WWF (comprising all members) meets periodically at forum headquarters both for review and for making policy decisions. Participatory decision-making processes ensure transparency and honest reporting about resource allocation and objective appraisal of achievements. This facilitates transparent judgment of whether the results achieved are satisfactory and provides a concrete mechanism for holding those responsible to account for their performance. Partnership, reciprocity, transparency, and independence are hallmarks of the forum. The general body elects a standing committee from within its own ranks every three years, which is then responsible for planning and managing all WWF programs. Credit groups have access to the forum's overall agenda through their area organizers, who relay any concerns to WWF staff or through the general body. Any disputes are referred to the standing committee.

Accountability in the Credit Program

The books of accounts that are maintained at the society office also help in the effective monitoring of loan repayment and in highlighting any discrepancies that may arise. These books also serve to maintain the WWF's accountability to the Indian government and to its donors. An independent evaluation team from UNFPA also visited WWF in 1992 and made its report public.

As stated above, all beneficiaries are made shareholders of the cooperative. They are required to hold shares to the extent of 10 percent of the loan obtained. Thus, when a larger loan is secured, shareholding also increases. Interest is charged on the loan at the rate of 18 percent. Coupled with the money received as share capital, this provides a capital base for the society to function independently of the funds provided by donors. The members are conscientious in repaying the loans because they want more of their community to benefit from the society's credit program. WWF organizers serve as a link between the forum and the beneficiaries and help maintain its accountability to members by virtue of belonging to the same community.

The functioning of the credit society is streamlined and its procedures simplified in order to facilitate the involvement of women who are largely illiterate. No forms have to be filled out (staff do this instead), and no security is demanded except for the personal security of the borrower herself. The credit program revolves around the economic empowerment of women so that they can help themselves. The government also conducts a periodic audit of the books of accounts of the cooperative, which furthers accountability to the authorities. The cooperative is supervised by a board of directors composed of share-holders and elected by them once every three years. Women from the grassroots level are thereby represented at the board level.

Accountability in the Health Program

WWF health workers who implement the family welfare project are also drawn from the community and receive training from the forum's training division and specialists in the field to enable them to function effectively. They are familiar with ground-level realities and tend to be more accepted by the community, since community members are able to relate more effectively to and accept the advice of one of their own. Members know and relate to WWF staff *personally.* As role models, they gain the trust of other women, who see them as "sisters" (UNFPA 1994, 12). Because they live in and come from the same community, WWF workers can be held accountable directly (though often informally) if anything goes wrong. The personal—rather than formal—relationships between members and workers have been a major factor in the success of the program as a whole.

The health workers maintain registers containing details of all the families living in their allotted areas (family planning methods adopted, immunization schedules, and so on). These records, combined with monthly review meetings at the forum office, provide for effective monitoring of the project (see Table 8.2). Problems faced by the workers in their areas are discussed and collective solutions arrived at. Periodic project advisory committee meetings also review project implementation.

Case Studies

The value of the WWF's activities to women, and the impact of grassroots-level monitoring and accountability in promoting effectiveness on a large scale, are illustrated in the following case studies.

Vijayarani, a health worker in Trustpuram, notes: "When I first went and visited the slum households for a survey, the people asked whether I had come to give them free gifts or ration cards. Men used to tease me and ask if I could do anything about the blocked drainage which was causing a lot of health hazards. To earn their goodwill, I engaged two persons as helpers and cleaned the drainage and asked the local municipal office to send corporation workers to remove the garbage. This incident evoked a great amount of support for my work in the neighborhood."

Likewise, Tulasi, a health worker in Vellore, notes: "Because they live in a squatter settlement, all the occupants in my service area were asked to

Table 8.2   Working Women's Forum: Progress Report of
Comprehensive Family Welfare Program,
January 1991–March 1994

Component (Total Number)	Madras	Kanchipuram	Vellore	Dindigul	Adirama-pattinam
Slums and villages	232	25	26	38	44
Workers	180	30	30	30	30
Families adopted for coverage of family planning methods	90,000	15,000	15,000	15,000	15,000
Population	432,169	71,758	74,500	68,146	65,221
Eligible couples	73,414	11,857	12,158	11,507	11,323
Children under 5 years	56,964	8,737	9,406	7,630	7,333
Permanent accepters	41,779	6,641	6,072	6,316	4,871
Temporary accepters	25,390	3,412	3,629	3,782	4,125
All family planning accepters	67,169	10,053	9,701	10,098	8,996
Total family planning area coverage (%)	91.49	84.78	79.79	87.75	79.44

vacate the site. An order to this effect was passed by the Taluk office. I immediately gathered a few women and wrote a petition and sent it to the collector through the president of Working Women's Forum. The collector immediately issued a stay order and prevented the evacuation. This incident has increased the popularity of all the programs of WWF in the community, and the clientele respect my work."

Chandra is a microentrepreneur from Dindigul who had pledged her jewels, borrowed money at exorbitant rates of interest, and carried on her business with extreme difficulty. Talking about her life, she says: "The interest charged by outside moneylenders is so high that I was not even able to meet the interest requirements from my profit. As a result, my jewels, vessels, and other tangible items at home were all under mortgage. I joined the WWF after the WWF family planning area supervisor talked to me about the organization. After the WWF training, I have become an active member of the local WWF group. We often sit down, talk about our problems, and also come up with solutions. We understand our mistake of borrowing money at very high rates of interest. We have also decided not to go to moneylenders anymore. In fact, when one moneylender approached me and asked me why I had not borrowed money from him this year, I told him about the WWF and its low-interest loan program. Further, along with other women, I saw to it that he did not ever enter our area again. But for the forum and its training, we would have neither realized that we were being exploited nor been able to overcome such exploitation."

Muniammal comes from Vellore. Her husband deserted her, and she and her two children earn their livelihood by rolling beedis (cigarettes). Her one daughter is married. Discussing her life, she says: "My neighbors used to look down on me and my children because of the simple fact that my husband deserted us. Their constant talking behind my back prompted me to go to my husband. I requested him to come back to the family. However, he refused and also advised me to work and earn a living. He further added that if I was not able to do this, I should commit suicide by jumping from the fort of the Vellore temple into the moat around it. This very nearly happened but for one person who saved my life. After this incident, I came to know about the WWF. I enlisted as a member, underwent training, and also received a loan. Being a part of the WWF has helped me forget my troubles. I have now abandoned thoughts such as suicide. Through the training and other meetings at the forum, I have been exposed to other women and their problems as well. I now understand that life is full of difficulties which need to be overcome. My life is now more meaningful despite my husband not being there. I certainly have the confidence and courage to face life as it comes."

In an area called Idayampatti (Vellore), the dwelling huts were to be destroyed. A notification to this effect had been issued by the local government authority (the Thasildar). The forum members decided to fight against this. They convened a set of training meetings to bring this issue to the notice of the women affected. After the meetings, it was decided to fight the demolition issue by giving a petition to the district collector. This timely response from the forum prevented the destruction of the dwelling huts in the area. Apart from dealing with the demolition issue, the training meetings also helped the women become more aware of other difficulties, such as lack of transportation, inadequate medical facilities, and the absence of labor legislation in the beedi-rolling industry. These grievances were voiced to the president of India and to the prime minister through a petition submitted to them in person. The women also staged a dharna (demonstration) outside the collector's office. It is to their credit that they now have special bus services for women, better working conditions, and plans for converting wastelands into dwelling sites.

Students and researchers from India and elsewhere are given free access to visit the forum and learn from its experiences. Worldwide sharing of such experiences takes place through Grassroots Organizations Operating Together in Sisterhood (GROOTS), a global network of like-minded NGOs. Future plans include establishing a training center for NGO activists.

The WWF has lent credibility and strength to the struggles of poor women in India by providing them with organizational backing. These women are the forum's greatest strength, since they provide the mass base that lends credence to the forum's existence. Today, the WWF operates with the same efficiency and speed as in earlier times. Organizational growth has not impaired its functioning, largely because of its decentralized structure and mode of operation. Member involvement at all levels of the organization provides the key to effective monitoring and strong accountability, both downward to members and upward to government and donors. The experience of the Working Women's Forum shows that donor funding and government regulation can be combined with accountability to the grassroots, and that credit provision, welfare work, and empowerment go together. The key to managing these multiple tasks and accountabilities lies in decentralization and member involvement.

Note

1. "Members" of the Working Women's Forum are defined as participants in credit and savings groups or as women who pay a membership fee.

References

UNFPA. 1994. *Income generation and family planning for working women in the urban slums of Madras and rural areas of Tamilnadu.* New York and Kanchipuram: UNFPA/Working Women's Forum.

NGO Accountability in Bangladesh

Beneficiaries, Donors, and the State

Syed M. Hashemi

NGO activities began in Bangladesh in the aftermath of the war of independence in 1971 and the famine of 1974 and were initially restricted to relief and rehabilitation. From the mid-1970s, there was a shift in focus to integrated community development programs. It was assumed that community development would benefit poor people within communities, but structural constraints prevented the trickle down of benefits. Through their own field experience, NGOs realized that "poverty [was] not simply a problem of income differentials but also of the power relations which constitute rural society" (White 1992, 12). NGOs therefore began to target specific groups left out of the development "net." The essential premise of the target group approach was that special programs were required to reach groups excluded by prevailing inequalities in resource endowments, power structures, kinship systems, and gender relations. NGOs in Bangladesh therefore shifted their attention from providing straightforward economic benefits to organizing marginalized sections of the population into self-reliant groups capable of resisting structural inequalities. Following the pedagogical approach of Paulo Freire, "consciousness-raising" was adopted as the underlying principle for organizing the poor.

The target group approach has allowed NGOs in Bangladesh to work with the rural poor and provide development inputs to a constituency generally bypassed by government bureaucracies. Donor agencies, concerned with the seemingly inescapable poverty of rural Bangladesh, have come to rely more and more on NGOs as a better mechanism for grassroots contact and a more effective safety net for the poor. However, larger-scale NGO development activity backed by increased donor funding has generated contradictions between the state and NGOs and has brought the issue of NGO accountability into the political discourse. This chapter examines the origins of these contradictions in Bangladesh. It also explores prevailing relations between NGOs and donors, and between NGOs and beneficiaries, to illustrate the need for, and nature of, NGO accountability.

Government-NGO Relations

Government-NGO relations in Bangladesh have moved through stages of indifference and ambivalence. However, in mid-1992, relations degenerated into all-out confrontation. Over previous years, government-NGO collaboration had increased in the spheres of relief distribution, family planning and health services, nonformal education, and microcredit. In fact, NGOs played an active role in the formation of a national health policy and in the national committee for the distribution of *Khas* land for the poor. However, government had also developed an increasing suspicion of NGOs, which led to a decision to institutionalize a control mechanism through the establishment of the NGO Affairs Bureau (NAB). The NAB was entrusted with the authority to grant permission for NGO operations. Although this represented an operational improvement over the previous system (in which the cabinet division bore responsibility for overseeing NGOs and granting clearance only after scrutiny by a large number of government departments), it also implied centralized control over NGOs.

The fall of President Ershad and the return to parliamentary democracy in Bangladesh (which was welcomed by most NGOs) could have been a signal to increase the freedom of grassroots organizations and NGOs to operate within civil society. However, the government reassessment of NGOs that followed the return to democracy was guided by bureaucratic imperatives (ensuring control) as well as by a lingering suspicion that NGOs had been too close to the Ershad government. In late July 1992, the NAB sent a secret report to the prime minister, accusing NGOs of "irregularities and corruption" and charging that their activities were "anti-state and dangerous." A series of condemnatory articles followed in the media. Matters came to a head when, on August 20, 1992, the NAB issued an order canceling the license to operate of the Association of Development Agencies in Bangladesh (ADAB), the coordinating body of NGOs, and one other NGO. Interestingly, however (for reasons explained later), the order was canceled by the prime minister's secretariat within a couple of hours of its issuance. Although the immediate conflict was resolved, antagonism remained beneath the surface.

The NAB's report to the prime minister accused many of the leading Bangladeshi NGOs of resorting to illegal activities. It stated that about fifty NGOs had secured foreign funds worth about 1.4 billion takas without the permission of the government. It also claimed that many NGOs maintained illegal bank accounts and spent money on high salaries, air-conditioned cars, and other luxuries, resulting in high administrative costs that amounted to 60 percent or more of their total budgets. The NAB accused many NGOs of being donor dependent and, at the behest of these donors, engaging in antistate activities such as publishing

magazines with political content, participating in politics and local government elections, engaging in religious conversions, and spreading fab-
ricated antinational propaganda abroad.

The NGOs immediately issued a rejoinder terming most of these
accusations "false and baseless." Some of the larger Bangladeshi NGOs,
with their fleets of air-conditioned four-wheel-drive vehicles and plush
offices, were easy targets for accusations of lavish lifestyles, particularly
since such "luxuries" are antithetical to the spirit of service that people
in South Asia have historically associated with organizations working
with the poor. The specifics of the NAB's criticisms suggested that NGO
personnel received high incomes and fringe benefits that were out of line
with salaries in other sectors of society. But in an earlier comparative study
of benefits packages, it was found that in terms of pay scales, accommodation, transport, pensions, and even foreign trips, high-level government
functionaries were better off than top-level NGO staff (Siddiqui 1987).
Contrary to popular expectations, NGO personnel do not receive higher
salaries or benefits than their counterparts in government.

This is not to suggest, however, that NGOs don't engage in a certain
amount of lavishness. If one compares the major NGOs in Bangladesh
with their counterparts in India, striking differences emerge in the level
of resources that are available to them. Compared with their Bangladeshi
counterparts, Indian NGOs seem more modest, down-to-earth, and
resource scarce. This is symptomatic of the general abundance of
foreign funds in Bangladesh. Although it may be argued that four-wheel-
drive vehicles, motorbikes, and computers are necessary for better performance, this has to be balanced by the search for low-cost alternatives
so that some degree of self-reliance may be achieved rather than constantly increasing dependence on donor funding.

But such differences (real or imagined) were not the most important
reason for the divergence in government-NGO interests; much more
central was the issue of political participation. NGOs are explicit in for-
going the roles of political parties—that is, competing for political power
at the level of state authority. However, when NGOs analyze poverty in
terms of structural causes and define their objectives in terms of structural transformation, they intervene directly within the political space
that defines the status quo. In so doing, development NGOs are clearly
"political." This is usually acceptable to government if it involves providing inputs such as literacy, credit, or employment, since these fall
within the domain of traditional (charitable or welfare) efforts to assist
the poor. However, when the poor are organized to articulate their
demands, fight for their rights, and struggle to change the structural basis
of their subordination, a challenge to the status quo is definitely implied.

Government agencies perceive their responsibility as maintaining law
and order in the prevailing status quo and therefore see NGO activity
directed at "empowerment" to be threatening. To a government that

strives to preserve the present (no matter how inequitable the system may be), such activities are akin to a political challenge that seeks to undermine the system itself. Hence the charges that NGOs were "being political." The case of Gono Shahajjo Shangstha (GSS), one of the most important NGOs in Bangladesh, illustrates this situation well.

Since its inception, GSS has been committed to raising the consciousness of the poor and assisting them to set up their own class-based organization, with the eventual aim of contending for political power. GSS sees NGO credit provision as an individualized attempt to promote economic welfare, which breaks down class solidarity and hence leads to the maintenance of the status quo. In early 1992, GSS felt that its membership in the district of Nilphamari (in North Bengal) was strong enough to challenge the prevailing power groups in local-level elections. GSS put up slates of candidates in five unions in the district of Nilphamari. Two features of this action were unique. First, GSS candidates (especially for the key post of chairman) were all from the poorest sections of the community. Other NGOs had at times supported candidates, but generally they had belonged to the better-off sections of the peasantry—people who would be socially acceptable. Second, GSS candidates ran on the organizational ticket and made a major statement of the fact that they were candidates of the organization of the poor.

Local-level elections in Bangladesh are staggered over several days. In the first day of voting, in one union, GSS members won the election for chairman as well as a majority of the ordinary seats for members. The prevailing power groups, which up to then had taken little notice of the attempts of the poor to run for political office, saw this as a real threat to their long-standing domination. They could not accept having to report to a day laborer as chairman. The dominant factions in all five unions (irrespective of their political affiliation) united to unleash a reign of terror. GSS schools were burned down, members (including women) were beaten up, and a house-to-house search to confiscate all GSS books was undertaken. In the elections in the other four constituencies, armed thugs ensured that GSS members could not reach the voting sites, and their candidates lost the elections.

The government administration sided completely with local elites. The police refused to take action against the armed thugs and instead filed charges against GSS members. In an interview with the author, the deputy commissioner of Nilphamari had this to say: "All of us want to help the poor and provide charity for them. But when the poor get uppity and want to sit in the head of the rich, when they want to dominate, that cannot be allowed." He accused GSS of "organizing the poor," an action that he thought was "tantamount to fomenting a revolution." He filed charges against GSS field-workers, saying that they belonged to underground revolutionary parties. The police conducted raids and arrested some GSS staff. Other GSS members left their villages and stayed in hiding for months.

The GSS experience in Nilphamari indicates clearly that the reaction of the government administration stemmed from GSS's challenge to the status quo, a situation that government functionaries depend on for containing rural unrest and for maintaining day-to-day governance. They saw in GSS a threat to the social and political order that provides them with the authority to govern. They saw GSS as attempting to subvert the structure of power that they were there to defend. GSS's functional literacy text (entitled "The Book of Learning for the Poor") was banned, and GSS was forced to move away from its strategy of confrontation. The new strategy involves working with civil society rather than helping poor people organize on their own. A model of class harmony has replaced the previous model of class struggle. GSS's economic activities now substitute for its previous political activities.

The NAB's accusations against NGOs in the summer of 1992 were predicated mostly on the threat presented by such strategies. Although on the surface the NAB backed off from its decision to revoke the operating license of ADAB, it succeeded in sending a clear message that set the political boundaries for NGO action. In fact, just a few months prior to the government's report, a few of the more "radical" NGO leaders had been called to the prime minister's secretariat and "scolded" for signing a statement demanding the death sentence for Golam Azam (the mastermind behind the murders of thousands of people during the war of independence). The NGO leaders were warned not to be "political."

Most NGOs in Bangladesh have given up strategies to organize the poor, sanitized their activities (if not their rhetoric), and chosen the path of delivering economic assistance. In fact, the Bangladesh Rural Advancement Committee (BRAC), which was using rhetoric similar to GSS's in the late 1970s, changed its emphasis in the 1980s to promoting credit-based economic improvements in the lives of the poor. Although government attempts to seek greater accountability from NGOs continue, the decision by some NGOs to deemphasize consciousness-raising signals that the government has already won the first round of the battle over accountability, since the consciousness-raising model must of necessity pit NGOs against government agencies unless the government itself is committed to structural transformation.

Beneficiary-NGO Relations

Although government-NGO conflict in Bangladesh arose from the government's determination to enforce greater upward accountability from NGOs, NGOs have never developed a countervailing system of downward accountability to the poor. It is interesting to note that although terms such as "grassroots" and "participation" permeate NGO rhetoric, the consciousness-raising approach is reminiscent of the vanguard party of the Old Left. The underlying assumption is that declassed, urban-educated, middle-class NGO workers from the outside must go to the villages to raise the consciousness of the poor so that they will organize to form their own class. This approach denies poor people their capacity to organize and struggle for themselves. Even a cursory look at the history of Bengal shows that the peasantry have organized themselves many times to fight against colonialism and feudal oppression. In NGO strategies, there has never been a sustained faith in the ability of poor people to bring about their own transformations. It is this perspective that has disallowed any real participation of the poor in NGO activities or the development of systems of accountability to them.

This does not mean that NGOs are not effective institutions in working with the poor. NGOs in Bangladesh are better able to reach people at the grassroots level because NGO workers are much more accessible. Generally, local government offices, with their "peons" and curtains on the door, act as formidable barriers to entry (real as well as symbolic) for poor people. In contrast, NGO workers mix freely with poor people, visiting them in their villages and talking with them about their lives and problems. In spite of this, only limited efforts have been made to make NGO operations truly participatory. Beneficiaries are seldom allowed to make decisions on programs or budgets or even to participate in monitoring and evaluation. Their participation is limited to relatively inconsequential areas of decision making. The solidarity and strength of groups of poor people are overshadowed by, and dependent on, the presence of the NGO. Members who want access to relief or who demand higher wages may do so less because of their own strength than because of the power of the NGO, which is more influential than the village landlord, the local contractor, or the government functionary. NGO directors and high officials belong to the same social milieu as top government bureaucrats, military generals, and ministers. New hierarchies and new lines of dependence are created (though less exploitative, certainly). A truly participatory development paradigm that integrates poor people effectively into the decision-making process remains largely unexplored in Bangladesh.

Donor-NGO Relations

Most Bangladeshi NGOs are totally dependent on foreign funds. The volume of foreign funds flowing to NGOs in Bangladesh has been increasing over the years and stood at just below 12 percent of all foreign aid to the country in 1992–93 (see Table 9.1). The high figure for 1989–90 is due to the amount of disaster relief aid disbursed through NGOs during the period after the cyclone.

Table 9.1   Flow of Foreign Funds to NGOs

Year	Number of NGO Projects Approved	Amount of NGO Foreign Aid (in Crores*)	Total Foreign Aid Disbursed (in Crores)	NGO Funds as % of All Aid to Bangladesh
1988–89	162	279.85	5,339.13	5.70
1989–90	189	1,088.26	6,031.26	18.04
1990–91	865	639.20	6,185.29	10.33
1991–92	695	576.12	6,146.14	9.37
1992–93	986	782.82	6,562.68	11.93

* One crore equals 10 million takas.
Source: Compiled from NAB records.

Donors increased their funding from 162 NGO projects in 1988–89 to 986 in 1992–93, a fivefold increase in five years. The total amount disbursed increased from 280 crores in 1988–89 to 783 crores in 1992–93, a 180 percent increase over the period. However, the disbursement of funds to NGOs is highly skewed. The top fifteen NGOs accounted for 84 percent of all NGO allocations in 1991–92, and 70 percent in 1992–93.

High levels of donor funding have had two major consequences. First, NGOs have become donor dependent, not merely in terms of the funding that is essential to their existence but also in terms of seeking donor assistance to legitimize their activities. Second, upward accountability to donors has skewed NGO activities toward donor-driven agendas for development rather than indigenous priorities.

These trends are exemplified by NGO responses immediately after the attack on NGOs by the NAB in 1992. Rather than mobilizing support from their own constituency (the rural poor), NGOs chose to seek the assistance of the donor community. In fact, it was strong intervention by donors that led to the immediate retraction of the suspension order by the prime minister's secretariat. When women from Nijera Kori (a Bangladeshi NGO that focuses on consciousness-raising) were involved in a violent conflict with shrimp cultivators in south Khulna, again it was the donors they turned to. The Dutch ambassador himself visited the area to give weight to the NGO cause. Even now, in the continuing struggle against religious fundamentalism, NGOs are actively seeking donor intervention.

NGO dependence on support from donors is ironic, given the fact that the Bangladeshi government also attempts to legitimize itself through donor support. The World Bank's approval of the government's structural adjustment policies, a greater quantum of aid obtained from the Paris Club, and the U.S. government's praise for the administration's handling of the economy are all publicized through the media to portray a government that is "successful."

Development agendas too are set in accordance with donor priorities. The emphasis on credit-based poverty-alleviation strategies in Bangladesh may have originated with the experience of the Grameen Bank, but moves among other NGOs to replicate this strategy stem from the easy availability of donor support. In fact, the emphasis on nonformal education, immunization, and diarrheal disease control is due to donor pressure. Conversely, the dropping of adult literacy from NGO agendas is due to the lack of donor interest in such programs. Now that donor interest has turned to HIV and AIDS, it is only a matter of time before large numbers of NGOs begin to integrate HIV and AIDS into their activities. This does not mean that donors are funding programs that are irrelevant or ineffective, but donor dependence creates a situation in which NGOs end up reprioritizing their own agendas. The shift in the focus of GSS from raising the consciousness of the poor to working to strengthen civil society seems also to be the result (in part) of donor-driven rethinking.

The term "civil society" is a new buzzword among donors. The U.S. Agency for International Development (USAID) is now gearing up to provide funding to strengthen civil society, perceiving this strategy as a logical element in its open market and open society program. Sanitized from its radical connotations, civil society has come to mean systemic class harmony in which the situation of less privileged groups can be improved through gradual readjustments in the system. Donor funding is therefore provided to groups in society that pursue "democratic" agendas. Explicitly (and deliberately) missing from this definition of civil society are the political parties, trade unions, and peasant organizations that have consistently fought against exploitation in Bangladesh.

Much of the debate concerning government-NGO relations centers on the regulatory powers of the state. The fundamental issue relates to the rights of NGOs to pursue their objectives unhindered by state coercion, and the state's authority to ensure the accountability of NGOs to specific laws. In Bangladesh, the NAB and the Foreign Donations Act specify a separate set of rules under which NGOs must operate. NGOs are regulated by the bureau, which provides licenses to operate and permission to receive foreign funding. This is, of course, necessary to ensure legitimate sources of funding as well as legitimate (nonprofit) avenues of expenditure. However, conflicts arise when the NAB extends its regulatory powers to determine which activities NGOs are allowed to pursue. Since there are already specific laws that can deal with NGO activities that *do* pose a threat to the public good (increasing pollution, for example) or are fraudulent (running off with funds, for example), the real purpose of the additional measures adopted by the NAB is to provide coercive authority to deny any serious challenge to the prevailing system of power. NGOs cannot remain fully accountable to government while simultaneously launching a challenge to government power.

Most Bangladeshi NGOs depend on foreign donors for most of their funding requirements. This has created relations of dependence. Although it is true that nongovernmental development interventions in Bangladesh cannot be financed completely by beneficiaries (because of their level of poverty) or by other domestic sources (at present), there must nevertheless be much greater efforts to mobilize local resources. No matter how strong an NGO might be, complete dependence on foreign funding will always pose a potential threat in the form of either acquiescence to donor demands (however subtle) or the termination of funding sources.

In reality, the only way to counter the influence of government and donors is through increased reliance on beneficiaries—the rural poor. Only through the development of a system of accountability to the poor can NGOs truly transform themselves into organizations of the poor. Only by becoming organizations of the poor can NGOs truly prepare for a sustained struggle for empowerment. This implies that NGOs have to make a choice—between the four-wheel-drive vehicle that comes with government licensing and donor funding and the much harder conditions involved in living alongside poor people. Whatever decision NGOs make, they should remember that poor people in Bangladesh have shown that they have a great capacity to rise up and shake the foundations of the kingdom of oppression. The choices made by NGOs will determine which side of this struggle they are on.

References

Siddiqui, K. 1987. *Benefit packages received by functionaries of government organisations and NGOs*. Dhaka: ADAB.

White, S. 1992. *Evaluating the impact of NGOs on rural poverty alleviation in Bangladesh*. London: Overseas Development Institute.

─── 10 ───

NGOs in Bangladesh

Issues of Legitimacy and Accountability

Mahbubul Karim

NGOs in Bangladesh embrace many fields but are largely geared toward alleviating poverty and promoting sustainable development.[1] Presently, they operate in more than 50 percent of all villages in the country, involving over 3.5 million families as beneficiaries of their work (Association of Developmental Agencies in Bangladesh [ADAB] 1994a). To the credit of NGOs in Bangladesh, there is a range of effective development approaches, models, and innovations, especially in the fields of microfinance and nonformal primary education; these have been recognized widely and in some cases adopted by official as well as private development agencies at home and abroad. Over the last two decades, the NGO sector in Bangladesh, as in many other places in the world, has also performed a major role in facilitating the process of institution building among the poor at the grassroots (Clark 1991). This is crucial if the 80 percent or more of the population currently living below the poverty line is to be empowered to participate meaningfully in national development and the process of democratization. There are, of course, many critics of NGOs in Bangladesh. They have expressed serious doubts about NGO performance, questioned their legitimacy and accountability, and argued strongly against their mode of operation (Muhammad 1988; Umar 1994). This chapter attempts to identify and assess some of these criticisms, especially those concerning legitimacy and accountability.

Genesis and Evolution of NGOs in Bangladesh

NGOs in Bangladesh have their roots in the liberation struggle for independence. During the liberation war of 1971, efforts were made by many concerned young people to render medical and other humanitarian services in the refugee camps across the border in India, as well as underground within the country, to alleviate the suffering of war victims (Wood 1994). In the postwar reconstruction period, several relief and rehabilitation programs were launched both with and without international assistance by freedom fighters in different parts of the country. They were the pioneers in setting an alternative development process in motion in Bangladesh. Interactions with poor people in the villages soon revealed to these pioneers the dynamics of poverty in rural areas, which gradually led to the transformation of their charity and welfare programs into participatory development actions for poverty alleviation (Report of Task Forces 1991).

If seen in terms of the four-generation model developed by Korten (1990), NGOs in Bangladesh are now in the third stage of their evolution. In the late 1970s, there was a gradual shift from first-generation strategies (relief and welfare services) to second-generation strategies characterized by small-scale, self-reliant, local development initiatives for building people's capacity. Throughout the 1980s, this thrust continued. Pursuing third-generation strategies that focus on achieving policy changes at different levels is a recent phenomenon, visible in Bangladesh since the early 1990s. This appears to be the first indication of Korten's fourth generation of NGO strategy, one that is characterized by a shift in emphasis from reform to transformational activity.

In terms of their origins, roles, and geographical locations, NGOs in Bangladesh are grouped into three major categories: local, national, and international. Both local and national NGOs are indigenous and are engaged mainly in organizing, mobilizing and empowering the poor, and simultaneously providing various services at the grassroots level. It is the scale of their operation that determines their status as local or national. In most cases, international NGOs provide support (financial, technical, or both) to local and national NGOs. The number of NGOs registered by the NGO Affairs Bureau (NAB) has risen rapidly in recent years, from 669 in 1992 to over 800 in 1994 (ADAB 1994a).

Government Control

The NAB, which functions under the prime minister's office, is the government agency charged with controlling the activities of those NGOs in Bangladesh that operate with foreign funds (which means most NGOs in the country). An NGO may be registered either with the Ministry of Social Welfare under the Voluntary Social Welfare Agencies (Registration and Control) Ordinance of 1961 or as a joint stock company by the Ministry of Commerce under the Societies Registration Act of 1860 or the Companies Act of 1913. If the NGO receives any foreign funding in cash or in any other form, it must be registered with the NAB first. To do this, it must operate under the Foreign Donations (Voluntary Activities) Regulation Ordinance of 1978 and the Foreign Contributions

(Regulation) Ordinance of 1982, as well as under rules that have been framed to carry out the purposes of these two laws (NAB 1993). According to these laws and rules, no NGO is allowed to undertake or implement any activity using foreign funds without the NAB's prior approval of both the project and the budget. Furthermore, clearance from the NAB for the actual amount to be received from the donor is required. NGOs have to submit a variety of reports and returns to the NAB in connection with their work.

Self-regulation

The Association of Development Agencies in Bangladesh (ADAB), an apex body of NGOs in the country, recently adopted a code of ethics (ADAB 1993) as a step toward self-regulation for its nearly 700 members. However, this has yet to be fully enforced, as mechanisms for monitoring compliance are still to be finalized.

The code, entitled "Declaration Regarding Definition, Statement of Purpose and Code of Ethics," defines NGOs as nonprofit organizations committed to the development of the underprivileged and underserved. To sharpen their identity within the private sector, they have been renamed private voluntary development organizations (PVDOs). The code specifies that the purpose of NGOs is to ensure sustainable development of the poor in Bangladesh through poverty alleviation, capacity and institution building among poor people, and increased participation in productive activities. The objectives of NGOs, as laid out in the code, are to raise the standard of living of the poor and to help them become worthy citizens of Bangladesh—more conscious and self-reliant and able to build and sustain the democratic process at the grassroots. The code posits that NGOs, besides generating their own funds, can accept resources and services from the public, the business community, the government of Bangladesh, and external development partners. But these resources are to be used exclusively for the development of the poor, not for any personal profit.

The code intends to establish self-regulatory practices and norms for the member NGOs of ADAB in relation to the people for whom they work, the government of Bangladesh, other NGOs, development partners, and their own staff. Members of ADAB, for whom this code of ethics is obligatory, commit themselves to working for solidarity among the poor, democratic leadership, and self-reliance, irrespective of caste, creed, religion, and gender. Signatories must also be accountable and transparent to the government with regard to their activities and use of funds. The code commits NGOs to enhancing solidarity with other NGOs by avoiding factionalism, divisiveness, and overlapping. They must also promote competence, professionalism, and the highest standards of transparency and honesty. The code makes explicit reference to the need to encourage democratic leadership, participatory management, and transparency, including "to the people."

Proshika: A Case Study

Proshika (a center for human development) was formed in 1976 with the aims of reducing poverty, protecting and regenerating the environment, improving women's status, increasing people's participation in public institutions, and enhancing people's capacity to gain and exercise their democratic and human rights. Proshika implements a wide range of activities geared toward facilitating people's access to public resources, services, and institutions to enable them to gradually become self-reliant. Its programs include building people's organizations; development education through training and theater; universal education; women's development; employment, income generation, and the provision of credit; environmental protection and regeneration; and health education and infrastructure. Proshika now operates in 6,006 villages and 108 slums in 35 districts, through a network of 72 of its own area development centers (ADCs). Facilitating people's organizations is the core of Proshika's activities. Poor people are encouraged to form primary groups (with an average membership of eighteen) in villages and then federate into broader organizations called coordination committees at the village, union,[2] and *Thana* (subdistrict) levels. To date, 41,205 primary groups covering 698,000 members have been formed, federating upward into 3,809 committees at the village level, 348 at the union level, and 48 at the *Thana* level. So far, around 1.58 million people have participated in Proshika's development education programs.

Proshika regards employment and income generation as crucial ingredients for empowerment. It assists groups to engage in agriculture, irrigation, livestock development, fisheries, sericulture, apiculture, small and cottage industries, and social forestry. These activities are facilitated by building up savings and providing credit, training, extension, and technical support. Thus far, Proshika has extended 1,010 million takas[3] in loans from its revolving loan fund to 49,492 projects undertaken by groups of poor people, who contributed 234 million takas of their own. These projects have generated over 373,000 employment or self-employment opportunities to date. In the health field, Proshika has assisted groups to install 10,590 hand tube wells for safe drinking water and 78,349 low-cost latrines. With the aim of expanding the literacy base in the country, Proshika's universal education program has set up 10,031 adult literacy centers and 301 nonformal primary schools from which 191,233 adult learners and 9,030 children have already graduated. Gender equity is a major focus of Proshika's approach to development.

Therefore, it ensures active and equal participation of women in every sphere of its activities. Women's groups constitute over 53 percent of all groups in the program.

Proshika is registered under the Societies Registration Act and with the NAB. The highest decision-making body of the organization is the general body, presently made up of thirty members from different groups and professions. In the annual general meeting, the general body approves the annual report, the audit report, and the budget; appoints auditors; and elects a nine-member governing body for a period of one year. The governing body makes major policy decisions within Proshika and sits at least four times a year to review the performance of the organization. It also has the authority to appoint the executive director.

Proshika practices a participatory planning process that begins at the grassroots level. Every year, the process starts in April with each primary group making its plan in terms of social, economic, and cultural programs, on the basis of performance in the previous year and assisted by Proshika staff. Each group's plan is taken to the village committee, where it is reviewed and approved, and a village plan is developed. A similar process operates at all levels, with plans at one level integrated into plans at the next higher level. Experience shows that each ADC gets to keep around 95 percent of its original plan at the end of this process. All levels of Proshika's management are assisted by a management information system (MIS) developed over a period of time by its impact monitoring and evaluation cell (IMEC). The MIS has been developed to fulfill two purposes: to monitor program targets and achievements in line with Proshika's core objectives, and to monitor day-to-day management (personnel, finance, and so on).

An impact assessment study conducted recently by Proshika in collaboration with Horizon Pacific International (HPI, Canada) shows that savings of group members have increased substantially over time. Women were found to be better savers and investors than men. The study also revealed that members are gaining increasing control over local-level arbitration systems and greater access to local government and public institutions. Over 90 percent of the women interviewed in the study reported a marked decrease in abuse and oppression (IMEC and HPI 1993). The report of a seven-member mission appointed by the Proshika donor consortium to appraise phase V by means of a review of phase IV of Proshika's work (July 1994–June 1999) observed: "progress in Phase IV has been satisfactory. Targets have in most cases been met, improvements have been made in programme operations, and there is emerging hard evidence of socio-economic impacts. The transition to starting programmes in the urban slums of Dhaka has been successful."

Proshika has built an organization that is open and self-confident and practices collective decision making. Proshika's management style will likely enable it to adjust to change without losing its basic vision or

reducing its effectiveness (Mitchell et al. 1994). As laid out above, Proshika is accountable downward via the participatory planning system at group, village, union, and *Thana* levels and upward to its general body, external donors, and the government of Bangladesh. It has to provide donors with semiannual performance reports and annual activity reports and an audit report and has to have its projects and budgets approved by the NAB. Proshika has worked out a strategy to reduce its dependence on donors. By operating its revolving loan fund in an effective and sustainable manner, Proshika should be able to cover 65 percent of its administrative and operational expenditures by 1999.

Criticisms of NGOs

NGOs in Bangladesh are viewed negatively by some individual members of the bureaucracy, the intelligentsia, and political parties and by a number of organizations. Some of these criticisms, such as duplication and overlapping of roles and lack of coordination, have some basis in reality, but others are far too generalized and are not substantiated in practice. One of the most common criticisms made about NGOs in Bangladesh is that their administrative costs are unacceptably high. From its inception in 1990 to November 1992, the NAB had approved 816 NGO projects. Only 14 percent of these projects had higher administrative costs than the generally accepted rate of 20 percent, and the administrative costs of 76 percent of the projects were below 15 percent (NAB 1992). Similarly, questions have been raised about the cost of NGO program delivery, despite general assumptions about NGO cost-effectiveness (Edwards and Hulme 1994). The evidence shows that NGOs in Bangladesh perform well in terms of costs. For example, the nonformal primary education program of the Bangladesh Rural Advancement Committee (BRAC) has a running cost that is 25 to 50 percent lower than that of the formal system (Smillie 1992).

Until recently, there existed a substantial gap between NGOs and other groups and institutions in Bangladeshi civil society, with many NGOs preferring to remain aloof. Perhaps they were under the impression that these groups and institutions had nothing to do with development. In retrospect, this was a great mistake on the part of the NGOs and has helped create confusion and suspicion about their activities. For example, the media in general became extremely critical and skeptical about the role and functions of NGOs, but the NGOs did not take account of the implications of this widening gap. The gap has also given rise to a great many stories (often invented) that have been damaging to the NGOs' image. For example, one of the allegations brought against NGOs is that they are involved in financing political parties. This is totally baseless (Report of Task Forces 1991). These negative experiences clearly

indicate a serious problem of information and communication. Fortunately, the popular democratic movement of 1990 helped bridge this gap
considerably.

Legitimacy and Accountability

The criticism that has been most uncomfortable for NGOs in Bangladesh is the question of their legitimacy and accountability. NGOs are
feeling uneasy about these questions, not because of the criticism itself
but due to the fact that historical weaknesses in the NGO sector are
often distorted to create confusion about their basic role. The most
important of these weaknesses is their dependence on external funds,
and it is this that makes NGOs vulnerable to such sensitive criticisms.
High levels of financial dependency exist in most Southern NGOs,
and the same is true of those in Bangladesh. It has proved extremely
difficult for NGOs to secure an alternative resource base inside the
country (though some progress has been made, for example, by BRAC,
which now generates over one-third of its budget from internal resources
[Edwards and Hulme 1994]).

When such dependence continues to characterize every sphere
of South-North relations, how can NGOs be expected to escape it? In
Bangladesh particularly, where both the public and the private for-profit
sectors rely heavily on foreign aid, is it realistic to ask or expect that
only the nonprofit development sector should be able to operate on its
own resources? Are NGOs illegitimate just because they rely on external funding? Legitimacy and accountability cannot be judged only in
terms of the funding context; the commitment of NGOs and the services
they provide to people are equally important. In a truly democratic
society, the people are the supreme authority in deciding who is legitimate and who is not. Therefore, why not leave this question to them?
The beneficiaries of NGO work were never consulted by those who criticize NGOs in Bangladesh; they have not been asked to express their views
about NGOs, despite the widely accepted fact that no development can
take place without people's participation. The Bangladesh Constitution
affords its citizens the right to form associations and organizations.
Legally, any organization operating in accordance with the provisions
of the law is legitimate. But of course, legitimacy is not simply a matter
of legality; it also rests on the role and contribution of NGOs, and their
relevance and effectiveness in the local socioeconomic context.

In terms of accountability, Bangladeshi NGOs are regularly answer-
able to at least four different authorities: to their boards of governors or
executive committees and, through them, to the general members, since
they are registered legal entities; to the government, which approves their
projects and budgets; to the people (both recipients and nonrecipients

of the benefits and services they provide); and to the donors that provide resources.

It is important to note that in a country like Bangladesh, where democratic norms, values, and institutions have yet to be firmly established, the term "accountability" has different meanings and connotations to different groups of people. In Bangladesh, even the accountability of civil servants and elected representatives at all levels is in a "diluted, diffused and fuzzy state" (Ahsan and Muslim 1994). In the name of greater accountability and transparency, attempts may therefore be made to impose unlimited control over NGOs. For example, NGOs in Bangladesh are now making painstaking efforts to mobilize public opinion against a move by the Ministry of Social Welfare to enact what is, according to them, a "retrogressive law" because some of its provisions contravene rights guaranteed by the constitution (ADAB 1994b).

Before the end of the Cold War, it was the leftist political forces in Bangladesh who opposed NGOs, identifying them as "agents of imperialism" (Umar 1989). In the post–Cold War period, it is the growing forces of fundamentalism who publicly demand a ban on the operation of NGOs, claiming that their activities are anti-Islamic (Rahman n.d.; Ahmed 1994). Criticisms of NGOs are invariably value laden and ideologically based. Therefore, *who* defines accountability, *for whom*, and *why* are questions that need to be analyzed very carefully.

This chapter is not intended to create the impression that NGOs in Bangladesh should continue to depend on foreign funding without making efforts to attain self-reliance, difficult as this may be within the existing world economic order; nor that current systems of accountability are satisfactory. The present arrangement cannot be preferred by NGOs for the simple reason that it is not sustainable (Holloway 1994). But what is the alternative? NGOs alone cannot find the answers. This is something that NGOs and donors must search for together, and this requires much greater interest and participation from the donors.

What NGOs should begin to do immediately is to build the capacity of people's organizations (POs) to enable them to take greater charge of their own development, so that POs that "graduate" can provide support to NGOs by paying for the various forms of assistance they need. This is not the only option to be pursued. There are several other possibilities and mechanisms of self and local financing that should be explored. For example, the general public, businesses, banks, and even the national government could be potential sources of local financing (Holloway 1994). Supporting appropriate and viable revenue-generating activities may be a meaningful option for certain types of NGOs. Donors could also provide endowment funds. The key point is that it is only by reducing their dependence on foreign funds that NGOs will be able to gradually overcome the questions of legitimacy and accountability thrown at them by their critics.

As an active group in civil society (Tandon 1994), NGOs must develop linkages, common understandings, and strategies for working together to strengthen the process of democratization and the development of society as a whole. This is essential if NGOs are to create greater acceptance and a more positive image for themselves. Like all organizations and institutions, NGOs in Bangladesh must be judged by their results, not on the basis of ideology.

Notes

1. In this chapter, the term "NGO" refers to intermediary development NGOs or to private voluntary development organizations as defined by the ADAB code of ethics.
2. The lowest level of local administration and government, respectively.
3. In April 1995, US$1 equaled 40 takas.

References

Ahmed, Noman. 1994. *NGOs, atheists and apostates.* Dhaka: Deshapremik Kishore Sangshad.

Ahsan, E., and S. N. Muslim. 1994. *Accountability in the Bangladesh civil service.* Report presented at ASEAN-SAARC Conference on Administrative and Financial Accountability, Dhaka, January 16–20 (quoted in the *Daily Star*, January 18, 1994).

Association of Development Agencies in Bangladesh (ADAB). (1993). Declaration regarding definition, statement of purpose and code of ethics. Dhaka: ADAB.

———. 1994a. Fact sheet on NGO activities [in Bengali]. Dhaka. ADAB.

———. 1994b. Position paper presented at press conference, Dhaka, June 4.

Clark, John. 1991. *Democratizing development: The role of voluntary organizations.* West Hartford, Conn.: Kumarian Press.

Edwards, M., and D. Hulme. 1994. *NGOs and development: Performance and accountability in the "new world order."* Background paper for the SCF/IDPM Workshop on NGOs and Development, Manchester, June 27–29.

Holloway, R. 1994. *Alternatives to donor funds for South Asian NGOs: What do we know and what do we need to know?* Paper presented at the South Asian NGO Research Project Meeting, Dhaka, March 6–10.

Impact Monitoring and Evaluation Cell (IMEC) and Horizon Pacific International (HPI). 1993. *Impact assessment and internal monitoring system of Proshika.* Implementation report: Stage one. Dhaka: Proshika.

Korten, David C. 1990. *Getting to the 21st century: Voluntary action and the global agenda.* West Hartford, Conn.: Kumarian Press.

Mitchell, Robert, et al. 1994. *Proshika manobik unnayan kendra, Bangladesh, phase V (July 1994–June 1999) Appraisal.* Dhaka: Proshika.

Muhammad, Anu. 1988. *Crisis of development in Bangladesh and NGO model* [in Bengali]. Dhaka: Prochinta Prokashani.

NGO Affairs Bureau (NAB). 1992. *NGOs in Bangladesh*. Dhaka: NAB.

————. 1993. *Rules and procedures to be followed by all foreign NGOs working in Bangladesh and Bangladeshi NGOs receiving foreign funds* [in Bengali]. Dhaka: Prime Minister's Office.

Rahman, M. H. n.d. *What the NGOs are doing in the pretext of service provision* [in Bengali]. Dhaka: Shibli Prokashani.

Report of the Task Forces on Bangladesh Development Strategies for the 1990's. 1991. *Managing the development process*. Vol. 2. *The role of NGOs*. Dhaka: University Press Limited.

Smillie, Ian. 1992. *BRAC at 20*. Dhaka: BRAC.

Tandon, Rajesh. 1994. Civil society, the state and the role of NGOs. In *Civil society in the Asia-Pacific region*, edited by Isagani R. Serrano. Washington, D.C.: CIVICUS.

Umar, Badruddin. 1989. The vicious circle of bourgeois politics in Bangladesh and what we need to do. In *Badruddin umar, military rule and politics in Bangladesh* [in Bengali]. Dhaka: Protik Prokashana Sangstha.

————. 1994. NGO-GO entente in Bangladesh. In *Economic-political situation in Bangladesh* [in Bengali], edited by Umar Badruddin. Dhaka: Jatio Sahitya Prakashani.

Wood, G. D. 1994. *Bangladesh: Whose ideas, whose interests?* Dhaka: University Press Limited.

11

"Return to the Roots"

Processes of Legitimacy in Sudanese Migrant Associations

David T. Pratten and Suliman Ali Baldo

In the current climate of state retrenchment and disengagement in Africa, attention has shifted to the development roles of alternative, nongovernmental forms of social organization. Indigenous or externally inspired institutions that aggregate demands and build capacities at the community level operate as empowerers and potential partners at a significant interface in the development process. Community-based organizations (CBOs) are mediators between state and society and between donors and households. The relationships created by this intermediary position highlight two areas of analysis within the wider debate on the legitimacy of development intervention. The first concerns the relationship between the organization and its community, which we call "internal" or "downward" legitimacy. The need here is to examine the claim that CBOs represent their constituencies effectively and provide appropriate and accountable services. The second, "external" or "upward" legitimacy, assesses the relationship between local organizations, the state, and other donors. The issue here is whether stronger linkages between state and civil society, or donor and community, will make governments and funders more responsive and thereby enhance their legitimacy.

This chapter explores the processes through which CBOs operate as legitimate local development agents for the communities they represent, in the context of migrant associations in Sudan. In particular, it examines the assumption that CBO legitimacy rests on two key features—closeness to the poor and popular support. It also analyzes the relationships between CBOs and the state (the principal external donor for these groups in Sudan) and questions the frequently proposed conflictual image of state and civil society. The case studies are from riverine groups in the north of Sudan (Ed Debba in Northern State and Shendi in River Nile State) and from communities in the west (Northern and Southern Kordofan States).

As migration increases and becomes more permanent, the connections between rural and urban communities in the Sahel become institutionalized. Associations formed by migrants in national and international urban centers and based on a shared community of origin are common forms of social organization. Set against a background of international isolation and the internal dismantling of civil society (Hamad 1993), migrant associations represent one of the most dynamic examples of community action in contemporary Sudan. Often referred to as ethnic welfare unions or *association d'originaires*, migrant associations can be defined as voluntary groups established by migrants to meet social needs in urban areas and to participate in the development of their home (rural) community.

In the urban environment, these associations perform two essential functions for their members, providing both social security and social differentiation. They maintain rural identities but also assist the migrant in adapting to an urban system. Migrant associations therefore represent the reconstruction of rural institutions to reinforce traditional identities in the urban milieu, for example, in lineage, burial, and dispute settlement. Yet although these cultural forms are persistent, they assume new meanings and functions in reorienting rural identities to urban life. In this way, migrant associations play an important role in familiarizing newly arrived migrants with urban status systems, particularly in endorsing achievements and achieving social recognition in the host society according to "modern" values. Migrant associations therefore represent intermediaries between rural and urban and between community and government and are, in this respect, "creative cultural combinations of old and new" (Jules-Rosette 1979, 20).

Although Sudanese migrant associations were generally established to provide for urban social needs, their orientation to rural development does not appear to have been inspired by the interests of an urban educated elite, as Little (1965, 29–30) suggests. Rather, in many cases, this is a reaction to rural needs. In this respect, CBOs can be seen as a cultural response to a rural agenda.[1] In the rural environment, Sudanese migrant associations are key actors in providing resources for local development projects, particularly infrastructure. Schools, clinics, mosques, and water supply networks have all been planned, funded, built, run, and monitored through urban-rural resource flows coordinated by the migrant community.

Legitimacy and Identity

Local organizations are representations of community; community and organization are not one and the same but are linked through shared identity and interest. An evaluation of the processes linking organization to community is central to understanding the representativeness and hence the legitimacy of CBOs. Concepts such as "closeness to the poor" and "extensions of base groups" (Carroll 1992, 12) are not wholly adequate in explaining the relationship between a community (however constituted) and the CBOs that represent them. As Uphoff (1986, 11) states, "many mistakes in development assistance derive from too gross an understanding of an apparently simple term—local." Yet the literature on local institutional development is occupied by typologies and definitions that, by their very nature, are decontextualizing. However complex, these typologies provide no real substitute for ethnographic analysis in assessing the influence of the dynamic construction of identity on local organizational processes. Sharing a community of birth and retaining familial and economic links give migrants authority in local decision making and in representing rural interests. Our analysis indicates, however, that the historical foundations and contemporary reconstructions of community identity are paramount in determining the internal legitimacy and performance of Sudanese migrant associations.

In Sudan, organizations formed on the basis of a shared community of origin represent the formalization of mutual support strategies among poor migrants. Associations from northern Sudan have developed from clubhouses built as social centers in neighborhoods (zawia) that are dominated by migrants from a particular rural area and that often assume their name. Many of these clubhouses were founded during the initial period of high rural-urban migration—for example, the Khartoum club, which was established in 1952 for migrants from Gilas. The clubs provide accommodation for newly arrived migrants, though it is common for them to stay for only a week before moving into an Azaba, a hostel for five to ten migrants from the same community who share the costs of food and rent. Clubhouses and associations also serve as a focus for maintaining rural ties and community identity. In addition to providing accommodation, the clubhouses are used by migrant families to celebrate religious festivals, cultural evenings, and fund-raising events and, in one case, as the bus stop for bus service to their home community in the north of the country.

For all Sudanese associations, the maintenance of rural attachment and identity is an important function, but for some it is absolutely crucial. One such group is the Shilluk from Upper Nile State, who are represented in Khartoum by the Fashoda Benevolent, Cultural and Social Association (FBCSA). The current war in southern Sudan has affected the livelihoods and social cohesion of the Shilluk, 300,000 of whom were estimated to be displaced in 1993. This upheaval has led to fears that the history and practices of the group will be lost. In 1986, the FBCSA was formed (as one member put it) "to preserve aspects of our cultural heritage which are still thriving, revive what is lost and develop the culture so that it may survive in a changing world." In addition to the distribution of relief supplies and petitions to international agencies for small-scale rehabilitation projects, the FBCSA received a video camera from its members working in the Gulf with which it was able to film the 1993 coronation of the *Ruth* (traditional leader) of Shilluk. The association now has a research and documentation unit that attempts to record burial, marriage, child-rearing, and other customary practices of the Shilluk clans.

The case of the Kanar Union from northern Sudan demonstrates both the shifting nature of community identity and the importance of self-identification in legitimizing local development activities. Northern Sudan is the seat of Arabism, Islam, and nationalism in the country. Few migrant associations from River Nile and Northern States are therefore based on ethnic loyalties, as is common in other regions of the country. Instead, associations are based on units of local administration—the village or a collection of villages called an *omodiya*.[2] Two such *omodiyas*, Kuri and Gilas, are located to the east of the urban center of Ed Debba in Northern State and are represented by clubs in Khartoum and other major towns in Sudan. The Kuri *omodiya* serves seven villages, but its association represents only three. Attempts to unite all seven in an *omodiya* club in Khartoum collapsed, and a new association (the Kanar Union) was formed in 1991 by the remaining four villages, with the intention of representing the whole region, including the *omodiyas* of Kuri and Gilas. The union recognized that its central activity (the introduction of a large-scale irrigated cooperative project) required the cooperation and participation of neighboring villages. Significant conflict around Kanar's identity has been generated in the process.

Kanar is not a place name and does not refer to an existing *omodiya*. Rival theories claim that the name Kanar is derived from letters of the names of the villages that founded the association or that it is the name of an ancient sheikhdom. While debates continue to rage as to Kanar's true identity, the majority of the neighboring villages have refused to join the union or the project and object to Kanar's regional pretensions. Fears that the Kuri and Gilas associations would lose their individual names on joining the union and be subsumed within a wider Kanar association have further heightened intervillage rivalry. There are, however, interesting exceptions to those communities that refused to join Kanar. One branch of the Kuri union is dominated by village members who, through intermarriage, retain strong links with a Kanar village and therefore support the union's project. The new proposals have also revealed rivalries within villages. In Kuri, the decision not to join the Kanar project was made by the democratically elected village committee (the rural branch of the urban association) in which an influential local family supported the motion in opposition to the family of the *omda*, the traditional village leader.

A significant consequence of these power struggles is the proposal by the Kuri union to codify the unwritten cooperation among its urban branches and to form a General People's Union, constituted on the same basis as the Kanar Union. Perceiving a threat to its identity, Kuri sought to reconstruct its community boundaries symbolically. Within the context of contested identity, it is also significant that of the thirty-five associations we encountered in Sudan, only the Kanar Union has engaged in community awareness raising (in the form of a newsletter). Until September 1994, the Kanar Union spent all its income (from membership dues) on travel and accommodation arrangements for annual meetings held at the village level. These meetings provided an ideal stage both to bolster support and to foster a new identity.

Based on residentially dispersed communities, migrant associations illustrate the fact that the legitimacy of local institutions rests not simply on proximity to rural constituencies but on shifting connections with the communities they represent. The case studies show that CBOs are engaged in a reciprocal relationship with their constituencies. They are based on and maintain a range of cultural and economic linkages with their community of origin and are instrumental in (re)defining the symbolic and geographical boundaries of that community.[3] Within Sudanese migrant associations and CBOs more generally, *legitimacy through community identification* precedes *legitimacy through participation*.

Legitimacy and Organizational Processes

Although the internal legitimacy of Sudanese migrant associations rests first on a secure (though shifting) understanding of a community's identity, popular support through processes of participation is a key legitimizing factor. Despite their community attachments, migrant associations elsewhere (notably in Nigeria) have been accused of using kinship and ethnicity as a cloak for the interests of their educated elite leadership. In this light, Nigerian "hometown unions" have been criticized for their orientation toward the "comparatively strong" rather than toward newly arrived migrants (Barnes 1975, 87) and are seen as platforms for rival urban businessmen (Trager 1994). Although Nigerian associations maintain their popularity, participation has been significantly curtailed. In contrast, the legitimacy of Sudanese migrant associations as participatory development organizations is enhanced by a series of checks and balances: an inclusive, broad-based membership and equitable, cross-community participation in fund-raising, implementation, decision making, and monitoring.

Migrant association membership procedures are open, flexible, and familiar. Although membership levels are high, the proportion of members who actually pay their membership fees is small. In the Kuri People's Union in Khartoum, only 23 percent contribute regularly. Elsewhere, different rates are applied to the employed, the unemployed, and students, to encourage their participation. Members of the Al Maghawir association in Khartoum, for example, are divided into high-, middle-, and low-income brackets and are expected to contribute up to 20 percent of their monthly income to the union. The collection of dues and donations among urban associations in Sudan reflects rural processes of hospitality such as *kashif* and *mujib*, in which neighbors and families contribute toward the expenses of burial ceremonies.[4] The characteristic equity of these membership arrangements is also apparent in the terms for shareholding in irrigation cooperatives initiated by associations in their home villages. Restrictions are placed on the number of shares allocated per person, a policy deliberately introduced to prevent control by elites.

Participation through self-financing is also a key factor in legitimizing CBO interventions, and although urban participation in fund-raising is culturally organized through customary practices, rural processes are also informal. In both northern and western Sudan, rural finances are raised through self-imposed taxes on sugar quotas. Ration cards were introduced in Sudan in 1990 to control the prices of wheat flour, oil, tea, sugar, rice, lentils, and soap. With most government subsidies now lifted, sugar remains a rationed commodity. In 1993 in El Duakhil (a village in Northern Kordofan State), villagers sold their sugar allocation to merchants and contributed cash and food to pay the 120,000 Sudanese pounds[5] required to hire a government bulldozer to dig a reservoir (*hafir*) as part of a plan to tackle the area's acute water shortage. The *hafir* was completed before the dry season, and each family is entitled to thirty-four jerry cans of water per month, for which they pay 5 Sudanese pounds. A village water committee guards the *hafir* and is saving the fees to extend its capacity.

Though their financial inputs are generally limited, rural communities are instrumental in providing labor for construction projects. In Mali, rural communities claim that their participation in migrant association projects is "not with our financial contributions but with our sweat" (Daum 1992, 81). The Sudanese context, in contrast, demonstrates that significant urban-rural labor movements are important in relieving or releasing villagers from additional burdens and dependence. Project implementation in Sudan is generally organized on the basis of *nafir* or *fa'za*,[6] a collective village work group. For instance, in Gilas village, the rehabilitation of an irrigation pump and drainage network inundated with silt by the floods of 1988 was initiated by the migrant association in Khartoum and the village cooperative but was carried out by eighteen successive *nafir*. It is common, however, for members of the migrant community to return to assist in projects and in *nafir*. In preparation for the flood of the Nile River in 1994, for example, the Kaboushia association called on unemployed members to travel to the town to participate in building *durab* (sand embankments) to prevent severe riverbank erosion. Other examples of collaboration include the building of a new mosque in Kuri village (Northern State), participation in brick making (often for the repair of damaged school buildings), and educational trips home during vacations by students.

Urban-rural links are also key features in the accountability of decision making in migrant associations. General assemblies for riverine groups are extensions of, and coincide with, migrants' annual return home in September to monitor their harvest and settle their accounts with casual laborers. General assemblies analyze local problems, set priorities, agree on an annual project agenda, and solicit official support from invited dignitaries; they also provide an opportunity for the rural community to voice its opinions and, if necessary, to reverse inappropriate "urban" planning. Extensive rural-urban dialogue generally ensures consensus in decision making, but the experience of the Kanar Union also illustrates the harder edge to accountability that general assemblies—the migrant association's "shareholder meetings"—can offer. For two years, the Khartoum-based leadership of the Kanar Union lobbied government for a large-scale agricultural rehabilitation and irrigation project to grow wheat on village *gusad* land.[7] The 1993 annual assembly was the scene of considerable conflict and a shift in priorities. Represented by a Kanar faction based in Port Sudan, villagers were frustrated by ongoing delays to the proposed 70,000-*feddan* project,[8] and the Port Sudan branch threatened to boycott the assembly if immediate action was not taken. An alternative irrigation scheme was therefore proposed that involved a more modest project using large pumps to improve the irrigation of the *jerif* land, where villagers grew date palms. This proposal was agreed on, a new pump was received with state funding for the original project, and the leaders of the Port Sudan branch stayed in the Kanar area to oversee preliminary work after the meeting. Importantly, the shift in priorities from wheat to date cultivation represents a manipulation of state funding. More significant, however, is the way in which the rural community (through the mediation of the Port Sudan branch) was able to postpone the large-scale irrigation scheme in favor of a project that met its immediate needs more directly.

General assemblies also provide an occasion to bring together the range of local structures and processes through which migrant associations plan projects, advocate policies, and mobilize participation. Migrant associations therefore act as a node or "apex" (Barkan, McNulty, and Ayeni 1991, 462) for intracommunity support groups that represent a range of local constituencies. Significantly, these linkages also reveal degrees of overlap between governmental and nongovernmental organizations. Through their branches, urban migrant associations link the migrant community with other affiliated organizations such as students' groups, cooperatives, and women's associations.[9]

Rural branches also oversee a network of organizations, including benevolent societies, subcommittees that monitor village projects, and a range of parastatal and religious groups such as *Shabab al Wattan* (the national youth organization), the Holy Koran Society, the Working Women's Association, and the Farmers' Union. The relative weighting attached to urban and rural branches is an important factor in the planning and decision-making process. When the rural branch is considered to be the headquarters, contact with the migrant community may involve funding requests only.

A number of checks and balances combine to encourage participation and enhance the legitimacy of migrant associations. The key features here are the absence of financial restrictions on joining, traditional mechanisms of self-funding, cross-community participation, project accountability through seasonal migrant returns and general assemblies, and interlinked urban and rural organizational processes. Crucially, in this context, these mechanisms are effective in counteracting the tendency for prestige projects or other "urban" agendas to dominate.

Legitimacy and the Development Discourse in Sudan

Although on occasion the urban migrant community may act as an external donor in funding village requests, and although certain projects are entirely self-funded, migrant associations are also intermediaries between the community and other development actors. This forms the second, "upward" axis of the legitimacy debate for CBOs: their relationship with external donors, including nongovernmental agencies and the various wings of the state. Northern nongovernmental organizations (NNGOs) have worked with Sudanese migrant associations only on a sporadic basis. Several, including ACORD, Band Aid, and Community Aid Abroad, have provided assistance to the Nuba Mountains Association in Port Sudan. Save the Children Fund–U.S. and SOS Sahel have also responded to migrant associations' requests in western and northern Sudan, respectively, but generally these groups are not involved in long-term NGO programs. Rather, migrant associations are linked personally, institutionally, and through policy and ideology to the Sudanese state, which forms their principal source of external resources.

It is the nature of these linkages and their potential role in holding the state accountable to local demands that are significant in this discussion. It is often argued that a strong civil society with access to state machinery can make governments more responsive to their citizens and, indeed, foster a notion of "citizenship" (Fowler 1993, 335–36). Although religious organizations, trade unions, bar associations, and independent student bodies have, since 1989, been subject to various strategies of state control—including monitoring, coordination, co-optation, and dissolution (Bratton 1989)—migrant associations have maintained their integrity. Their immunity may be attributed to a low profile (particularly among groups from Northern Kordofan), institutional and personal connections with the state (most pronounced in associations from northern Sudan), and, most importantly, their invaluable role as public service providers.

Cliental contacts and state approval further enhance migrant associations' own authority and effectiveness in representing their rural communities, but their role in holding the state accountable to local interests is debatable. Geographically dispersed, without a federated superstructure, and with differential access to state offices and officers, Sudanese migrant associations' demands are irregular, isolated, and uncoordinated. Migrant associations do not challenge or influence government on a policy level but rather respond to opportunities afforded by the state agenda. They are key participants in a bargaining process for services and amenities that would not otherwise be implemented, and in this sense, they effect a degree of state accountability. But this role should not be exaggerated; overall, Sudanese migrant associations are important actors both in providing appropriate project solutions to state programs and in attaching local meaning to government policy. The following examples illustrate this point.

Responses to rural emergencies are particularly notable in relief efforts by migrant associations during the floods of 1988 and 1994 in northern Sudan. The *El Siyasa* newspaper reported that, "during the rains and flood disaster of 1988, the state apparatus stood like a mud-house in the middle of a sea of water and inertia." Meanwhile, migrant associations were instrumental in providing relief supplies. For example, the Nubian organizations from Wadi Halfa, Sakout, and Ma' has established an operations room in their shared clubhouse. In Northern State, migrant associations lobbied government ministries for supplies, rented trucks or planes, and transported medical personnel, drugs, food, and shelter to their rural communities, where committees, were established to target and monitor distribution. Preparations for the 1994 floods were substantially better. The government provided early warning of flood levels, and the associations organized work groups of returning migrants to build flood defenses. Nevertheless, relief supplies were still required, and it is significant that on this occasion, associations in Northern State attempted to coordinate their actions. Speakers from different migrant associations at planning meetings held in Khartoum echoed the sentiment of the Al Barkal Union, whose representative said, "we need solidarity to mobilize government support." As a result, a joint committee was established to collect damage- and needs-assessment reports, which were presented to the relevant ministers.

Projects in the health sector sponsored by migrant associations provide further evidence that, although access to the state and its limited resources is problematic, CBOs are able to provide effective and sustainable services according to local capacities and practices. Plans for upgrading the clinic in Al Maghawir, a village in River Nile State, were established at the local association's general assembly held in 1992. The design for the clinic was drawn up by an architect-member of the association, and temporary accommodation was provided by another. Personal connections with the Ministry of Health proved important for the association in identifying and recruiting a doctor, especially at a time when the exodus of trained medical staff from Sudan to the Gulf States was so acute that legislation had been passed to prevent it. In order to retain the doctor, the association offered to supplement his state salary with 50 percent of the profits from the clinic's private evening surgeries. The clinic's operation is monitored by a subcommittee of the rural branch of the migrant association.

In education, too, migrant associations have lobbied for resources to maintain local capacities in line with national standards. Financial support for *khalwas* (Koranic schools) in the 1930s and early 1940s was followed in the 1970s by support to upgrade primary schools after government attempts to increase the number of years spent in primary education. Reforms in 1992 increased the time spent in primary school even more and called for the construction of additional classrooms. Parents and communities were called upon again to provide these facilities. In response, the Kuri association in Khartoum, for example, coordinated a fund-raising campaign and "general return" to the village, in which forty migrants traveled to participate in work groups to construct the classrooms. Clearly, migrant associations provide services that the government is unable to offer, and the view expressed by a member of the Al Maghawir students' association, which runs literacy classes in the village during vacations, is not uncommon: "education is the responsibility of the state, but it is lagging behind, so we had to do something."

The patterns and themes discussed above are crystallized in the way in which migrant associations and the state appear to be engaged in a common discourse on national self-sufficiency called "return to the roots." Whereas infrastructural projects demonstrate the role of migrant associations and CBOs in public service delivery, "return to the roots" sees a shift toward a closer partnership between these associations and the state. In official discourse, "return to the roots" implies a search for the roots of Arabism and Islam and a quest for self-reliance. The policy manifests itself in a number of ways that draw on traditional processes and self-help organizations. For example, state-level funding campaigns advertised as *nafirs* (work groups) have sought to encourage private and commercial investment in infrastructural development, such as the administrative headquarters for El Metemma Province in River Nile State and the road from Omdurman to Dongola—*Tarid El Tahida* (the Challenge Road).

Since 1990, national self-sufficiency in food supply has been a key feature of this campaign and has focused on increasing agricultural production (particularly of wheat) in the northern region. The underlying message from the government is illustrated in comments made by the vice president, Major General Al Zubeir Mohamed Salih, during a visit to agricultural schemes in River Nile State in August 1994: "The Salvation Revolution is keen to prepare all lands in the state for wheat cultivation with a view to reaching self-sufficiency in this strategic food crop which is being used as a weapon against the Sudan by the forces of arrogance in the world" (*SUNA Daily Bulletin*, August 23, 1994). The lifting of subsidies on basic commodities and the extension of credit and investment funds through cooperative societies and the Agricultural Bank of Sudan have all been instigated to further this policy.[10]

For the migrant associations themselves, however, the policy of "return to the roots" has a different set of connotations. It is seen as an opportunity to take advantage of state funding, as expressed in the following statement by the president of the Kanar Union: "The government is advocating agricultural development, and there are schemes in the government's agenda targeting Northern State. We thought that we should step in and join hands with the government and implement these plans: to be the implementers and beneficiaries." As a result of this policy, the Kanar Union, along with at least ten other associations from the northern region, is planning a large-scale land rehabilitation and irrigation project. A significant implication of how this proposal ties in so closely with the state agenda is that the project monitoring committee is composed of national and provincial ministers as well as officials from the union. A further indication of the dynamism of associations in responding to funding possibilities is the growth of agricultural investment companies such as the Wifaqq Company for Investment and Development in Northern State, in which the Gilas association intends to participate.

At the same time, regional interpretations of "return to the roots" have added a fuller dimension to its meaning. Faced with ever more marginal urban employment opportunities and a chronic shortage of agricultural land and rural labor, the Kanar Union sees the national self-sufficiency campaign as an opportunity to encourage urban-rural return migration. The definition of "return to the roots" offered by the union's president also highlights the significance of urban-rural linkages in maintaining community identity: "The slogan 'Return to the Roots' we are advocating is literally meant to incite people to physically go back and develop the area and preserve rural values and heritage, it is a matter of preserving identity in a changing world."

Government policies and migrant association strategies represent a "meshing" of national and local interests (Barkan, McNulty, and Ayeni 1991, 463). Yet rather than defining priorities, migrant associations are engaged in a discourse with the state in which both the associations and the government are able to attribute their own meanings to the same process. Indeed, these examples indicate that "development" itself is an idiom that provides "an opportunity to perform joint acts in which each party can pursue its own initiatives" (Lithman 1984, 263). Furthermore, the case studies outlined in this chapter suggest that a dichotomous view of state and civil society is untenable and that, analytically, space should be left for engagement and disengagement, congruence and conflict (Bratton 1988, 418).

The two axes of legitimacy outlined in this chapter—internal and external—are central concerns in the wider debate on the performance and accountability of intervention by the nongovernmental sector. As potential partners for NGOs, which are increasingly concerned with institutional capacity building in the South, CBOs are assuming greater importance as representative, participatory, and accountable intermediaries. In the wider political debate surrounding democratization, "good governance," and the potential for a strong African civil society to hold states accountable to their citizens, the brokerage role of CBOs is also significant.

As we have attempted to illustrate, however, the internal legitimacy of CBOs, which is often assumed or glossed over in terms of membership control, self-funding, and popular support, rests on culturally organized processes. Foremost among these processes are the construction and negotiation of community attachment and identity, and the network of social checks and balances that enhances CBO participation and accountability. In terms of voicing local priorities in national or international agendas, the experience of migrant association–state relations in Sudan is cautionary. Although Sudanese associations exert some accountability in the bargaining process for social facilities, their current impact on state policy is limited. Sudanese CBOs do not act as bulwarks against the state but as intermediaries in negotiating and interpreting development in local terms.

Notes

This chapter draws on a study entitled "Rural-Urban Linkages: The Role of Migrant Associations in Sudanese Development," conducted jointly by SOS Sahel and Al Fanar Centre for Development Services. SOS Sahel is a U.K.-based NGO specializing in natural resource management and working in Sudan, Ethiopia, Mali, Niger, and Eritrea. Al Fanar is a research and consultancy group based in Khartoum. The research in Sudan is funded by the Ford Foundation. The study in Sudan forms part of a pan-Sahelian study also assessing local institutional dynamics in Mali and Ethiopia.

1. This is evident most dramatically in the formation of the Halfa National Committee in 1959, when the governments of Sudan and Egypt signed the agreement for the construction of the High Aswan Dam, which had significant consequences for local resettlement and rehabilitation.

2. The system of native administration, abandoned by Nimeiri in the 1970s and recently revived, is based on a positional hierarchy of sheikh, *omda,* and *nazir,* each representing corresponding areas—village, *omodiya, and nazara.*

3. These cases provide further evidence of contemporary settlement theories that indicate that local communities (the village or village group) are constructed as much by shared institutions (meeting places, markets, projects, and associations) as by physical features, and that in this respect, community should be seen as "a locus for discussing and implementing" (see Massaro 1994).

4. *Kashif* literally means "list." In rural areas, a person sitting in the *furash,* the male section of the compound, makes a record of names and donations. *Mujib* is the equivalent process for women. In urban areas, it is common for a *kashif* list to circulate among fellow office workers.

5. At the time of writing, US$1 equaled 380 Sudanese pounds.

6. *Fa'za* literally means "emergency call" and is the term most commonly used in northern regions of Sudan. Customarily, *nafir* are called for agricultural production in the fields of villagers unable to weed or harvest due to household labor shortages.

7. Located on the banks of the Nile River, villages in northern Sudan cultivate both land in front of the settlements (*jerif*) and land stretching behind the village itself (*gusad*).

8. A *feddan* is equal to 0.42 hectare or about one acre.

9. Migrant associations are male dominated, a reflection of a conservative Sudanese culture. In urban centers, women (a migrant minority) form mutual support groups, participate in students' associations, and, in a few cases, are represented on migrant association executive committees. In rural areas, women participate in the religious and women's branches of national parastatals and in *nafir,* where they prepare food for the labor groups.

10. Branches of the Agricultural Bank of Sudan have grown significantly from 34 in 1989 to 118 in 1994 (23 are located in Northern State).

References

Barkan, J. D., M. L. McNulty, M. A. O. Ayeni. 1991. "Hometown" voluntary associations, local development, and the emergence of civil society in western Nigeria. *Journal of Modern African Studies* 29:457–80.

Barnes, S. T. 1975. Voluntary associations in a metropolis: The case of Lagos. *African Studies Review* 18(2):75–87.

Bratton, M. 1988. Beyond the state: Civil society and associational life in Africa. *World Politics* 41(3):407–30.

———. 1989. The politics of government-NGO relations in Africa. *World Development* 17(4):560–87.

Carroll, Thomas F. 1992. *Intermediary NGOs: The supporting link in grassroots development.* West Hartford, Conn.: Kumarian Press.

Daum, C. 1992. *L'immigration ouest-africaine en France: Une dynamique nouvelle dans la vallée du fleuve Sénégal?* Paris: Institut Panos.

Fowler, A. 1993. Non-governmental organisations as agents of democratization: An African perspective. *Journal of International Development* 5(3):325–39.

Hamad, A. Z. 1993. Dismantling civil society: Suppression of freedom of association in Sudan. *Censorship News* (London) 27, art. 19.

Jules-Rosette, B. ed. 1979. *The new religions of Africa.* Norwood, N.J.: Ablex.

Lithman, Y. G. 1984. When tomorrow is today: Development as the idiom of routine. *Ethnos* 3–4:250–65.

Little, K. 1965. *West African urbanization: A study of voluntary associations in social change.* Cambridge: Cambridge University Press.

Massaro, R. J. 1994. Still searching for the missing link: Tanzanian national settlement strategies. Paper presented at the annual meeting of the African Studies Association, Toronto.

Trager, L. 1994. Rural-urban linkages and local "development": Whose agenda? What impact? Paper presented at the annual meeting of the African Studies Association, Toronto.

Uphoff, Norman T. 1987. *Local institutional development: An analytical sourcebook with cases.* West Hartford, Conn.: Kumarian Press.

─────── 12 ───────

NGOs and Development in East Africa

A View from Below

Zie Gariyo

This chapter summarizes some of the experiences of different types of NGOs in their attempts to improve the livelihoods of poor rural and urban communities in Africa. Based on evidence from fieldwork in Kenya, Tanzania, and Uganda, the discussion highlights the percep- tions of NGOs and grassroots organizations (GROs) toward development issues; discusses how support from Northern NGOs (NNGOs) influences the activities of Southern NGOs (SNGOs); and analyzes the extent to which state action and policies affect development programs and strat- egies in the region. During fieldwork in 1993, a total of ninety-five NGOs were surveyed, including twenty-one apex NGOs, twenty-five intermediary NGOs, thirty-six grassroots organizations (GROs), and thirteen NNGOs (Table 12.1).[1] Their activities ranged from service delivery (credit, health, and so on) to action-oriented research and lob- bying (human rights, environment, and so on).[2] A number of methods of data collection were used, including questionnaires, face-to-face interviews, and visits to project sites to ascertain the views and activi- ties of NGOs in East Africa and their perspectives on development and welfare issues.

As Table 12.1 shows, only a small number of GROs were surveyed in Tanzania and Kenya, because of the limited time available for field- work (five weeks in Tanzania and three weeks in Kenya). Since more GROs were surveyed in rural Uganda, the conclusions of the research on GROs are based largely on Ugandan experience. In Uganda, there are a few large apex NGOs, but intermediary NGOs tend to predominate. The many GROs we visited in Uganda are also affiliated with apex and intermediary NGOs. In Tanzania (where the formation of NGOs is a more recent phenomenon), development work is dominated by the three major churches; discussions held in Tanzania were with church (or related) development program officials in Arusha, Moshi, and Dodoma.

Table 12.1 Number and Type of Organizations Surveyed, by Country

Type of Organization	Tanzania	Kenya	Uganda
Apex (Southern) NGO	7	7	7
Intermediate NGO	6	6	13
Grassroots Organization (GRO)	4	3	29
Donor (Northern) NGO	7	6	–

Contextualizing NGOs and Development

Historically, most development programs at the community level in Africa have been dominated by the state. More recent intervention strategies are different because they have largely been promoted by foreign or foreign-sponsored agencies and because they rely on financial and material resources supplied from outside the country. This has important implications. Previously, most development initiatives were subordinated to state control; now they tend to be subordinated to foreign agencies. Both the design and the implementation of development programs are largely dominated by external development agencies. Fieldwork revealed that SNGO development programs (whether service delivery or otherwise) are heavily influenced by NNGOs. NNGOs have their own agendas and often specialize in particular activities or approaches: relief, environment, child sponsorship, health services, human rights, credit programs, training, and so on. Poor people themselves have little influence over most of these programs, as in other areas of aid policy and practice. As Bratton (1990, 90) noted, "Poor people have no control over the material and institutional conditions under which they exist . . . the poor lack the political 'clout' to make their own preferences stick." In addition, development programs have tended to target individuals rather than community problems: poverty alleviation programs tend to target women as beneficiaries but do not tackle women's subordination, nor do they transform "the systems and structures which determine the distribution of power and resources within and between societies" (Edwards and Hulme 1994, 13). The issue of women's empowerment is part of the larger process of social transformation, to which the response from the state remains muted at best and oppositional at worst.

The influence of NNGOs over development programs has also meant that issues of accountability have been transferred from the realm of bureaucratic reports to state functionaries to the realm of evaluation and monitoring reports to the headquarters of NNGOs in foreign capitals. Until recently, popular participation was not regarded as an essential component of NGO development programs. The African Charter for Popular Participation drawn up in Arusha in 1990 was in part a response to this situation. It called for a new era in Africa "in which democracy, accountability, economic justice and development for transformation become internalised" and stated that "the empowerment of the people, initiative and enterprise and democratisation of development are the order of the day in every country." Crucially, the charter noted that development cannot be divorced from the wider economic, social, and political processes in African societies; that for development and transformation to take place, community initiatives must be placed at the forefront; and that the development process is inescapably a part of the democratization process in Africa. These strictures have yet to be internalized in North-South NGO relations.

NGOs and Donor Dependence in East Africa

The links between NNGOs and East African NGOs are mainly financial. Financial assistance is, however, limited to the better-organized and more easily accessible apex and intermediary NGOs. Although some apex NGOs claim to have a paid membership, contributions from members are mainly token payments. Of the sixty-two NGOs and GROs in East Africa that responded to a questionnaire on their sources of funding, thirty-six reported that they depended on foreign donations for between 75 and 100 percent of their funding, and another seven received between 50 and 75 percent. The eighteen organizations that received less than 25 percent foreign funding were mainly GROs that have limited access to foreign donors or whose funding is mediated through apex and intermediary NGOs. Such high levels of foreign funding tend to deprive NGOs of a strong base in their own societies and contribute to their inability to plan for the long term.

Compounding this already difficult situation is the issue of accountability or, more precisely, the demand for strict accountability by external donor agencies. This comes in two forms. First, demands for strict financial accountability do not allow for flexibility in switching funds between alternative uses. Second, the demand for continual reports monitoring program activities, implementation, and the evaluation of achievements is extremely time-consuming. On lack of flexibility, an official from one NGO in central Uganda complained thus:

> We want to start our own income-generating projects so as to sustain our programs when the donors stop giving us financial assistance one day. The area we are in has rich fertile soils which can be used to grow food crops for sale in the main urban centers. Our donors cannot allow us to use part of the money they give us to purchase land and start an agricultural project. When donations stop this year, we would have wanted to be able to continue some form of assistance from our own

sources, but now it will be difficult. We shall have to close unless we get another donor.[3]

An official of another NGO in Nairobi involved in credit delivery had this to say:

They [the donor agencies] should give us money but should not dictate what we should use the money for. Sometimes we want to set up our own income-generating activities such as consultancies, training centers, or services such as accommodation units, but donors would not hear of it.[4]

Such views may appear utopian, but they are not isolated. They pervaded most of our discussions with the numerous NGOs we visited in all three countries. To break its dependence on donors, KENGO (the Network of Kenya Energy and Environmental Non-Government Organisations) has acquired a plot outside Nairobi to construct a training center and establish a business bureau to undertake consultancies to generate its own sources of funds in support of its environmental programs. Nevertheless, demands for strict accountability and adherence to rigid terms of reference limit the extent to which NGOs are able to shift development funds to related activities that are not specified in the initial program document. Much of the disillusionment of SNGOs with donors stems from their lack of control over their financial resources. In the long term, this limits their ability to create an independent source of material support for their programs. Above all, it reflects the influence of complex demands for financial accountability by NNGOs and official donor agencies (Edwards and Hulme 1994).

What is more difficult to explain is the level of bureaucracy that exists in many local NGOs, which donor agencies are also opposed to. Some donors insist that at least 75 percent of project funds go directly to beneficiaries or projects. However, evidence from the field revealed that salaries and other operational expenses often push the cost of administration to as high as 60 percent. For example, analysis of one proposal by TANGO (the umbrella organization for NGOs in Tanzania) revealed that out of a total package required for a three-year training program, less than 20 percent was directly allocated for training. Salaries and consultants' fees were allocated 14.2 percent and 29.2 percent, respectively; equipment and travel 19.6 percent; rent 3.0 percent; and other miscellaneous charges 15.5 percent.

Apex NGOs, GROs, and Village-Level Development

Apex NGOs are networks of member organizations formed partly at the initiative of NNGOs to coordinate development activities at the grassroots level. However, the membership of apex NGOs in East Africa remains limited to GROs that are easily accessible or to intermediary NGOs that are more highly organized. Part of the explanation for the weak links that exist between apex NGOs and their members is that membership is based on co-optation rather than being a response to pressure from below. Thus, NGOs such as KENGO and the National Union of Disabled Persons of Uganda (NUDIPU), despite being membership networks, tend to operate more as national registration centers and clearinghouses for other organizations. Other apex NGOs have been formed in response to hostility and pressure from the state. TANGO, formed in 1989, and the Development Network of Indigenous Voluntary Associations (DENIVA) in Uganda, formed in 1992, were both established to provide a protective shield and a united voice for their members.

In both TANGO and DENIVA, however, financial contributions from affiliates and member organizations represent only a token amount of their total budgets. This has important implications. First, it reduces the potential influence of member organizations on decision making. Second, because they are themselves dependent on foreign funding, the activities of apex NGOs (such as networking, training, and research) may be determined not by the demands of their members but by the amount of financial support available from outside. Accountability may not respond to demands for effective representation from below. Weak links between the grassroots and the apex body restrict the developmental impact of NGOs, because of "the failure of NGOs to make the right linkages between their work at microlevel and the wider systems and structures of which they form a small part. . . . In other words, small-scale NGO projects will never be enough to secure lasting improvement in the lives of poor people" (Edwards and Hulme 1992, 13–14).

Because most apex NGOs are dependent on donors, they are less able to support independent GRO initiatives and tend instead to integrate them still further into the world of foreign aid. This is summed up by the comments of the chairperson of a grassroots women's organization in Mbale, eastern Uganda:

> We were told to form a group so as to obtain financial support. We went for training seminars on project proposal writing, project planning, and implementation. When we came we wrote a proposal. It is almost a year; we have not received any money.[5]

Further problems arise because of internal organizational, structural, and institutional weaknesses in GROs. In most cases, GROs are too small, too poor, and too weak institutionally to take on larger and longer-term development programs. They are loosely organized and have little influence over the larger urban-based NGOs and institutions. Most are located in remote areas and are therefore unable to benefit from the information systems available to apex and intermediary NGOs. Small GROs also tend to take on a wide range of unrelated activities, thus stretching their own meager resources too thinly.

Another disturbing aspect of GRO-NGO relations concerns the erosion of voluntary participation. Historically, the strength of village-based GROs has been their reliance on voluntary participation and contributions in the form of funds or labor from their members. This had several advantages. Accountability (in terms of decision making and project implementation) had a popular mandate, and the organization was accountable to the membership and not to any outside authority. Projects acknowledged and built on existing initiatives within communities. As a result of externally derived initiatives, this perspective is slowly being eroded. Presently, most development programs consist of either elaborate project proposals seeking foreign funding or donor-derived projects such as credit schemes, income-generating projects, and health or child sponsorship schemes seeking local participation. Membership lacks real strength and permanence. Of the twenty-nine GROs surveyed in Uganda, fewer than ten (mainly savings cooperatives) could claim a membership of more than ten registered and fully paid-up members. With such a limited membership, it is difficult to move accountability from being donor driven to being membership driven.

The State, NGOs, and Development: Collaboration or Recognition?

Bratton (1990, 95–96) has argued that "selective collaboration between NGOs and the state is likely to be more productive than confrontation." Relationships between NGOs and the state in East Africa remain cold. Most African governments remain suspicious of any independent initiative that attempts to mobilize and provide services to disadvantaged communities without the direct involvement of the state. Because increasing NGO involvement in development has been conceived as a challenge to state hegemony and a response to state failures, this has intensified such suspicions. In a report to a workshop on NGOs, an official of a Ugandan NGO commented:

> In some cases relationships with government are characterized by suspicion and mistrust. Some government officials are fearful that as NGOs gain greater recognition by donor agencies, they will begin to compete with government for outside funds. . . . NGOs on their part lack knowledge of and access to government aid priorities and programs due to the tight secrecy that surrounds them.[6]

There is also a tendency to characterize NGOs as collaborators of state functionaries. In Tanzania, TANGO noted:

The general attitude of government towards NGOs in the country is that these are collaborators in development and have a role to play. . . . It is held, from official point of view, that NGOs will not work against government policies but will help in achieving the social goals and objectives which are pronounced from time to time. (TANGO and AMREF 1992)

Governments tend to see NGOs as an extension of state policy. They are expected to implement government policy instead of charting their own independent agenda. This undermines the social base of NGOs in their efforts to pursue an alternative development path for the poor and marginalized sections of East African societies, in the face of the failure of state-centered development. Generally, NGOs are not opposed to implementing government policy. Most, however, are opposed to deliberate frustration by state functionaries and to increasing state monitoring, control, and direction. Sections of the state leadership have occasionally branded NGOs as "foreign agents." For example, at the height of multiparty debates in Uganda in 1992, the Foundation for African Development (FAD), an indigenous NGO, was accused by the president of Uganda in a statement to Parliament of serving "foreign interests." In its defense, FAD took out a newspaper advertisement that stated:

Our attention has been drawn to a statement dated 6th August 1992 presented to the National Resistance Council (NRC) . . . also attributed to the President. In the statement reference is to made to 'Certain Foreign Groups, e.g., FAD' . . . having persistently not heeded advice that the interim period be a time of national recuperation and of allowing the population of Uganda to chart their own future. . . . The Foundation for African Development is *not a foreign group*. It is an organisation which was founded in Uganda by Ugandans way back in 1979.[7]

FAD continued:

Reference has been made about FAD receiving foreign assistance. This is not a secret. . . . This is not peculiar to FAD . . . we do not need to mention the so many Ugandan NGOs which depend entirely on foreign donations and assistance without being subjected to the kind of accusations FAD is constantly subjected to. The Government itself is depending on foreign assistance.

These are not isolated incidences. They depict the precarious situation in which NGOs work if they intend to pursue programs independent of those sanctioned by the state. Some East African governments have turned suspicion and mistrust into an attempt to extend direct control over NGO activities. In Uganda, for example, all NGOs (both foreign and local) are required to register with the NGO Registration Board under the Ministry of Internal Affairs. NGO Statute No. 5 of 1989 states: "No organisation shall operate in Uganda unless it has been duly registered with the board." One of the functions of the board is "to guide and monitor organisations in carrying out their activities." The membership of the board includes officials of the two major intelligence organizations. Statutory Instrument No. 9 of 1990 further states that "an organisation shall in carrying out its operations comply with the following: it shall not make any direct contact with the people in any part of the rural areas of Uganda unless it has given seven days notice in writing of its intention so to do to the Resistance Committee and the District Administrator of the area." Compounding the complexity of control is the fact that coordination and monitoring of NGOs fall to the prime minister's office, where NGOs are "expected to register and declare their project proposals and to require an endorsement for their correspondence with foreign donors to solicit for funds."[8] Like most Ugandan government policies, however, these laws have not been implemented, largely because the board "has no resources to guide and monitor NGOs. . . . There is one full time officer and a clerk, no office equipment and transport, and an inadequate budget" (Ratter and Kwesiga 1994, 17).

As a response to the power of the state, some NGOs have chosen the path of collaboration in order to survive both financially and politically. The co-opting of politicians onto NGO boards and management committees has been used to secure additional protection. In turn, NGOs are allowed access to information about government programs and policies, for example, via NGO representatives at meetings of local and national planning authorities. Some of the large NGOs, such as KENGO and Maendeleo ya Wana Wake in Kenya and the Community Development Trust Fund (CDTF) and the Family Planning Association (UMATI) in Tanzania, have appointed prominent politicians and senior public officials to their boards.

This research does not, however, suggest that the situation for NGOs in East Africa is hopeless. Indeed, to emphasize their independent existence, attempts are being made to forge regional linkages between NGOs in eastern and southern Africa, to "harness the capacities of NGOs in the region to articulate and implement an African development agenda rooted in on-going experiences and analyses, with a sensitivity to both the realities and aspirations of African societies."[9] The NGOs that participate in such networks are both indigenous and foreign. The extent to which such efforts can forge an economic, social, and political development agenda for transformation, participation, and democratization remains to be seen, but seeking recognition from (rather than collaboration with) the state seems to be a better strategy for NGOs in the region.

There are a number of lessons to be learned from the research presented above. First, there is an obvious need for African NGOs to become less dependent on foreign initiatives, which tend to bring only short-term benefits. Second, NGOs and GROs in East Africa have yet to come to terms with a context of development assistance that emphasizes projects and programs to the exclusion of social and economic transformation. Development assistance that seeks to solve the immediate problems of individuals can succeed only in the short term. Long-term development requires that development be viewed as a process that seeks to overhaul the present social and economic structures that are responsible for the destitution and deprivation of poor people in rural and urban areas. For some time now, NGOs have merely responded to the crisis of poverty and deprivation; they need to go beyond this narrow perspective.

Within this context, it is pertinent to note that NGOs are not a substitute for the state in the process of development in Africa. Nor are they to be conceived simply as partners of government. The state and NGOs have different perspectives on development. Development cannot ignore politics, and in order to facilitate transformation, NGOs must pursue an agenda that seeks to democratize both economic and political power. Thus, the development of organizational capacity and skills among poor people should be enhanced within the NGO agenda. Last, NGOs need to enhance their struggle for recognition as independent organizations with a specific agenda of their own, and not organizations to be tolerated by the state or subordinated to its interests.

Notes

A more detailed version of this chapter was published as a Working Paper of the Centre for Basic Research, Kampala.

1. Apex NGOs are usually hierarchical, urban-based organizations formed (partly at the suggestion of donors) to act as a link between NNGOs and SNGOs. Intermediary NGOs are dependent on donor funds and are often formed by university graduates, as a form of employment for themselves and as a response to the harsh socioeconomic climate resulting from the structural adjustment programs implemented in Africa since the early 1980s. GROs are village-based groups formed to pursue the interests of their members.

2. Thirteen other organizations were included in the survey from government training institutes and trade unions in Kenya, Tanzania, and Uganda. They do not form part of the analysis for this chapter.

3. Fieldwork interview, administrator, Senyange Project, Masaka, Uganda.

4. Fieldwork interview, credit manager, Kenya Rural Enterprises Programme.

5. Fieldwork interview, chairperson of Muyembe Women's Cooperative Society.
6. Report by Ssentamu-Makumbi, executive director, Joint Energy and Environment Projects (JEEP), Kampala, 1992.
7. The full-page statement appeared in *New Vision*, August 28, 1992.
8. *New Vision*, May 16, 1992. Statement by Dr. Madraa, national coordinator of NGOs in the prime minister's office, to a meeting of indigenous NGOs in Lira, northern Uganda. This directive has largely remained unimplemented. With more than 1,000 registered NGOs by 1994—most of them seeking foreign assistance for projects—the administrative costs of such an undertaking would be very high.
9. This policy framework is contained in a workshop report titled "Consultation on a Research and Advocacy Agenda for African NGOs," prepared by Mwelekeo wa NGO, or a Vision for NGOs (MWENGO), an eastern and southern African reflection and development center for NGOs, held at Nakuru, Kenya, July 26–29, 1991.

References

Bratton, M. 1990. Non-governmental organisations in Africa: Can they influence policy? *Development and Change* 21(1):87–118.

Edwards, M., and D. Hulme, eds. 1992. *Making a difference: NGOs and development in a changing world*. London: Earthscan.

————. 1994. *NGOs and development: Performance and accountability in the "new world order."* Background paper for the SCF/IDPM Workshop on NGOs and Development, Manchester, June 27–29.

Ratter, A., and J. B. Kwesiga. 1994. *Realizing the development potential of NGOs and community groups in Uganda*. Report for the Ministry of Finance and Economic Planning, Kampala.

TANGO and AMREF. 1992. *Strengthening the efficiency and development impact of TANGO and its member NGOs in Tanzania*. TANGO policy paper. Dar es Salaam: TANGO.

Part III

Ways Forward

13

Assessing NGO Performance

Difficulties, Dilemmas, and a Way Ahead

Alan F. Fowler

The 1990s have witnessed a significant increase in efforts to assess the performance of nongovernmental, nonprofit development organizations (NGOs). This trend can be traced to a number of factors. First, since the early 1980s, a growing proportion of financial resources used by NGOs has derived from the official aid system, overtaking, in terms of rate of growth, their income from public giving (Fowler 1992a). Public funds are accompanied by more stringent "contractual" demands for financial accountability and the realization of agreed-on impacts (Hawley 1993). Second, the post–Cold War rationale for official overseas development assistance is further accelerating shifts in donor priorities toward the institutional restructuring of recipient countries, with a corresponding push on NGOs to alter their role in society. Effective management of such organizational transformations requires sound and timely information about achievement. Third, NGOs tend to argue that they are more cost-effective than governments in reaching and serving people who are poor or marginalized and they are now being called upon to demonstrate that this is indeed the case (UNDP 1993; van Dijk 1994). Fourth, there is a growing realization that organizational effectiveness is positively correlated with an ability to learn from experience (Senge 1990). This insight is argued to be of particular relevance for NGOs because, as entities dedicated to social change, they predominantly function as natural open systems (Scott 1987, 105–15; Fowler, Campbell, and Pratt 1992, 17–19), in which performance is dependent on and sensitive to instability and rapid change in the external environment. Such situations are common in both the South and the North. Learning requires data about all aspects of organizational functioning, prompting greater attention to the need to gather evidence of impact and to assess the capacity to adapt.

NGOs have always understood the need to assess their performance. However, the growing internal and external pressures sketched above are bringing to light serious inadequacies in past attempts to do so—

169

inadequacies that stem from fundamental difficulties inherent in the development approach adopted by the aid system, the concept of performance when applied to nonprofit organizations, and the way developmental NGOs need to profile themselves in order to secure and maintain public support and funding.

This chapter reviews the difficulties and dilemmas that accompany attempts to determine NGO effectiveness and charts some practical ways ahead. The first section looks at the basic problems of performance assessment that arise as a result of contradictions between the principles underpinning international aid and the nature of sustainable change that aims to benefit poor people. The intrinsic difficulties of identifying performance criteria for nonpublic, nonprofit organizations are examined in the second section. This analysis identifies the challenges to be overcome in designing approaches to NGO performance assessment that are sound, practical, and cost-effective, approaches that are the subject of the third section. The concluding section of the chapter offers some speculative observations on ongoing attempts by NGOs to gain more insight into what they are achieving.

Factors Affecting the Assessment of Project Performance

Figure 13.1 provides an overview of the factors that condition NGOs' ability to determine what impact they are making in terms of the people they are established to serve. It shows the interconnections commonly found in the project flow of international development resources; the interfaces where one organization's ends become another's means; the factors that influence the flow of resources; and the different points at which performance can be assessed in terms of outputs, outcomes, or impacts.

Development as a Linear Process

The international aid system was initially premised on the notion of underdevelopment as a "deficit" in capital, knowledge, and technology. The transfer of such resources from richer to poorer economies would, it was believed, enable or speed up economic growth, leading to an improvement in the material circumstances and well-being of poorer strata within recipient societies. Projects—discrete packages of resources and activities—were the mechanism chosen to achieve this outcome. The project mode of development, sometimes called the "blueprint approach," assumes that it is possible to predetermine a set of cause-and-effect relationships that will turn resources, knowledge, or technology into desired and sustainable human change. In other words, this approach assumes that it is possible to predict and create a knowable future (Roling and de Zeeuw 1987).

Figure 13.1   NGOs in the Aid Chain

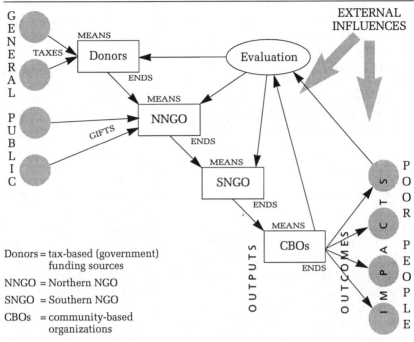

Donors = tax-based (government)
        funding sources

NNGO = Northern NGO

SNGO = Southern NGO

CBOs   = community-based
         organizations

The notion of prediction and a controllable future underpins "hard" science and its application to the physical world. It also determines what is considered to be valid knowledge and dictates the methods by which such knowledge can be gathered and validated. Most critically, knowledge must be objective in the sense that it is derived from observation in the real world that can be demonstrated to be independent of the persons doing the observing. Under these assumptions, it should be possible to define and plan a project as a linear process of causes and effects, using resources in a predetermined sequence of activities to produce the desired outcome. Logical framework analysis is an instrument now commonly used for designing this type of development.

Putting project development into practice requires action by a number of organizations that are tied together like a chain between the resource provider and those intended to benefit. Figure 13.1 shows the typical setup for NGOs. From left to right in the diagram, resources move either directly (as gifts from constituents in the richer North) or indirectly (from taxes through governmental donors) to Northern NGOs (NNGOs), to Southern NGOs (SNGOs), and then to community-based organizations (CBOs) comprising poor people and households. Each organization obtains resources (or "means" in Figure 13.1) to fulfill its role while its processes and capacities are tailored toward goals (or "ends") that are set in relation to an overall mission and the specific objectives of the project. If all goes well, the result of this joint endeavor is the realization of a predefined impact on human well-being.

Despite attempts at rigorous study, there is far from unanimous evidence that project-based aid achieves the intended effects reliably (Cassen 1986; White and Woestman 1994). In fact, some analysts argue that 60 percent or more of such aid is ineffective (Hancock 1989). If this is the case, there must be something essentially questionable about such an approach to development.

Development as Complex, Contingent Change

Accumulated experience shows that the principle and practice described above are seriously flawed for most types of human and social change. First, the concept of a knowable future is highly questionable, as is the validity of the notion of objective knowledge (Long and Long 1992; Wolpert 1992). Second, the blueprint approach requires an ability to control all the factors outside of the project that may influence its outcome. This degree of control is possible in only a limited number of instances, usually where technology is dominant, such as with road and bridge construction or telecommunications.

At least five other factors work against the linear approach to realizing what is intended. First, as one moves along the chain in Figure 13.1, the number of actors involved increases, and each has its own perspective and set of interests that are not static. Second, each actor's behavior is conditioned to a greater or lesser degree on external forces, with NGOs particularly dependent on the vagaries of external finance for the maintenance of their core functions (Hudock 1994). Third, the increase of contingent factors in project progress gives rise to greater levels of uncertainty and unpredictability. In addition, the timescale required for observing effects or changes tends to lengthen. For example, reducing infant mortality rates cannot be seen from the life or death of one child. Only after a longer period does this type of change become apparent. Fourth, human well-being is determined by many external elements that are integrated within an individual. Improving access to potable water, although useful in itself, will not mean much if food intake is diminishing, nor will economic investment mean much if there is no political or financial stability, nor will education mean much if it cannot be applied to anything tangible. Finally, getting returns from external flows of financial investments, knowledge, or technology is determined by how people use them (their behavior), whereas who benefits is determined by people's ability to organize and by the basis on which power, influence, and control over resources are distributed.

An example can help illustrate what these factors mean in terms of practical impact assessment. Assume that a particular population group suffers from poor health due to inadequate nutrition. One reason identified for this situation is the high percentage of harvested crops lost in storage. A project is defined and designed by an NGO to introduce improved grain stores. The *output* of the NGO's work can be measured in terms of the number of stores built and at what cost. However, the *outcome* of the project will have to be measured in terms of a reduction of crops lost during storage (which may take more than one season to determine), which, in turn, will be critically affected by how the grain stores are used from one season to the next (by people's behavior). The nominal value of the crops saved can be set against the cost of the store to calculate a financial cost-benefit, but this will be possible only some years after project completion. Project *impact* must be sought in the improved nutritional status of the population, which is unlikely to be determined by grain alone and will require distinctive non-agricultural or economic measures, such as improvement in anthropometric status and reduced incidence of nutrition-related illnesses such as kwashiorkor. Further, the spread of impact on human well-being will be determined by the differential ability of household members to gain access to the increased food supply, and experience shows that women and children tend to have the weakest entitlements.

To all the above must be added the fact that, although varying significantly between countries, overall international aid is only a tiny proportion of the flow of resources and knowledge between countries and levels within societies. For example, the World Bank's total lending in 1993 was the equivalent of the amount transferred by international capital markets in the space of nine minutes.[1] The idea that aid can, will, or does "make the difference" to world development or the distribution of poverty is illusory; far larger forces are in play.

Together, these factors, and the interplay between them, reduce the validity of predictive change as an appropriate approach to socioeconomic development. Indeed, it is increasingly argued by even the most hardened physical scientists and economists that development at all levels of the natural and social order is the product of complex and contingent processes that are only partially amenable to prediction and control (Anderson, Arrow, and Pines 1988; Waldrop 1993; Lewin 1994; Gell-Mann 1994). They point out that as component systems of the world evolve, they interlock and give rise to new (emergent) properties. For example, computerization and communication technology are creating new ways of organizing, including "virtual organizations." Similarly, localized environmental degradation caused by myriad individuals struggling to survive across all the continents of the world can combine to destabilize whole patterns of weather or lifestyles of the better-off. Simple rules employed by billions of people operating in parallel can lead to dramatic, unexpected outcomes.

In sum, the basic linear principles on which development aid is allocated do not correspond to the complex, contingent way that development actually occurs. This fundamental mismatch complicates performance assessment, particularly when it comes to attributing causes to effects and working out what would have happened anyway (the "counterfactual" case). This realization has increased the call for a new sort of development professionalism not premised on linearity (Chambers 1985, 1993). The gap between the principles of aid and the nature of poverty creation and alleviation makes life particularly difficult for NGOs, which need to convince their supporters and funders that *they* have made the difference to people's well-being. Because they cannot levy taxes, NGOs (more than official aid agencies) face a major problem of public persuasion if performance assessment cannot attribute effects to causes.

Assessing NGO Organizational Performance

NGOs must contend with the fact that they belong to a category of organization with no straightforward or uncontested measure of organizational, as distinct from project, effectiveness. In other words, unlike governments and businesses (which can be assessed, respectively, in terms of political support and financial returns) nonprofits have no readily acknowledged "bottom line."

A "Bottom Line" for Nonprofit Organizations

By nature of their (social) function, NGOs provide services to a segment of the population that is unable to meet the full cost of what it receives: if the poor could afford the services, they would go to the market as consumers (Fowler 1989; Leat 1993). Financial returns cannot, therefore, serve as a measure of organizational performance. Likewise, as self-established entities not owned or mandated by those they serve, NGOs cannot use feedback from political processes such as those intended to legitimize governments. What approach can be adopted to establish the standards against which nonprofit organizational performance can reasonably be assessed?

Measuring the performance of nonstate, nonprofit development organizations, rather than of the projects they implement, is a relatively new issue in the development arena. Its arrival is tied to the growing concern, associated with increased aid from official sources, that their organizational capacity is inadequate for the expanding role they are expected and funded to play (Campbell 1990). At present, therefore, an analysis of the problems associated with measuring the organizational performance of developmental NGOs must draw mainly on work focusing on nonprofits operating in the North.

Some fifteen years ago, the well-known organizational analyst Rosbeth Moss Kanter (1979) reviewed the wide range of conceptual dilemmas, practical difficulties, contending principles, and different methods adopted in attempts to determine nonprofit effectiveness, productivity, and performance. She concluded that:

1. The measurement of effectiveness must be related to a particular context and life stage of the organization.

2. Rather than seeking universal measures, the need is to identify appropriate questions reflecting multiple criteria.

3. The concept of assessment of organizational goals should be replaced with the notion of organizational *uses*; in other words, to recognize the fact that "different constituencies use organisations for different purposes." (Kanter 1979, 36)

Drucker (1990) reaches essentially the same conclusions, namely, that:

1. Performance must be determined and interpreted contextually.

2. Questions should form the base of the assessment approach.

3. Standards must derive from the various constituencies that the organization serves.

4. The process of organizational assessment should be participatory.

Another approach to performance assessment of nonprofits working in the North relates to the "contract culture" that is shaping their role, position, and behavior (Smith and Lipsky 1993) and rapidly permeating the aid system (OECD 1993). This approach focuses on the quality of service provided. Lawrie (1993, 19) identifies four types of performance indicator in this respect: (per unit) cost, take-up or "occupancy," impact or result, and user reaction. Each has different applications and levels of difficulty in terms of definition, the ability to obtain the needed information, and degrees of precision and tangibility. He stresses the distinction between performance indicators as unambiguous (or what he calls "dials") and as contestable (or "tin openers").[2] Lawrie notes the bias that funders have toward "dials" and the insufficient time available to negotiate "tin openers." Organizational effectiveness (in terms of quality of service) is determined by measuring gaps that exist in the expectations and perceptions of different stakeholders. What might all this mean for development NGOs?

The "Bottom Line" for Development NGOs

Each of the analyses noted above highlights the difficulties involved in identifying a nonprofit "bottom line," even when the purpose is reasonably straightforward, for example, providing a direct welfare service such as running a home for elderly people or a shelter for the homeless. Developmental NGOs are faced with an additional obstacle because, as shown in Figure 13.1, the "product" of their endeavors (sustainable development for poverty alleviation) *is not produced by NGOs but by (poor) people themselves* (Lewis et al. 1988). In other words, at best, NGOs can facilitate and support the process of people's own development and need to be assessed in how well they do this, in addition to what their work realizes in terms of material change.

Yet another complication arises because the funds that SNGOs employ are normally derived from foreign sources. This separates the political relationship between giver and receiver and means that there is no recognized system by which the satisfaction or dissatisfaction of those served can be fed back to the funder independent of the NGO itself.[3] This situation does not arise in the North, where local or national political processes can serve to monitor the performance of nonprofit organizations.

These problems have resulted in performance appraisal for most NGOs being stuck at the point of comparing outputs with intentions, that is, with (negotiated) plans such as the number of wells built, number of people attending training activities, and repayment rates for credit. Crucial elements of development processes, such as people's degree of control over decisions or the capabilities of community-based organizations (CBOs), are seldom assessed at all. There is a general consensus that this situation is neither adequate nor acceptable (Marsden, Oakley, and Pratt 1994). How can this accumulation of obstacles be overcome? Is there a way forward?

A Way Ahead in NGO Performance Assessment

The problems recounted above are not new; for a number of years, both researchers and practitioners have recognized them and have been actively looking for ways to overcome them. However, more progress has been made in assessing project performance than in assessing the performance of NGOs themselves. These two strands are tied together, only weakly if at all, with the measurement of project impact separated from organizational appraisal. However, a common principle underlying both is the need to involve stakeholders more systematically.

A Unifying Principle: Engaging Multiple Stakeholders Structurally and Systematically

Attempts to reconcile the contradictions of linear versus contingent development, as well as to assess NGO effectiveness, share a common principle—that of structured multiple stakeholder involvement.[4]

In relation to project performance, a promising direction for impact assessment appears to lie in the application of frameworks and methods that allow all interested parties to have a say in defining means and ends. Causes and effects are negotiated, monitored, and evaluated from the perspectives of the actors who can be reasonably assumed to have an influence on both progress and impact. One approach of this sort that has been tested in practice is the marrying of logical framework analysis and objective-oriented intervention planning (INTRAC/South Research 1994). Over a period of time (up to a year), the goals, objectives, existing context, and processes to be used are discussed with the stakeholders whose involvement will be critical to a project's definition and implementation. Differences in motivation and perceptions underpinning what is to be achieved, who is likely to benefit, and how they will benefit become apparent early on, so that compromises can be negotiated. Rather than crippling a project later on, conflicts can be identified and a decision made whether the preconditions exist for the initiative to be viable.

In terms of organizational appraisal, involving stakeholders in this way calls for some form of social accounting of multiple interests (Epstein, Flamholtz, and McDonough 1977, 76, cited in Kanter 1979).[5] One recent application of these principles—known as a "social audit" and derived from a process of independent social accounting—is being tested by Traidcraft and the New Economics Foundation (Traidcraft 1994; see also Chapter 17 of this volume). Here, performance criteria are negotiated with four key stakeholders: producers, staff, consumers, and shareholders. In parallel with the financial audit, an independent person obtains feedback on stakeholders' views about the degree to which Traidcraft has fulfilled the standards agreed on.[6]

More recently, Oxfam (United Kingdom and Ireland) initiated an "assembly" of some 250 diverse stakeholders—partners, advisers, associates, volunteers, staff, senior managers, donors, "friends," and others—to deliberate and provide advice on strategic issues facing the organization, such as whether or not to work in the United Kingdom (Oxfam 1994). The assembly is advisory and not a formal part of Oxfam's organization. Yet the step taken by Oxfam contains a clear moral imperative to take the assembly seriously or risk being publicly derided and written off as a dishonest organization.[7]

It is too early to ascertain what the influence of these initiatives will be for the overall performance of these organizations.

The Importance of Process

It is beyond the scope of this chapter to detail precisely how multiple stakeholder involvement is obtained. However, some points are worthy of note. First, stakeholder input is not an on-off affair but a continual process within the organization's functioning. One option being adopted by some NGOs is to establish a permanent advisory body composed of different stakeholders whose task is to monitor organizational performance in meeting standards that have been agreed on and modified by mutual consent.

Second, creating a systematic way of engaging multiple stakeholders is unlikely to be free of conflict and risk, especially when different levels of authority and power exist. In this situation, the weighting of different stakeholders is important. Additional pitfalls can arise when there is a significant disparity in understanding between donor, NGO, and recipients about what development is or entails. For example, in NGOs funded by child sponsorship, a donor may wish its sponsored child to receive direct handouts, as may the child's parents. In these circumstances, how can the organization justify a nonwelfare, community-based approach? Bringing parties together as stakeholders invites organizational disturbance![8]

Third, the process of stakeholder engagement should help build the capacity of the parties involved, particularly the poor and marginalized, whose ability to put forward their interests is most likely to be constrained. In sum, to be useful and meaningful, obtaining stakeholder engagement must be matched by the right processes.

NGO Performance Assessment as Combined Social Judgment

Multiple stakeholder engagement allows the performance of NGOs (as organizations dedicated to social change) to be defined as the (often contested) outcome of the social judgments of the parties involved, using criteria that are important to them. The methods set out above help temper the shortcomings of "linear" approaches by:

1. Contextualizing assessment and hence taking account of contingency;

2. Making the interpretation of events more objective as multiple perspectives are brought to bear; and

3. Contributing to cost-effectiveness by combining capacity building with performance monitoring.

In sum, the key to NGO assessment appears to lie in identifying and using as performance standards the criteria or factors that relevant people are likely to use when making a judgment.

Herman and Heimovics (1994) describe and examine how this can be done in practice by constructing and employing "vignettes." A vignette is a picture built up from criteria (and values attached to them) that relevant stakeholders would use to judge the organization. For example, as measures of effectiveness, they may include the percentage of income spent on fund-raising, the proportion made up by contributions from volunteers, the percentage of revenue coming from government, the profile of those the organization actually reaches, the gender divisions within the organization, and so on. Vignettes, describing what interested parties consider to be signs of effectiveness, can help construct a bottom line.

Uniting the Strands: Performance as an Expression of Organizational Capacities

A key weakness in today's practice of NGO performance assessment is the separation of project evaluations from features of the organization itself, as if each has relatively little or nothing to do with the other, which is patently not the case. For example, one recent comparative impact assessment of NGO work in credit provision did not take organizational variables into account when explaining differences in performance (Riddell and Robinson 1992). One way of bringing together the major facets of NGO performance is to use the concept of organizational capacity. Neither NGOs nor donors have a uniform definition of "capacity" (James 1994). However, current uses of the term imply that capacity can be understood as a number of core abilities, together with the means and relationships through which they are expressed. Analysis of the NGO sector in Africa indicates that, to be effective, three principal areas of ability are required:

1. An ability to *be*, that is, to maintain its specific identity, values, and mission.

2. An ability to *do*, that is, to achieve stakeholder satisfaction.

3. An ability to *relate*, that is, to manage external interactions while retaining autonomy.

When combined, these three areas of organizational ability determine the overall performance of NGOs as well as their role and institutional position as civic actors (Fowler 1992b; Fowler, Campbell, and Pratt 1992). Figure 13.2 is a schematic presentation of the above.

A significant amount of effort is presently being applied to the identification of appropriate indicators of capacity and effectiveness in each of these areas, although endeavors are biased toward measures of achievement in various types of poverty-reducing sectoral investments (Carvalho and White 1993).[9] Progress in locating indicators of organizational capacity in terms of "being" and "relating" is less advanced, in part because of the relatively recent concern about them, and in part due to the inherent difficulties described above.

The design and practical testing of organizational assessment indicators and methods currently undertaken with NGOs reconfirm that question-based approaches are likely to be the most viable.[10]

Figure 13.2   Types of Performance as Factors in
NGO Organizational Capacity

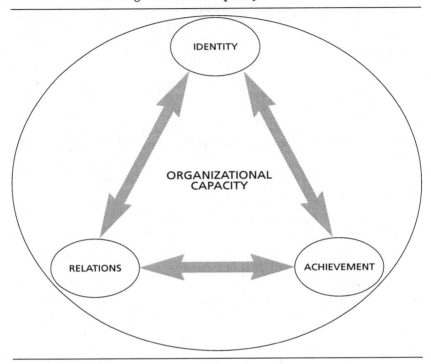

Drucker (1993) believes that there are five key questions an NGO should ask itself:

1. What is our business (mission)?

2. Who is our customer?

3. What does the customer consider valuable?

4. What have been our results?

5. What is our plan?

From these derive all sorts of subquestions, which must be answered by the organization in a participatory way, involving all levels of staff as well as the board, facilitated by a skilled, independent outsider. However, interpreting the answers to these questions requires that users have a firm understanding of the nature of nonprofit organizations. Bringing staff up to the necessary level of insight, often including the cross-cultural dimensions of organizational behavior, requires significant investment and guided application. More often than not, it appears that time and other resource constraints present the major hurdle to NNGOs when carrying out a thorough organizational assessment of or with their partners. Although some Northern agencies have involved their partners in policy formulation and "reverse evaluations" (with mixed success), there is little evidence to date to suggest that many NGOs are aware of the potential of, or are actively moving toward, a set of standards and measures for performance appraisal negotiated among their stakeholders.

Easing Management Tensions:
Linking Performance and Accountability

A final, and perhaps most significant, feature of structured stakeholder performance assessment is that it simultaneously resolves some of the difficulties faced by NGOs in satisfying the multiple demands for functional and strategic accountability (Edwards and Hulme 1994). NGO stakeholders are commonly characterized by contrasts in their attitude toward, power over, or reliance on the organization. Typical differences include understanding about purpose or role; perspectives on development; ability to sanction; levels of understanding about the organization itself; and diverse expectations about responsiveness, acceptable levels of service, timescales for results, and impact. To some extent, these differences derive from basic contradictions between the role of aid and the functioning of the global political-economic system, of which poverty and marginalization are but one product. Perspectives in the North and South certainly differ considerably.

In organizational terms, these and other differences translate into more or less permanent tensions that have to be managed; most cannot be "developed" away or resolved solely by the action of the NGO itself, because their origins lie deep within the institutional structures of society. Be that as it may, although not without risks in the short term, structured engagement with stakeholders can externalize, make transparent, and hence ease the tensions and associated management stresses that NGOs currently internalize. Enabling stakeholders who seldom if ever meet to come together and listen to the incompatibility of the demands they are placing on an NGO can be both a salutary experience and good education for all concerned. If located within the right process, such encounters can make a significant positive difference to NGO functioning and can help transform North-South NGO relationships into effective partnerships.

There is little doubt that external pressure and internal concerns (both opportunistic and professional) will continue to push NGOs to demonstrate their effectiveness and hence their value as agents of development. Given the consistent trend to include more nonstate actors in development, it is likely that the methods adopted will stretch along some form of continuum from simple participatory project appraisal at one end to full stakeholder determination of NGO performance criteria and judgment at the other. The factors that will determine which NGOs end up where on the continuum are not easy to discern. One guess is that an NGO's position will be related to the profile of its funding, its ability to retain autonomy, and its particular ideology or analysis of the causes of poverty and marginalization.

Because of the rationale and expectations associated with tax-derived finances, NGOs relying on this type of income are more likely to adopt a contracting role than are those financed by the gift economy (such as Oxfam) or their own market-oriented activity (such as Traidcraft) (Fowler 1994a). In the former case, projects will probably remain the primary mode of operation linked to government agreements, treating beneficiaries as inputs rather than actors central to the development process (World Bank 1994). Autonomy is a more complex factor because it is determined by an NGO's ability to maintain its own policy development and decision-making processes unimpeded by other agencies. Although sources of finance play their role, the strength and unity of the constituency that "owns" the NGO are significant factors in helping to maintain independence of policy and action. NGOs that benefit from greater autonomy are usually better able to include a broad range of stakeholders in any or all aspects of their work.

Surprising as it may seem, relatively few development NGOs have a coherent and well-articulated understanding of why the problems they seek to address actually arise. Put differently, they lack a theory or analysis of why poverty exists as a global phenomenon. Dealing with symptoms and effects is still a sufficient justification for the existence of many NGOs. This means that they are unlikely to consider or seek to counter the structural nature of impoverishment (in the North as well as the South) in what they choose to do. This appreciation is more likely to be found in NGOs treating poverty alleviation as a global civic endeavor requiring international solidarity and mutual responsibility. The latter type of NGO may be more inclined to recognize the interests of stakeholders outside of a project framework.

The existing literature on NGOs and development, together with the few impact studies that exist, suggests that by the end of the century, most NGOs will be found clustering between the "people as project input" end of the performance assessment spectrum and a middle point pivoting around the logical framework analysis–objective-oriented intervention planning approach, which itself may have evolved to embrace organizational as well as project performance. It is doubtful that many NGOs will be found operating on the basis of performance criteria and standards negotiated with and among their diverse stakeholders, unless this is recognized as the real "bottom line" for demonstrating both performance and accountability.

Notes

1. Estimate of John Clark, NGO Unit of the World Bank, Washington, D.C. (personal communication).
2. "Dials" are supposedly unambiguous standards and measures of performance, such as the temperature shown on a thermometer. "Tin openers" are measures of performance that are contested, such as the minimum acceptable waiting time for an operation or for an ambulance to arrive at an emergency.
3. Independent evaluations are the normal way of providing funders with alternative feedback on the work of the NGOs they finance. There are many limitations on the utility of this instrument, including (1) delay in gaining information, (2) contention about the definition of terms of reference and competing paradigms used for interpretation of results, (3) critical dependence on who is selected to do the work, (4) difficulties in gaining "objective" involvement of those served, and (5) transience of staff involved over the duration of the project and hence consistency of ideas (Marsden and Oakley 1990; Howes 1992; Cracknell 1983; Carlsson, Kohlin, and Ekbom 1994; Marsden, Oakley, and Pratt 1994). There are now a number of initiatives, such as the Aga Khan Rural Support Programme in Pakistan, dedicated to improving on this situation using participatory and other people-centered mechanisms.
4. Stakeholders could be regarded as the groups or entities to which an NGO is accountable. For an overview of who they might be, see Edwards and Hulme (1994, 18–24). For a discussion on the principle of stakeholders in relation to (development) organizations, see Fowler (1994b).
5. Commercial corporations appear to be rediscovering the merits of social responsibility and social change as components of their overall goals and strategies (Smith 1994).
6. More information can be obtained directly from Traidcraft Exchange, Kingsway, Gateshead, Tyne and Wear, Newcastle NE11 0NE, UK.
7. The political risk taken by Oxfam in constituting the assembly was highlighted when the gathering's advice to commence work in its home country made front-page headlines in the *Guardian* newspaper, which argued that prevailing government policies had turned the United Kingdom into a developing country in need of Oxfam's attention. Personal communication from Max Peberdy, assembly organizer.
8. I am grateful to Wendy Crane of Plan International for this observation.
9. In May 1994, the World Bank hosted a meeting with NGOs to compare notes on impact assessment that focused almost exclusively on technical interventions at the project level.
10. These findings result from experience in designing and running courses on organizational assessment and organizational development with INTRAC, attended by staff of over fifty Northern and Southern NGOs, as well as in-house consultancy work and personal communications from Piers Campbell, Peter Baas, Rajesh Tandon, David Harding, Daudi Waithaka, Dr. John Hailey, and others of the growing but limited number of specialists in this area.

References

Anderson, P., J. Arrow, and D. Pines, eds. 1988. *The economy as an evolving complex system.* Redwood, Calif. Addison-Wesley.

Campbell, P. 1990. Strengthening organizations. *NGO Management* 18: 21–24.

Carlsson, J., G. Kohlin, and A. Ekbom. 1994. *The political economy of evaluation: International aid agencies and the effectiveness of aid.* London: St. Martin's Press.

Carvalho, S., and H. White. 1993. *Performance indicators to monitor poverty reduction.* Washington, D.C.: World Bank.

Cassen, R. 1986. *Does aid work?* Oxford: Oxford University Press.

Chambers, R. 1985. Normal professionalism, new paradigms and development. Paper for the Seminar on Poverty Development and Food: Toward the 21st Century, Institute of Development Studies, University of Sussex, Brighton.

————. 1993. *Challenging the professions: Frontiers for rural development.* London: Intermediate Technology Development Group.

Cracknell, B. 1983. *The evaluation of aid projects and programmes.* Proceedings of a conference organized by the Overseas Development Administration in the Institute of Development Studies at the University of Sussex, April 7–8. London: Overseas Development Administration.

Drucker, P. 1990. *Managing the nonprofit organization: Principles and practices.* New York: HarperCollins.

————. 1993. *The five most important questions you will ever ask about your nonprofit organization: Participant's workbook.* San Francisco: Drucker Foundation/Jossey-Bass.

Edwards, M., and D. Hulme. 1994. *NGOs and development: Performance and accountability in the "new world order."* Background paper for the SCF/IDPM Workshop on NGOs and Development, Manchester, June 27–29.

Fowler, A. 1989. Why is managing social development different? *NGO Management Newsletter* 12:18–20.

————. 1992a. Distant obligations: Speculations on NGO funding and the global market. *Review of African Political Economy* 55:9–29.

————. 1992b. *Prioritising institutional development: A new role for NGO centres for study and development.* Gate Keeper Series no. 35. London: International Institute for Environment and Development.

————. 1994a. Capacity building and NGOs: A case of strengthening ladles for the global soup kitchen? *Institutional Development* 1(1):18–24.

————. 1994b. *The World Bank and its stakeholders: Who are they and why?* Discussion paper, Human Resources Vice Presidency. Washington, D.C.: World Bank.

Fowler, A., P. Campbell, and B. Pratt. 1992. *Institutional development and NGOs in Africa: Policy perspectives for European development agencies.* Oxford and The Hague: International NGO Training and Research Centre and NOVIB.

Gell-Mann, M. 1994. *The quark and the jaguar.* New York: Freeman.

Hancock, G. 1989. *The lords of poverty: The power, prestige, and corruption of the international aid business.* New York: Atlantic Monthly Press.

Hawley, K. 1993. *From grants to contracts: A practical guide for voluntary organisations*. London: National Council of Voluntary Organisations/ Directory of Social Change.

Herman, R., and R. Heimovics. 1994. A cross-national study of a method for researching non-profit organisational effectiveness. *Voluntas* 5(1):86–100.

Howes, M. 1992. Linking paradigms and practice: Key issues in the appraisal, monitoring and evaluation of British NGO projects. *Journal of International Development* 4(4):375–396.

Hudock, A. 1994. Sustaining Southern NGOs in resource-dependent environments. Paper presented at the Development Studies Association Annual Conference, University of Lancaster, September.

INTRAC/South Research. 1994. *A tool for project management and people driven development*. Reports of a Workshop on LFA/OIP, Leuven, Belgium. Oxford and Brussels: International NGO Training and Research Centre/ South Research.

James, R. 1994. *Strengthening the capacity of Southern NGO partners*. Occasional Papers Series, vol. 1, no. 5, Oxford: International NGO Training and Research Centre.

Kanter, R. M. 1979. *The measurement of organizational effectiveness, productivity, performance and success: Issues and dilemmas in service and non-profit organisations*. PONPO Working Paper, no. 8. New Haven, Conn.: Yale University, Institution for Social and Policy Studies.

Lawrie, A. 1993. *Quality of service: Measuring performance for voluntary organisations*. London: National Council of Voluntary Organisations/ Director of Social Change.

Leat, D. 1993. *Managing across sectors: Similarities and differences between for-profit and voluntary non-profit organisations*. London: VOLPROF, City University Business School.

Lewin, P. 1994, *Complexity*. London: Phoenix.

Lewis, J., et al. 1988. *Strengthening the poor: What have we learned?* Overseas Development Council, U.S.–Third World Policy Perspectives, no. 10. New Brunswick, N.J., and Oxford: Transaction Books.

Long, N., and A. Long. eds. 1992. *Battlefields of knowledge: The interlocking of theory and practice in social research and development*. London: Routledge.

Marsden, D., and P. Oakley. eds. 1990. *Evaluating social development projects*. Development Guidelines no. 5. Oxford: Oxfam.

Marsden, D., P. Oakley, and B. Pratt, eds. 1994. *Measuring the process: Guidelines for evaluating social development*. Oxford: International NGO Training and Research Centre.

OECD. 1993. *Non-governmental organisations and governments: Stakeholders for development*. Paris: OECD.

Oxfam. 1994. *Oxfam assembly (1994): Talking, listening, sharing*. Oxford: Oxfam.

Riddell, R., and M. Robinson. 1992. *The impact of NGO poverty alleviation projects: Results of the case study evaluations*. Working Paper no. 68. London: Overseas Development Institute.

Roling, N., and H. de Zeeuw. 1987. *Improving the quality of rural poverty alleviation*. Final report of the Working Party on the Small Farmer and Development Cooperation. Wageningen: International Agricultural Centre.

Scott, W. 1987. *Organisations: Rational, natural and open systems*. Englewood Cliffs, N.J.: Prentice-Hall.

Senge, P. 1990. *The fifth discipline: The art and practice of the learning organization*. New York: Doubleday.

Smith, C. 1994. The new corporate philanthropy. *Harvard Business Review* (May–June):105–116.

Smith, S., and M. Lipsky. 1993. *Nonprofits for hire: The welfare state in the age of contracting*. Cambridge: Harvard University Press.

Traidcraft. 1994. *Social audit report 1993*. Newcastle upon Tyne: Traidcraft Exchange.

UNDP. 1993. *Human development report*. Oxford: Oxford University Press.

Van Dijk, M-P. 1994. The effectiveness of NGOs: Insights from Danish, British and Dutch import studies. *Schriften des Deutschen Ubersee-Instituts Hamburg*. 28, pp. 27–42.

Waldrop, M. 1993. *Complexity: The emerging science at the edge of order and chaos*. New York: Simon and Schuster.

White, H., and L. Woestman. 1994. The quality of aid: Measuring trends in donor performance. *Development and Change* 25(3):527–54.

Wolpert, L. 1992. *The unnatural nature of science*. London: Faber and Faber.

World Bank. 1994. *The World Bank and participation*. Washington, D.C.: World Bank.

14

Painting Canadian Roses Red

Ian Smillie

This chapter deals with the strange phenomenon of a multi-billion-dollar international endeavor that is poorly understood and, despite fast-growing interest in the subject, very poorly evaluated: the work of Northern nongovernmental organizations (NNGOs). It draws in part on an extensive twelve-country study in which the author participated, conducted by the Development Centre of the Organization of Economic Cooperation and Development (OECD) in 1993 (Smillie and Helmich 1993), but focuses specifically on the case of Canada, where NGO evaluation is considerably more advanced than in most other OECD countries.

The OECD study observed that NNGOs are in trouble. Collectively, they spend an estimated US$9 billion to $10 billion annually[1] but live with a level of financial insecurity that would drive most private-sector firms into bankruptcy. Increasingly criticized by governments for their lack of professionalism, they are accused of bureaucratization when they do professionalize. With very few exceptions, governments refuse to contribute seriously to financing professionalism, insisting on unrealistically low overheads and on putting NGOs through long, inefficient approval processes. Many governments are locked into an outdated project approach, which also works against professionalism. Despite the fact that they spend tens of millions of dollars annually through their NGO communities, few governments have taken evaluation seriously, with the result that NGO survival has been almost completely delinked from performance.[2] Perhaps most fundamentally, NGOs have a growing identity crisis in relation to their increasingly effective Southern counterparts, most of which want money rather than interference and support rather than secondhand rules and regulations passed on from government donors in the North.

Just as the North-South NGO identity crisis began to peak in the early 1990s, it became clear that official development assistance itself was in serious trouble. Report after report on official development assistance scandals (such as the Pergau Dam affair in the United Kingdom) and

World Bank performance (the "Wapenhans Report") has damaged public opinion, encouraging recession-plagued governments to cut aid budgets and retreat behind "new" concepts of accountability, participation, and the role of "civil society." Adding to the burden these shifts place on NGOs, many governments actively poach on NNGO territory, dealing directly with Southern NGOs (SNGOs) as though they have nothing better to do with their overstretched bureaucracies.

Some SNGOs, tired of the paternalism and the financial limitations of their erstwhile NNGO "partners," have welcomed the change. Adding to the confusion, many governments have restricted their matching or "responsive" NGO funding programs, while providing massive funding increases—on highly favorable terms—for emergency and refugee work. Most governments have also thrown in special funds for AIDS, women, democracy, and a variety of other issues, as though NGOs—which first brought some of these issues to the attention of governments—needed special prodding to take them seriously.

A high proportion of NGOs, suffering from recession and dysfunctional competition, have flocked like swallows toward the easier money. Not content with the huge sums available from governments for emergencies, however, too many have turned up the "starving baby" fundraising, adding to a widespread Northern image of the Third World as a wholesale disaster area. The public, confused by highly competitive fund-raising appeals, unsubstantiated NGO claims, and unremitting horror stories from the South, can perhaps be forgiven for its ignorance of what is going on and for a growing antipathy toward any kind of aid but for the most heart-wrenching plights.

The Failure to Learn from Failure

In discussing NGOs, it has become fashionable to move quickly from their positive attributes (increasingly referred to as "unproven"[3]) to their obvious weaknesses. The 1993 United Nations Development Program (UNDP) *Human Development Report*, which devotes an entire chapter to NGOs, is one of the most recent and dismaying examples of this. Ten of its fifteen pages are devoted to debunking—with faint praise and outright condemnation—the effectiveness of NGOs in tackling poverty, providing credit to the poor, reaching the poorest, empowering marginal groups, challenging gender discrimination, and even delivering emergency relief.

Development is, or should be, a knowledge-based endeavor. Learning what works, and why, is essential to success. Knowing what does not work is almost more important. Knowledge, however (too often confused with information), involves awareness, consciousness, and the familiarity that develops with experience and learning. Just as messages sent are not always received, lessons taught—in school and in life—are not always learned. This is particularly true at an institutional level; the inability to learn and remember is an acknowledged and widespread failing of the development community as a whole. For NGOs, it represents a particular dilemma, because there are few reasons (and no money) to disseminate the positive lessons of development and many more powerful reasons to conceal the negative lessons than to institutionalize, remember, and disseminate them.

Part of the problem has to do with the expectations of supporters—the public at large and governments. NGOs have long prided themselves on reaching the poorest quickly, effectively, and efficiently. In the 1960s, when much NGO work was relief oriented, this was certainly true. It is still true in emergency work today. As NGOs became more involved in development work, however, their advertising messages remained the same: speed, effectiveness, and efficiency. As more NGOs came onto the Northern scene, competition for funding increased, and promises escalated.

But development is not speedy, and NGOs—working with the very poor in resource-deficient, marginal regions of countries in great distress—know that effectiveness and efficiency are far less easy to deliver and to measure than, say, infrastructure development. Having promised too much to donors and the public, however, NGOs are trapped in a vicious circle. If funding is to be maintained or is to increase in the face of growing demands, success is essential. Often it is exaggerated, while failures are downplayed or concealed. Important lessons are not learned, and only successes—often highly situational—are disseminated, usually in a public-relations format.

Part of the solution to this problem has to do with public perception. Much has to do with the development of transparency, accountability, and, ultimately, greater credibility through appropriate types of evaluation, research, and dissemination of findings.

Duplication at the Expense of Replication

NGOs repeat the same types of projects time after time. There is little effective coordination at home and less overseas. NGOs pride themselves on, and are rewarded by donors for, "innovation," but often innovation is simply a reinvention of old wheels. "Pilot projects" and demonstrations demonstrate only that the NGO can do it. Uptake by others is limited. Despite the admirable push-start provided by the first Manchester Conference on "scaling up" (Edwards and Hulme 1992), government support remains limited for the widespread replication of successful programs—for the complex set of activities that Norman Uphoff calls "extendability": institution building, linkage to government services, and broad-based empowerment (see OECD 1988, 57). This is true in part because many NGOs are not interested in, nor are they capable of, scaling up. But the way in which NGOs are funded by governments is also a factor. NGO budgets in most government agencies have little flexibility, are often tied to a historical rather than a developmental reality, and have no capacity to help move real success stories to full-scale application.

Evaluation

The country studies in the 1993 OECD report demonstrate that although NGO evaluation is rising rapidly on the agendas of many OECD governments, it is still very much in the elementary stages in most countries.[4] In those where it has advanced to a relative degree of sophistication (such as the Netherlands, the United States, and Canada), it is used more as a control and justification mechanism by the donor agency than as a tool for learning or for disseminating findings.

There are examples of attempts to expand and enhance approaches to NGO evaluation: for example, the rapid and participatory rural appraisal techniques developed at the Institute for Development Studies (IDS) in Brighton and the International Institute for Environment and Development (IIED) in London; a Norwegian Agency for International Development (NORAD) study series; and the Overseas Development Institute working paper *Judging Success* (Riddell 1990). A handful of NNGOs have asked their Southern partners to evaluate *them*. Other suggestions include comparative cross-national and sectoral evaluations. Generally, however, the relatively few serious NGO evaluations that do exist remain confidential. Government agencies, faced with the same public expectations as NGOs, with added and often conflicting demands from their legislators, become partners in the cover-up, burying their own failures and shortcomings in similar public-relations exercises and obfuscation.

Development, especially human development, is not easy; it is not quick; it is not cheap. If it were, NGOs and foreign aid would have disappeared with the Marshall Plan. Failure should be regarded as a bad thing only if the same mistake is made over and over. But when evaluations are rare and secretive, when lessons are not shared, not learned, and not remembered, repetitive mistakes are almost guaranteed.[5]

A related issue has to do with the conspiracy of silence that prevails within most NGO communities. NGOs rarely challenge one another openly; there is little, if any, regulation of NGOs by NGOs (unlike other professionals such as accountants, architects, and engineers); and the NGO codes of conduct that do exist (in Australia, the European Union, and the United States) are usually not enforced in any serious way.

Canada: Evaluation Off the Rails?

Hard Choices in Hard Times

One of the findings of the OECD study was that both official and unofficial statistics on NGO funding are unreliable. There is no doubt, however, that a high proportion of the cash income of most Canadian NGOs is derived from the Canadian International Development Agency (CIDA). For some (such as Foster Parents Plan and World Vision) the proportion is low, but for most it is well over 50 percent, and for some it is more than 80 percent.[6] Therefore, when CIDA sneezes, Canadian NGOs reach for their vitamin C.

The pace of change at CIDA between 1991 and 1994 (including a series of major budget cuts, three presidents, and three ministers) was bewildering. Much of the change has focused on structures, on systems, and on what CIDA now calls "stakeholders"—NGOs, the private sector, and others with a financial stake. This is perhaps understandable. CIDA's rapid budget growth throughout the 1970s and 1980s was not accompanied by a concomitant growth in its human resources. As development needs grew and became more complex, CIDA relied more heavily on others—consultants, the private sector, NGOs, and professional institutions—to do the work that its officers and contract employees once did. Gradually, much of the initiative for Canada's development work, especially in the social sector, seemed to fall away from CIDA.

In the early 1980s, CIDA began to place increasing importance on evaluation, and for most NGOs, a comprehensive institutional review every three or four years became a feature of the relationship. These reviews, always conducted by external consultants, are lengthy and complex, delving into overseas program effectiveness as well as questions of organizational management. Views on the quality and usefulness of the evaluations vary, according to the stance of the beholder. Because they are directly related to the renegotiation of a block grant, many NGOs approach them with considerable fear and loathing. For CIDA, however, they perform an important function. Because of declining human resources, CIDA officers can no longer examine their clientele as thoroughly as they once did. In the almost total absence of any NGO self-evaluation, the institutional reviews provide the only serious government window into what an NGO does. The evaluations are rarely used, however, to modify CIDA funding, and certainly no evaluation in recent memory has resulted in the cessation of funding to an NGO. The evaluations are, in a sense, a corroboration of CIDA's decision to support an NGO in the first place.

Ultimately, most of the evaluations are weak when it comes to questions about an NGO's program impact. This is partly because the generic methodology for NGO evaluation is weak. It also has to do with poor or nonexistent baseline indicators around which an evaluation can be framed. And it is partly because—despite the large CIDA evaluation budget—the time and resources available for individual NGO reviews are usually inadequate.

Institutional Funding

"Institutional funding," introduced by CIDA in 1993, is the newest approach to dealing with some of these problems.[7] Institutional funding means that CIDA funds the "institution" rather than a collection of projects and programs. It is assumed that mature NGOs, if well-managed and founded on clear development principles, will have the sort of impact that they and CIDA espouse. Much of the evaluative function can actually be carried out by the NGO itself. To put it simply, detailed, third-party overseas impact evaluation is not necessary. In principle, institutional funding makes sense. At first glance, it appears to reduce CIDA's involvement in the routine administrative and programming work of the NGO; it places less emphasis on "blueprint" planning; and it emphasizes *development* work overseas and puts new emphasis on development education in Canada, merging this with regular program approvals.

Institutional funding, however, means that the *entire* NGO will now be open to full CIDA scrutiny: its structure, management, programs, policies, and attitudes. Current institutional assessments cover many aspects of an NGO's persona, but the new approach guarantees that *all* will now be addressed. Although the implications for some NGOs are not great (and the sacrifice small), for others they are significant. Institutional funding represents a step forward in the ability of government to manage and control Canadian NGOs and a step backward from the concept of NGOs as independent expressions of civil society.

The NGO must now spell out its "understanding of the development challenge," work through its goals and objectives, establish a strategic approach, provide details on the scope of work envisaged, describe the implementation structure and the partnership relationship, and develop or describe a monitoring and evaluation plan. In return for much greater openness, the only actual promise from CIDA is a more critical application of its cost-sharing formula.

That CIDA wants to encourage greater self-evaluation and better strategic thinking among NGOs is a positive feature of the new arrangement. But CIDA still intends to conduct its own formal institutional assessments "to thoroughly assess the organization and its continued eligibility" every three to five years. It may conduct midterm reviews; it will do an "annual financial assessment" (with the possibility of "more extensive monitoring"). CIDA managers will continue to make field trips "to review activities of organizations and their southern partners on the ground"; there will be regular discussions and contact with the NGO, and CIDA program managers will attend the NGO's board meetings "at least once a year to discuss issues of mutual concern." In short, there is considerably more work for the NGO, and more CIDA intrusion than in the past, and there is likely to be at least as much work as before for CIDA managers, if not more.

How to Evaluate a Canadian NGO

CIDA's new institutional funding arrangement is based on a comprehensive checklist of characteristics and practices that form the basis for evaluation and funding allocations. Of course, CIDA (and any other institutional support agency,) *should* have clear funding priorities for NGOs. These should be based on an organization's developmental cost-effectiveness. In order for criteria to be used effectively, they must be clear, and the application must be seen as fair. A difficulty with the new CIDA approach, however, is uncertainty about its basic objective. It is no secret that CIDA is in a period of contraction; the irony is that contraction, rather than expansion, seems to have bred a stronger interest in good management and good programming. This makes the need for clarity and fairness essential if CIDA is to avoid the lobbying, grantsmanship, and grandstanding that has marked the rise of Canada's 200 or 300 NGOs over the past thirty years. It is absolutely essential if good work is to be rewarded—if the intent is to create something more than a paring knife.

At this level, CIDA's new criteria largely fail. Take the simple question of governance, for example: one of the criteria is "reasonable staff turnover relative to the needs of the organization." What is "reasonable"? Who will judge? In some categories, there is a clear requirement: defined evaluation plans, an explicit policy and strategy on gender, and training in environmental assessment. In others, despite a listing of categories, there is none: for example, "nature and extent of the donor base; nature and extent of the volunteer base; nature and involvement of the constituency." "Nature" means what? What is good? What is good enough? What is bad? Who decides?

There are some excellent and innovative points in CIDA's new policy. Unfortunately, many of these are buried in vague and repetitive lists based on current aid enthusiasms: the environment, gender, sustainability, human rights, democratic development, and "good governance." The imbalance in priorities is extreme: there are over two pages on the environment and gender, fewer than two explicit lines on poverty, and no description of what is meant by "democratic development" or how NGOs might contribute to it.

Another confusion, common to most NGO support institutions, is the conflation of innovation and replication, as though they were the same thing. This criterion is a serious contradiction in terms. Replicate means to make a copy of, to reproduce. Innovate means to invent. This needs to be thought through. "Innovation" appears on almost every list of funding criteria for NGOs worldwide. Why? Innovation certainly has its place, and many accepted development lessons have come from NGO innovations. But too many NGOs reinvent too many wheels in the name of innovation. Ironically, there is less and less money available for replicating or taking the innovations to scale. Donors should think carefully about the trade-offs involved here, and they should make sure that they know what they really want to foster.

The word "sustainable" is used in the new CIDA policy twenty-five times. The words "poor" and "poverty" appear once each. Although the word "development" is used liberally, there is no definition of it, other than what might be inferred from the sum of the parts. If development is the intended whole, however (and there is no explicit assurance that it is), it comes off as considerably less than the sum of its parts.

In sum, Canadian NGOs now have a suggested and reasonably clear formula for good management, but of what? An NGO with competent staff, a good board, and a constituency? An organization that understands gender and environment, one that gets along well with its partners and whose staff works as a team? In one document, it is stated that "development performance will be given the most weight" in determining budgetary allocations, but this is not borne out in the text. Program impact is placed last, after governance, management and delivery, Canadian constituency, and identity.

The section on impact is, in fact, the foggiest part of the new policy. It is as though we no longer know what development is about, as though long, jargon-laden checklists about environmental or social sustainability are a substitute for the hard question: what is this organization doing to reduce poverty in the short and long run? The impact section of one document uses the word "sustainable" nineteen times, breaking it up into myriad vague proxies that ultimately mean very little. For example:

> Extent to which the organization has demonstrated an understanding of the key factors which contributed to social sustainability, such as improved income distribution, social equity (gender, class, race, religion, etc.), empowerment of women and men in directing their own growth, emphasizing participation of beneficiaries, and access to productive resources.

Apart from the redundancy, this is a fairly tall order, one that has baffled and defeated many organizations, including the Soviet Union, the United Nations, and CIDA itself. Many paragraphs in the new CIDA policy documents are like that, and yet there is something missing from all of them: NGOs have to *understand* empowerment, access, etc. ("etc."

is used seven times in one paragraph); they have to *demonstrate* an understanding of key environmental sustainability factors, of gender, of political sustainability. They have to *incorporate* these into their policies and strategies, but there is little suggestion anywhere that anyone really has to *accomplish* anything.

Funding Criteria

The documents say that when an NGO's performance is deficient in two out of the sixteen new funding criteria, reductions in funding will be "indicated." The fundamental problem is that when lists of criteria are lengthy and vague, they can be taken to mean anything. How will reduced funding be "indicated"? If an organization does not have a strong environmental assessment capacity, for example, and if the "nature and extent of its volunteer base" is deemed inadequate, would a 10 percent reduction be indicated? Eleven percent? Thirty percent? Who will make this decision? Precisely how important are things like human rights and democratic development? In the absence of any real development performance indicators or comparative impact evaluation in the field, CIDA managers will end up with a stew that simply encourages the arbitrary decision making that these documents seek to alter.

The dictionary defines a "professional" as one who is extremely competent in a job. The voluntary sector has a number of inherent weaknesses that work against professionalism: a dependence on what Salamon (1987) calls "the particularism and favoritism of the rich," an inability to generate adequate or secure resources, and a proclivity toward self-defeating paternalism. Too often, however, governments tend to see professionalism in terms of their own standards and procedures. The more an NGO acts like government, the more "professional" it is. Some NGOs have conformed, becoming as bureaucratic internally and with their Southern partners as they are forced to be with their funders. Others, reacting against this trend, throw the baby out with the bathwater and refuse to take the issue of professionalism seriously.

Some constraints to NGO professionalism are a reflection of the NGO community as a whole. For example, the vast and increasing number of small, generalist NNGOs almost guarantees a high level of amateurism. The OECD directory of NGOs listed 1,600 NNGOs in 1980 and 2,500 in 1990. In the 1993 twelve-country OECD study, some 2,970 NGOs were identified, a number that is probably on the low side.

A strong concern expressed in many countries has to do with the growing level of financial dependence that many NGOs have on government. Governments are torn: They are eager for NGOs to do more but want them to raise the necessary funds from a public that may be unable or unwilling to contribute more. Governments want ready and compliant NGOs that can go where governments cannot, but they worry about amateurism, and they dislike the grasping, commercial mentality that seems to have infected many NGOs. Most governments claim to value NGO independence, but they insist that NGOs conform to government norms and priorities and are resentful of NGO criticism.

Several suggestions for consideration emerged from the OECD study, and they are compatible with the situation in Canada. The most basic is that the *learning* aspect of evaluation must be stressed. If evaluation fulfills this function properly, the other major function of reassuring the donor (which until now has received top priority) will take place naturally. If learning is to take place, the implied financial threat that accompanies failure must be removed. This should not absolve NGOs from responsibility for preventable errors and inefficiencies; rather, it would help ensure that the preventable becomes more predictable and therefore more avoidable.

But evaluation is only part of the learning process. NGOs also have an important research function that is barely acknowledged and poorly supported. For thirty years, NGOs have been valuable laboratories for public health, credit for the poor, the involvement of women in development, environmental issues, and a wide range of other initiatives that have gradually been taken up by governments and donor agencies. Much of this has happened, however, by osmosis and by accident, and with much needless trial and error. Research and dissemination could and should be a much greater part of the NGO agenda. A few positive examples stand out, but they are the exception rather than the rule: *The Oxfam Field Director's Handbook*; *Making a Difference* (Edwards and Hulme 1992) and the research programs of Save the Children–U.K. that spawned it; the sustainable agriculture program of IIED; and the publishing houses of the Intermediate Technology Development Group, Earthscan, and Kumarian Press.

Only recently has the NGO phenomenon itself been seen as a subject worthy of academic research. Growing interest on the part of universities and research institutions will undoubtedly help build awareness, understanding, and support for the movement as a whole. Ultimately, however, the survival of an independent NGO community as a source of development learning and as a genuine weapon against poverty will depend on its own willingness to confront questions of quality, cost-effectiveness, and impact head-on, openly, and by itself. Evaluation in most countries has not been given the same priority as in Canada, but it is rising rapidly on the agenda of many governmental support institutions. If NGOs are to avoid the confusion, the contradictions, and the hijackings that have occurred in Canada, they would be well advised to take the matter in hand themselves, before it is too late.

Notes

1. Accurate statistics on NGOs are elusive. This figure is therefore an esti-mate. Reasonably accurate U.S. figures, however, which show a total flow of $5.8 billion for American NGOs in 1991, would suggest that a total of $10 billion is probably not an exaggeration.
2. This divorce of funding and performance is discussed by Singh (1987).
3. This sort of terminology can be found in reports that use Judith Tendler's largely outdated 1982 study as a source, including the 1993 *Human Devel-opment Report*. Although her work was important in many ways, Tendler pulled a lot of wings off NGO butterflies by debunking what she called NGO "articles of faith."
4. New evaluation procedures for NGOs are being developed in Britain, Canada, the United States, and Australia. Broad overview studies of the NGO community have recently been conducted or are under way in Nor-way, Sweden, and the United States. A limited survey on NGO evaluation was conducted by the OECD/DAC Expert Group on Aid and Evaluation in 1992.
5. Sweden and Norway publish (in English, so beneficiaries can read them) a wide variety of often critical evaluations of projects undertaken by their bilateral agencies, SIDA and NORAD. Ironically, both governments have only recently decided to undertake comprehensive reviews of their NGO sectors.
6. CESO 1992, 48 percent; Canadian Hunger Foundation 1991, 70 percent; CARE Canada 1992, 71 percent; CODE 1992–93, 83 percent; CUSO 1992–93, 83 percent.
7. The following sections are based on four CIDA documents: "Institutional Review: Issues for Consideration" (1992); "Eligibility Criteria for Partners" (1992); "NGO Program: Program Criteria" (1992); and "NGO Division Allocation Process for 1994/95."

References

Edwards, M., and D. Hulme, eds. 1992. *Making a difference: NGOs and devel-opment in a changing world*. London: Earthscan.

OECD. 1988. *Voluntary aid for development: The role of NGOs*. Paris: OECD.

Riddell, R. 1990. *Judging success: Evaluating NGO approaches to alleviating poverty in developing countries*. London: Overseas Development Institute.

Salamon, L. 1987. Partners in public service: The scope and theory of government-nonprofit relations. In *The nonprofit sector: A research handbook*, edited by W. Powell. New Haven, Conn.: Yale University Press.

Singh, B. 1987. NGO self-evaluation: Issues of concern. *World Development* 15 (Special Supplement on NGOs).

Smillie, I., and H. Helmich. 1993. *NGOs and governments: Stakeholders for development*. Paris: OECD.

Tendler, J. 1982. *Turning private voluntary organizations into development agencies*. Washington, D.C.: U.S. Agency for International Development.

UNDP. 1993. *Human development report*. New York: UNDP.

15

Accountability and Effectiveness in NGO Policy Alliances

Jane G. Covey

At the beginning of the last decade of the twentieth century, there was much talk of the emerging advocacy role for NGOs in both North and South. Debates about the propriety, legality, and safety of NGO lobbying were in the air. Now, only a few years later, advocacy activities with governments, donors, multilateral development agencies, and publics are assumed to be a crucial ingredient in enhancing the position of NGOs as key players in the diffuse social movement loosely labeled "sustainable development." The United Nations Conference on Environment and Development (UNCED) in the summer of 1992 undoubtedly helped turn the tide from the "should we?" line of questions regarding NGO roles in policy influence to the "how do we do it?" discourse now emerging.

Democratization, in its messy evolution in societies around the globe, tugs NGOs toward a more active policy-influencing role as more political space opens for people's voices in public affairs. The promise of democracy becomes a reality, however, when groups (especially marginalized sectors of society) participate effectively in the marketplace of competing interests. Inclusion in political systems long dominated by elites depends on the institutional strength of policy newcomers and the perceived legitimacy of their participation. The challenge of building an effective policy-influencing organization increases as groups seek to shape positive policy environments as well as protest against negative ones. For example, winning policy advantages requires that mobilized public opinion be accompanied by convincing analysis that is at least on a par with the analytic capability of the decision makers NGOs are trying to influence (Clark 1992). The dual challenge of mobilizing arguments as well as people is great. Arguments that gain the attention of policymakers call for "expert" knowledge of both the issue and the decision-making process; public outcry and protest actions that constrain decision makers' power call for an active and organized grassroots constituency.

Policy-influencing efforts may or may not create conditions that foster greater popular participation in the future. A movement may not achieve its immediate policy objectives, but getting its issue on the public agenda expands the range of voices engaged in the political process, and so expands political space. Attempting policy reform through protest and advocacy that threaten vested interests dramatically may engender a dangerous backlash from social and political elites, a problem of special importance in less open political regimes. Similarly, campaigns can be carried out in ways that strengthen grassroots organizations (GROs) and their voices, or they can be implemented by intermediaries with grassroots "clients." The latter can lead to the evolution of a civil society with a strong professional advocacy sector and a weak grassroots base (Jenkins 1987).

The status of poor and marginalized groups is a poignant reminder of their lack of power in society. GROs seldom (if ever) achieve policy change in their favor without the participation of other social groups such as NGOs, churches, professional groups, and academia. The small literature on the policy-influencing work of NGOs in Southern countries reports a strikingly similar pattern of organization. Some sort of alliance emerges to bring together grassroots groups, intermediary NGOs, allies from academia or the church, and (more frequently than perhaps expected) allies from the state or official development agencies. Hall (1992) notes, for example, that the success of the Itaparica hydropower campaign in northeastern Brazil can be attributed to a combined bottom-up and top-down strategy involving local communities, a regional NGO formation, the church, international NGOs, and the World Bank.

Multiorganizational, multisectoral alliances are complex. Questions of how interests, participation, and power are balanced among members typically arise in alliance formation and during the course of a campaign. They reflect the challenges inherent in forging alliances across groups that differ in wealth, class, culture, and resources. Fundamentally, these questions have to do with finding the right balance between bottom-up and top-down forces in an alliance. The process of finding this balance is directly related to the questions central to this book: What does an alliance need to be effective? How is alliance accountability to its members maintained, especially to the grassroots interests it purports to represent? This chapter explores the questions of effectiveness and accountability in policy alliances. It is a preliminary exploration of data from two Institute for Development Research (IDR) studies, one looking at national policy-influencing campaigns promoting a wide variety of development issues, and another examining transnational NGO alliances formed to influence World Bank projects.[1]

The Concepts: Effectiveness and Accountability

Looking at policy alliances in terms of effectiveness and accountability is important for NGOs that seek to promote sustainable development and more open societies through popular influence on decision makers. Together, effectiveness and accountability reflect the character of a policy-influencing campaign and the nature of relationships among the parties in an alliance. By developing clarity about what effectiveness means and understanding how and to whom accountability flows, those who pursue development through policy influence may achieve greater success and avoid some unintended consequences of their actions.

Effectiveness of Policy Alliances

Basically, the success of a policy alliance is measured by the degree to which its stated policy goals are achieved. Did the alliance win desired policy advantages for those it represented? How significant were its compromises? Even if the gains were small, were they consistent with longer-term objectives, or was the alliance co-opted? Is the bureaucracy implementing the policy as it was designed? Answers to these questions depend on one's interests, point of view, and subjective judgment. Nevertheless, they are the measure of the alliance's policy achievements.

A second dimension is less explicit. It is often assumed that policy efforts intended to benefit underrepresented groups also strengthen the capacity of these groups to advocate for their own interests. Expanding people's consciousness and empowering community-based organizations is not an automatic outcome of policy work. However, strengthening community-based institutions so that grassroots groups can be more effective actors in the policy arena is crucial to long-term alliance effectiveness.

Analyses of the Southern development experience conclude that, although presumptions of grassroots association presence and strength are often ill founded, institutions for popular participation are essential for sustainable development (Cernea 1987; Bratton 1989). Likewise, policy alliances must strengthen grassroots participation if people are to develop the staying power required to build democratic societies. A second set of questions emerges from the role of policy alliances in strengthening civil society. To what extent has the alliance, through its organization and campaigns, strengthened the institutional base for citizen action? Has it nurtured informed grassroots participation for the long haul, not simply mobilized groups for acts of protest? Has it contributed positively to an inclusive political culture and to public resolution of conflict through peaceful means?

Accountability in Policy Alliances

NGO policy alliances typically include a constellation of community-based organizations; organized social movements such as peasant federations; local, national, and international NGOs; and allies from the church, academia, business, government, and official agencies. A set of crosscutting social and power relationships is therefore established that forms a bridge between the grassroots and elite groups. Structurally, alliances incorporate many of the inequalities in wealth, power, knowledge, and resources that they are trying to reshape (Brown and Tandon 1993). When many actors are involved, to what and to whom is the alliance accountable? Each member has unique interests in addition to those encompassed by the shared agenda. Competing interests must be negotiated and renegotiated in some fashion as the alliance carries out its campaign. As the alliance interacts with policymakers and opponents, goals and tactics must be changed. Decision making reflects the power dynamics of the alliance itself. To what extent do these dynamics perpetuate existing patterns of influence in society, albeit in the service of a shared purpose? To what extent is the alliance internally democratic?

Alliance accountability rests partly on formal representational and decision-making structures that characterize membership-based community organizations. However, even when representative democratic structures exist, organizations may not be democratic because, over time, the "iron law of oligarchy" presses for bureaucratization and concentration of power at the center (Fox 1992). Accountability between NGOs and the communities they work with is similarly elusive. Despite the growing consensus that people's participation is a hallmark of good development projects, NGOs are seldom formally structured to ensure their accountability to GROs. In fact, NGO accountability procedures are most often designed to meet donor needs rather than grassroots objectives. Edwards and Hulme (1994) point to "the paradox of organizations promoting democratization which are themselves only weakly democratic." Carroll (1992) offers alternatives to direct or representative democracy by which NGOs can be held accountable to the grassroots. His findings suggest that an open collegial NGO style, and an ethos that encourages community participation, can help create sensitive and accountable organizations.

The following analysis asks two questions: (1) what factors increase the effectiveness of policy alliances in achieving policy outcomes and strengthening civil society? and (2) what factors enable alliances to be accountable to their members, especially grassroots groups?

The Cases

The analysis is based on two cases of national-level policy change in the Philippines and two cases of transnational alliances that aimed to influence World Bank projects. The cases were chosen from a larger body of IDR work to illustrate how structures and processes within alliances lead to different levels of effectiveness and types of accountability. Both national and transnational alliances are examined because each has important consequences for the lives of people in developing countries. The Philippine cases involve community-based organizations, NGOs, NGO coalitions, and other allies. The transnational cases involve all these actors plus international NGOs focused on World Bank environmental policy reform. Together, the four cases offer contrasting examples of alliance effectiveness and patterns of accountability.

The Philippine Campaigns

The first Philippine alliance, the Urban Land Reform Task Force (ULRTF), arose from more than twenty years of community efforts to protect the rights of the urban poor. It is the first attempt by urban people's organizations to influence policy through the parliamentary process rather than through open confrontation and mass protest. The alliance, which also included policy-oriented NGOs, a progressive church-related business group, and leaders of the Catholic Church, came together in 1991 when a weak urban land reform Bill was drafted by the legislature. The task force's goal was to improve the quality of this legislation. It built on the strength of its key players: the mass base of urban people's organizations, the business council's experience with and access to the legislative process, the bishop's political clout, and the NGO secretariat's technical and professional expertise. Governance and decision making in the alliance were fairly loose. Over the course of the campaign, trust and flexibility increased significantly within the alliance as more ideologically radical community groups withdrew. The alliance won passage of an amended legislative agenda and enhanced the legitimacy of urban land concerns of the poor. Furthermore, participation strengthened the ability of grassroots member organizations to negotiate with powerful groups.

The second case is the Task Force for a Total Commercial Log Ban (TCLB), formed around 1990 when a small number of Manila-based environmental groups, concerned with the rapid depletion of Philippine forests, came together with related NGOs and community organizations to launch a coordinated legislative campaign to protect the remaining forest cover. As it reached out to other groups around the country, the alliance incorporated grassroots economic concerns about equity and community use of forest resources. As a result, its initial call for a total ban on logging was modified to call for a ban on commercial logging. The national campaign was coordinated by a secretariat and a set of operational committees run on a part-time basis by staff from the Manila-based groups. Diverse community and regional log-ban campaigns functioned simultaneously but autonomously from one another. The task force succeeded in placing environmental concerns on the national agenda and strengthened NGO commitment to the issue. However, its limited resources and a lack of effective coordination among members reduced its ability to influence outcomes.

The Transnational Campaigns

The Sierra Madre Forestry Project involved a protest against a World Bank–Mexican government venture intended to modernize the forestry industry of northern Mexico. A local church-based human rights organization began tracking this project because of concerns over its environmental and social impact on the indigenous groups in the area. This group initially worked with a Texas-based policy group and an environmental advocacy group in Washington. Later, other U.S. regional and national NGOs exerted pressure on the World Bank to cancel the project due to concern about its effect on the Rio Grande watershed and plant and wildlife populations. The aim of the local NGO was to redesign the project to increase economic benefits for the area. However, after a second environmental impact assessment was released, international NGOs increased pressure on the World Bank to cancel the project altogether. Meanwhile, macroeconomic factors associated with trade liberalization undermined the project's financial viability, and at this point it was canceled. The forest dwellers (Tarahumara Indians) were largely absent throughout this campaign, even though the Mexican Department of Indigenous Affairs secured extra funds to consult them, and the local NGO had previously worked closely with them on human rights and land tenure issues.

The Mount Apo Geothermal Plant Project was also contested by local, national, and international groups whose goal was to persuade the World Bank not to finance a large-scale energy project in Mindanao (Philippines). In 1983, the Department of Environment and Natural Resources (DENR) denied the Philippine National Oil Company's exploration request on the grounds that this type of development was prohibited in national parks. However, in 1985, the Bureau of Energy Development issued an exploration permit without an environmental impact assessment or public hearing. DENR declared the action illegal. In spite of this, the project got under way.

The concerns of indigenous people centered on the desecration of sacred sites and the violation of tribal self-determination, whereas local farmers were worried about downstream pollution. Joined by the local Catholic church, these groups formed a task force that took the initiative in opposing the Mount Apo project. They solicited assistance from regional advocacy NGOs and obtained help from Manila-based national advocacy groups. Through their various solidarity networks, this alliance of local, regional, and national groups brought the project to the attention of counterparts in Europe and North America. The project was suspended in 1989 but resumed in 1992 as pressure to meet growing energy needs mounted. At the suggestion of a U.S. environmental NGO representative, a campaign began to pressure the World Bank and International Monetary Fund through close coordination between the Manila-based NGOs and a Washington-based advocacy network. The World Bank rejected the environmental impact assessment approved by the DENR. Subsequently, the government withdrew its loan request but is seeking alternative funds to complete the project.

Analysis of Alliance Effectiveness

This section examines the four cases with respect to their effectiveness on policy outcomes and their impact on civil society (Table 15.1).[2] Policy effectiveness involves the extent to which the alliance achieved its policy goals through either direct or indirect influence on decision makers. The civil society dimension of effectiveness involves two measures: the alliance's impact on the strength of local institutions, and the nature of community participation in the process of policy influence.

Policy Outcomes

In none of the cases was there total victory. Influence often comes through compromise, as in the urban land reform case. The task force modified its goals during the campaign and, as a result of these compromises, won solid but only partial reform. When multiple policy goals are pursued, outcomes are likely to be mixed—the alliance wins some but loses others. In the Mexican forestry case, project abandonment achieved the alliance's environmental goals but simultaneously made the economic development goals of the local NGO impossible to achieve.

The log ban case illustrates that policy outcomes often occur at various levels. The coalition failed to get national legislation passed because the national campaign was technically and politically unable to counter the weight of the commercial logging lobby. However, local groups did succeed in stopping some commercial logging and in gaining some reforestation projects. When alliance members pursue different levels of policy action (local, national, and international), gains at one level do not necessarily flow to others. Determining when to compromise and balancing trade-offs among different goals and different policy levels pose major challenges to NGO policy alliances.

Finally, effectiveness in influencing multiple actors also needs to be considered. The Mount Apo campaign skillfully pressured the World Bank to reject the environmental impact assessment performed by the Philippine government, which caused the government to withdraw its loan request. In this instance, however, the alliance did not gain sufficient

Table 15.1 Policy Alliance Effectiveness

Case	Policy/Project Outcome	Civil Society Outcome
Urban land reform	Achieved its legislative goals	Involved urban poor in legislative and bureaucratic advocacy
Logging ban	Concrete gains at local level; no national reform	Built environmental constituency
Sierra Madre forest project	Project canceled	No involvement of local people
Mount Apo geothermal plant	Philippine government withdrew World Bank loan request; project will probably be completed	Increased strength of existing local and regional groups and their relations to support networks

bargaining power to dissuade the government from going forward with alternative funding.

To what extent are the alliance's efforts responsible for the policy outcome? In the urban land reform and community-level log ban campaigns, the alliances can clearly take credit for the outcomes. However, positive outcomes are not always a direct result of alliance activity. Even though the result for some alliance members in the Mexico forest case was positive, the alliance's efforts were secondary to economic and political forces that made the project undesirable to the Mexican government. When policy gains are not achieved (as in the Mount Apo and national-level log ban campaign), larger forces tend to overwhelm the interests of grassroots groups. For example, energy demands carried great economic and political weight with the new Philippine government elected on a platform of economic success by the year 2000. Similarly, the economic and political clout of commercial loggers outstripped the influence of environmentalists whose ideas were not firmly rooted in broad public acceptance.

Impact on Civil Society

There are clear positive outcomes in two of the cases. Local organizations were strengthened in some fashion in the urban land reform and Mount Apo cases. The presence of preexisting GROs is a critical element in both. In the Mount Apo case, locally initiated action was reinforced and linked to provincial, national, and international resources. This was made possible in part by the active role played by the federation of indigenous people's organizations at the national level. Because the federation was coordinating national and international lobbying efforts, grassroots leaders were able to keep attention focused on community issues during the course of the campaign. The ULRTF also included strong GROs, but some of them left the alliance in protest against compromise. During the legislative campaign, local organizations were active, citizen participation was high, and grassroots leaders developed new skills. However, when the task force later took on the role of monitoring implementation, local organizations became overextended and had difficulty delivering basic services and benefits to their members. None of the cases illustrates a clear negative impact on grassroots groups. However, in the Sierra Madre case, the indigenous people affected were used briefly to lend legitimacy to the environmental campaign. They felt exploited and withdrew from further involvement, and so lost an opportunity to pursue their interests.

Seeking Impact on Both Policy and Civil Society

Figure 15.1 depicts the degree to which each alliance changed policy and strengthened civil society. The four cases plotted on the two dimensions show strikingly different patterns. The urban land reform and Sierra Madre campaigns were more effective in terms of policy gains but differed in the degree to which they promoted stronger grassroots groups. In contrast, the Mount Apo and log ban cases were both lower on policy outcomes, but Mount Apo supported greater local involvement; the national log ban campaign was unable to engage with local groups successfully.

Because the ebb and flow of a successful campaign must match the rhythm of the political process, it often appears that trade-offs must be made, at least in the short term, between policy gains and strengthening grassroots associations. Lobbying actions sometimes cannot wait for slower-paced grassroots education and participation efforts. Sometimes, the strategies preferred by the grassroots frame the issues so that they are hard to win. However, the urban land reform example shows that effectiveness on both dimensions is possible. It illustrates the potential for educating and involving grassroots groups in campaign decisions and strengthening alliance capacity to achieve policy outcomes. The alliance's strategy simultaneously increased the commitment of the poor to support legislation through mass action, expanded their understanding of political decision-making processes, and increased their confidence and repertoire of skills for dealing with the government. Through the active involvement of grassroots and other members, the alliance had the ability to influence at many points of leverage and through multiple channels.

At the other extreme, the log ban alliance achieved neither its policy goal nor a positive impact on civil society and citizen participation. In

Figure 15.1   Effectiveness in Achieving Policy Gains and
Strengthening Civil Society

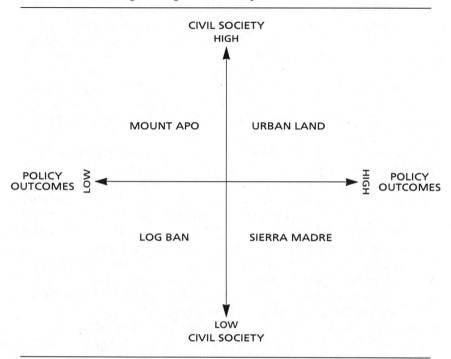

fact, efforts to engage local organizations in the commercial log ban campaign were unsuccessful largely because the national environmental NGOs could not forge a genuine alliance with grassroots groups. They were unsuccessful at forging a campaign to encompass both livelihood and environmental issues. There were, in fact, two campaigns being waged—one at the national level that had little popular support, and another at the grassroots level in which people struggled with some measure of success to secure more control over their livelihoods.

Characteristics of Alliance Effectiveness

Among the many factors that influence the outcomes of a policy alliance, four alliance characteristics stand out from these cases as fundamental to success. Two influence effectiveness in terms of policy change; two others affect strengthening civil society.

Fundamental to the accomplishment of policy gains is a coherent campaign strategy coupled with adequate resources to influence decision makers. The urban land reform alliance included a policy research center capable of critiquing legislation and offering sound alternative proposals. Businessmen lobbied the realtors and developers, Cardinal Sin lobbied key players in Congress, and the community groups mobilized their constituents at critical junctures. The task force brought together excellent access and strong technical capability, with well-organized and well-informed, active grassroots constituents. In contrast, the TCLB alliance had too few organizational resources to design and implement a campaign strategy or build a coalition successfully. It was particularly limited because it failed to build a strong grassroots constituency and so was vulnerable to charges that it represented the interests of elitist conservationists.

Second, a campaign's ability to win policy advantages depends on its ability to counter the forces of opposition. Framing a winning issue requires that the alliance define the debate in terms that are compelling to grassroots groups and that limit the opposition's ability to mobilize its own forces. In the log ban case, the alliance modified its initial stand from a call for a *total* logging ban (which directly threatened forest dwellers) to a *commercial* logging ban. However, community groups had difficulty grasping the difference, and the opposition successfully portrayed the issue as one of jobs versus environmental conservation. The log ban task force was also not able to gain favorable media coverage—a crucial ingredient to the successful framing of any issue.

Third, a commitment to strengthening civil society and democracy is essential if an alliance is to have a positive impact on citizen participation and building grassroots institutions. This is particularly clear in the international alliances. The Mount Apo case represents a network that was strong on commitment to citizen participation and close coordination of campaign strategies with grassroots groups. This alliance cared deeply that affected people be centrally involved.

Consequently (and fourth), Mount Apo offers a clear example of grassroots groups having a significant influence on the structure, goals, and strategies of the alliance. Other alliance members followed the lead of the local groups because of the quality of their organizations and their legitimacy as primary stakeholders. In contrast, the Tarahumara in the Sierra Madre case were powerless. They expressed disapproval and dissent by withdrawing after being used to lend legitimacy to the campaign. In some circumstances, this "exit" option can limit the effectiveness of an alliance. However, the NGOs were not limited by the Tarahumara's absence, since their primary target (the World Bank) did not require local representativeness when considering the merits of environmental issues.

This analysis suggests that an alliance can achieve both policy and civil society outcomes if it aspires to do so, includes the appropriate social groups, and has access to the necessary resources. Perhaps the most important element is whether or not the alliance *actively seeks* both policy outcomes and increased citizen participation.

Figure 15.2   Alliance Accountability to Grassroots Groups

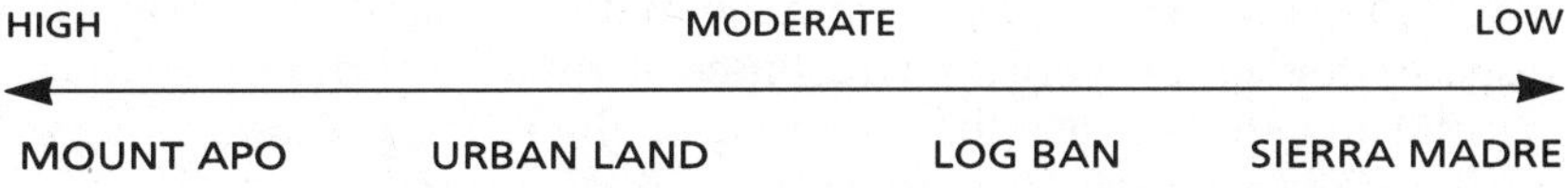

HIGH	MODERATE		LOW
MOUNT APO	URBAN LAND	LOG BAN	SIERRA MADRE

Analysis of Alliance Accountability

Policy alliances involve multiple members who expect the alliance to be accountable to their interests. Since there is never a perfect fit among the expectations of alliance members, the task of being accountable to all is challenging. As microcosms of the larger society, alliances can easily replicate unbalanced patterns of influence and so give their grassroots members short shrift. This section identifies how alliances are accountable to the grassroots as well as to other members. Indicators of accountability include inclusion in decision making, access to alliance resources (especially information), and division of roles and responsibilities (for example, who the spokespeople are).

Figure 15.2 shows the four cases arrayed on a continuum of accountability to the grassroots. High accountability is associated with alliances in which grassroots groups have access to key information, participate in strategic as well as tactical decision making, and play leadership roles in the alliance.

The Mount Apo case has a high level of grassroots accountability. It was structured so that the regional, national, and international task forces and networks supported the goals defined by indigenous people and farmers. When alliance members held different institutional priorities (for example, environmental protection versus indigenous people's rights), they resolved conflicts arising from these interests in an agenda set by indigenous people's and farmers' concerns. In contrast, in the Sierra Madre case, there was little accountability to affected people. NGOs pursued their own priorities and solicited only token input.

In the urban land reform case, local groups were active decision makers and implementers of the national campaign strategy—a task relatively easy to accomplish logistically, since Manila was the focus of the national campaign. The secretariat was strongly committed to the inclusion of all parties and was especially sensitive about legislative proposals being put forward only when they had strong grassroots support. Grassroots outreach and education enabled active and informed participation by grassroots leaders in decision making. In addition, the secretariat was highly accountable to all parties through direct member participation in key decisions.

In the log ban campaign, the rural members of the alliance were geographically, organizationally, and ideologically diverse, with no framework or mechanism for common representation in Manila. Local groups did not have an active presence in Manila, where national campaign decisions were made. This, coupled with the task force's limited resources and its inexperience with the concerns of local groups, produced significant gaps between the intentions of the task force concerning inclusion and accountability and its actual performance.

Factors Affecting Alliance Accountability

These cases suggest several factors that affect an alliance's accountability. Inclusion is the prerequisite for accountability to the grassroots, so the composition of the alliance is a fundamental defining characteristic. The diversity of interests and organizations within an alliance also affects its accountability. If the alliance has many and diverse members, the task of accountability is more complex. The ULRTF illustrates a heterogeneous alliance that cuts across many sectors of Philippine society, from poor urban communities to the highest ranks of the Catholic Church. Significant differences in wealth, culture, and power existed among these groups. Even though they came together to seek benefits for the urban poor, their inherent social differences made accountability a complex task. From the beginning, the alliance recognized that community groups had important resources to contribute as well as the primary stake in the outcome of its work. This realization, coupled with a strong community empowerment ethos, led it to seek high levels of accountability to the grassroots.

The Sierra Madre alliance excluded indigenous people, but it included a Mexican human rights organization, U.S. regional environmental organizations, and a Washington-based advocacy NGO. Despite differences among these NGOs, the alliance remained unisectoral. It left out other interests such as business, the church, and professional groups. Balancing accountability in this type of alliance is simpler than in one that includes NGOs, community-based organizations, and representatives of other social sectors.[3]

The legitimacy and resources each member brings to the alliance shape the power dynamics of the alliance itself (Brown in press). When the grassroots is organized, respected, and has considerable resources, it has power relative to other members. In this instance, other members are likely to be more accountable to grassroots interests, as in the Mount Apo and urban land reform cases. When grassroots groups cannot assert their legitimacy or other groups hold most of the resources, as in the log ban and Sierra Madre cases, grassroots accountability will be minimal. The power of each member also depends on its role and function in campaign strategies. In the Sierra Madre case, the Tarahumara lent symbolic legitimacy to the campaign. There was no need for them to be active participants, since the target of the campaign, the World

Bank, was interested in the technical merits of the argument rather than the political base from which it came. The strategies of the Mount Apo and urban land reform cases, however, relied heavily on demonstrating to the Philippine government that a political constituency demanded a response to their concerns. Community groups in these instances had resources that were critical to success.

Institutional mechanisms for information sharing and decision making are fundamental to fostering accountability to the grassroots. In the urban land reform alliance, the secretariat played a pivotal role. It was an ideologically neutral, technically competent, professional NGO secretariat committed to supporting grassroots participation. This secretariat was instrumental in negotiations between community organizations and the business group on specific legislative strategies and goals. It helped balance power in these negotiations by informing the community about options and by educating the business group about the core concerns of the community. The Mount Apo alliance involved a series of sub-coalitions at local, regional, national, and international levels, each with different roles and decision-making responsibilities. National groups had primary responsibility for linking local, national, and international strategies. But this was done with strong local representation in Manila through the indigenous people's coalition and through systematic consultation with all parties.

The log ban case illustrates that resources and experience in managing multiorganizational, multilevel alliances are necessary for the successful inclusion of all parties in decision making. Lapses in consultation with the grassroots and in the formulation of a cohesive strategy resulted from limited time, personnel, and skills in the coordinating bodies. Alliances that were more successful in accounting to all their members, especially the grassroots, had both formal and informal mechanisms to ensure good information flows and the inclusion of all members in decision making. Some form of structured representation of grassroots groups in decision-making structures, coupled with a secretariat that has a commitment and the resources to encourage community participation, seems to be essential for accountability to the grassroots.

NGOs have growing opportunities to be involved in policy alliances as states gradually open themselves to greater citizen participation and as donors learn the value of including the grassroots as a legitimate stakeholder. NGOs also can take an active role in supporting grassroots involvement when the state and donors are not open to popular participation. In these instances, confrontation is the likely course of events. Whether the context is cooperative or confrontational, alliances may take one of three basic forms, characterized by different goals, influences, and accountability: grassroots-centered alliances, NGO-centered alliances, and mixed alliances.[4]

Grassroots-centered alliances, such as the Mount Apo coalition, define the policy question from the grassroots point of view. NGOs and NGO coalitions join the alliance based on their affinity with the issues framed by the grassroots and their willingness to play a supporting role. Established primarily on principles of solidarity, these alliances may forgo policy gains to strengthen civil society. For example, NGOs with expert resources may defer to goals and strategies devised by the grassroots, even when their skills and insights could improve strategies for policy change.

NGO-centered alliances are exemplified by the log ban and Sierra Madre cases. In these alliances, NGO definitions of the problem shape the alliance agenda and strategy. If grassroots groups are involved, they play a supporting role to NGOs (providing information, staging local protests, or lending legitimacy to NGO-designed actions). Accountability to the grassroots tends to be weak, since the alliance is formed primarily to achieve NGO-defined policy goals. These alliances are well suited to achieving policy change with institutions that themselves have low levels of public accountability, such as multilateral development banks. They may also be useful for incremental policy change (Jenkins 1987), but they have little positive impact on deepening civil society and broadening democratic participation.

Mixed alliances such as the urban land reform coalition link poor people, middle classes, and elites in pursuit of a common objective. They have the potential to build civil society and to enhance policy outcomes simultaneously. However, this type of alliance offers the greatest challenge as well as the best promise for combining concrete policy benefits with increased participation of marginalized groups in the institutions of civil society. Success requires the alliance to have a bridging mechanism that is capable of spanning ideological differences and balancing power.

In a study of NGO roles in community-government partnerships in several Asian and African countries, Brown (in press) draws lessons that are highly relevant to mixed alliances. He concludes that NGOs balance power in multiorganizational alliances "by controlling important resources, shaping participants' awareness of their own and others' interests, and defining and enforcing the rules of the game to promote mutual influence." The ULRTF secretariat played this role by being an honest broker between grassroots and elite groups. The secretariat's sensitivity to and respect for the interests of all members was largely responsible for the alliance's success in balancing local needs with the interests of the business community and church. In the urban land reform alliance, the NGO secretariat had important resources itself (technical and policy analysis skills), but it also provided others with access to resources that they did not have (infor-mation about political processes to community members; "expert" community knowledge to businessmen). The secretariat urged the urban groups to understand their interests in new ways that enabled them to reframe their demands. It also facilitated the creation and implementation of decision-making rules that increased mutual influence.

Brown (1991) suggests that this "bridging" function is extremely demanding of the organizations and individuals who perform it, and that NGOs are uniquely able to fill the role. In a policy alliance, the bridging agent must not only help others establish mutual goals and reconcile differences but also manage its own interests and priorities. The bridging agent must have strong skills to facilitate mutual influence and assist alliance members in finding common ground. When the bridging agent has a strong stake in the alliance's policy outcome (as did the environmental NGOs in the log ban case), those interests may undermine its ability to balance information and decision-making processes. However, the urban land reform and Mount Apo cases illustrate that it is possible for NGOs to be effective intermediaries in developing multisectoral and international policy alliances that influence policy *and* strengthen civil society at the same time.

Notes

This chapter draws heavily on the joint analysis of the Philippine cases done by Valerie Miller, Dina Abad, David Brown, and myself. Their contributions are crucial. I am also indebted to Scott Kennedy for his editorial assistance in preparing this chapter.

1. IDR is researching NGO policy influence efforts at the national level in several countries in Asia and Africa. A comparative analysis of cases in the Philippines is under way, and new case studies are beginning in Indonesia and India. The study of transnational NGO influence efforts looks at large projects with environmental consequences as well as World Bank operational policies. These studies work with NGO communities to identify and build capacities necessary for effective and accountable policy influence. Support for these case studies comes from the Ford Foundation, the Moriah Fund, the Joyce Mertz Gilmore Foundation, the Asia Foundation, the Social Science Research Council, and the Canadian International Development Agency (CIDA).
2. The analysis of alliance effectiveness draws on Miller (1994).
3. Differences between the desired outcomes of the Mexican and U.S. advocacy groups undoubtedly affected accountability. This analysis will be refined when the final draft of the Sierra Madre case is completed.
4. A second form of grassroots-centered alliance, not represented in the cases here, is a grassroots movement that has little if any direct involvement of NGOs. National federations of peasants, unions, or women's groups often fit into this category.

References

Bratton, M. 1989. Nongovernmental organizations in Africa: Can they influence public policy? *Development and Change* 12(21):81–118.

Brown, L. D. 1991. Bridging organizations and sustainable development. *Human Relations* 44(8):807–31.

———. In press. Creating social capital: Nongovernment development organizations and intersectoral problem-solving. *Private action for the public good*, edited by W. W. Powell and E. E. Clemes. New Haven, Conn.: Yale University Press.

Brown, L. D., and R. Tandon. 1993. *Multiparty collaboration for development in Asia.* New York: United Nations Development Program.

Carroll, T. F. 1992. *Intermediary NGOs: The supporting link in grassroots development.* West Hartford, Conn.: Kumarian Press.

Cernea, M. 1987. Farmer organizations and institution building for sustainable agricultural development. *Regional Development Dialogue* 8(2):1–24.

Clark, J. 1992. Policy influence, lobbying and advocacy. In *Making a difference: NGOs and development in a changing world*, edited by M. Edwards and D. Hulme. London: Earthscan.

Edwards, M., and D. Hulme. 1994. *NGOs and development: Performance and accountability in the "new world order."* Background paper for SCF/IDPM Workshop on NGOs and Development, Manchester, June 27–29.

Fox, J. 1992. Democratic rural development: Leadership accountability in regional peasant organizations. *Development and Change* 23(2):1–36.

Hall, A. 1992. From victims to victors: NGOs and the politics of empowerment at Itaparica. In *Making a difference: NGOs and development in a changing world,* edited by M. Edwards and D. Hulme. London: Earthscan.

Jenkins, J. C. 1987. Nonprofit organizations and policy advocacy. In *The nonprofit sector: A research handbook*, edited by W. W. Powell. New Haven, Conn.: Yale University Press.

Miller, V. 1994. *NGOs and grassroots policy influence: What is success?* IDR Working Paper, vol. 11, no. 3. Boston: Institute for Development Research.

16

Participatory Methods for Increasing NGO Accountability

A Case Study from India

Parmesh Shah and Meera Kaul Shah

This chapter explores the participatory methodologies used to increase the accountability of one NGO to the village institutions and communities it professes to support and serve. The case study used is the Aga Khan Rural Support Programme in India. The problems that are likely to occur in using these methods are highlighted, and mechanisms are explored that may help NGOs introduce and increase accountability to grassroots institutions.

Accountability: Multiple Dimensions

Accountability is generally understood as a means by which individuals and organizations report to authority (Edwards and Hulme 1994). However, in development programs at the grassroots level, accountability relates to the wider process of information exchange, decision making, management, negotiation, and bargaining that takes place between different stakeholders. Accountability exists between peer groups and operates at many levels. For example:

Membership organizations——→ Members

Community organizations——→ Community

NGOs————————————→ Community organizations

Membership organizations

Village institutions

Local government

State and central government

Donors

Other competing and
complementary NGOs

This chapter focuses mainly on the accountability of Southern intermediary NGOs (or grassroots support organizations) to community organizations and membership organizations (Carroll 1992). It also examines the suitability and relevance of participatory methods tried out at the grassroots level for introducing accountability at other levels—between Southern NGOs, Northern NGOs, and official donor agencies.

In the past, accountability has been used to introduce control mechanisms linked to hierarchy and authority. In contrast, we consider accountability to be a reciprocal process in which multiple actors are accountable to one another. Accountability does not mean just reporting; it means a process of information exchange, consultation, and joint decision making.

Current experience shows that accountability is mostly upward, toward donors and governments. In the context of development programs, NGOs have undertaken limited consultation with community institutions before making strategic decisions that affect them. We use the term "reverse accountability" to emphasize the need to reorient the flow of accountability, reporting, and decision making toward community institutions. An overemphasis on mechanisms for introducing upward accountability has led to weak links between accountability, performance, and impact in Southern NGOs. If Southern NGOs have limited personnel and scarce resources, they should spend more time introducing mechanisms to increase accountability to community institutions. However, evidence shows that the time and resources spent by Southern NGOs on improving accountability to donors (including Northern NGOs) have reduced their capacity to do this. Participatory methods provide fertile ground for increasing the accountability of Southern NGOs to the community institutions and membership organizations they support.

Participatory Methods to Increase Accountability

Participatory methods have been used by NGOs in development programs to increase the participation of local communities in the development process and support the formation of accountable local institutions. NGOs have used methods such as participatory rural appraisal (PRA) to increase the accountability of office bearers and leaders in community institutions to members, and of members to one another. However, these methods have rarely been used by NGOs to develop accountability mechanisms to the local institutions they support or to facilitate peer evaluation of NGO performance. Most NGOs are happy to involve community institutions in program monitoring and evaluation, but they are less active when it comes to evaluating the performance of the NGO itself as a support institution. There is considerable scope for using participatory methodologies to develop reciprocal accountability between NGOs and community institutions.

The Case of the Aga Khan Rural
Support Programme–India (AKRSP–I)

AKRSP–I is an NGO that has been working in western India since 1985 to create an "enabling environment to enable local communities to develop and manage their local natural resources in a productive, sustainable and equitable manner through their own local institutions." It has catalyzed the formation of a range of village membership organizations by agencies with elected office bearers and leaders. AKRSP has been using PRA to enable communities to participate in program appraisal and planning and to develop their own institutions and paraprofessionals to manage development programs.

The programs implemented by village institutions (VIs) involve watershed management, forestry, small-scale irrigation, the rehabilitation of tanks, agriculture, savings and credit, animal husbandry, marketing, and energy conservation. AKRSP provides training, technical, financial, and management support to the community institutions, based on the appraisal and planning process carried out by the villagers. Budgeting is carried out by the program, based on a participatory planning process at the village level. AKRSP is currently funded by a number of donors, including the state and central governments and bilateral agencies.

The initial strategic planning and budgeting exercise for preparing proposals for funding was largely carried out by AKRSP professionals, based on limited consultation with the community. The donors to AKRSP relied heavily on an external evaluation to determine their support and funding for the next phase. The internal review of the first phase clearly showed that many assumptions made by NGO staff and the external evaluation team were not valid, and that inadequate consultation had led to unrealistic planning. AKRSP therefore decided to involve VIs more actively in strategic planning and the evaluation of its performance. It also decided to precede any future external evaluation of the program by an internal evaluation of AKRSP carried out by community institutions. The areas to be covered included not only program performance but also NGO management, the process of decision making, and the nature of support provided by AKRSP. Community institutions were asked to develop criteria for assessing the effectiveness and performance of AKRSP as a support organization.

The Development of Performance Criteria for AKRSP

The VIs were asked to devote one session of their regular meetings to brainstorm criteria for evaluating AKRSP's performance. This exercise was carried out with all VIs to avoid selecting institutions with a bias. The discussions varied considerably among VIs, and the criteria evolved after animated discussion. The major criteria developed by VIs were as follows:

- Process of consultation
- Management style of NGO (bureaucratic, participatory)
- Relationship with VIs (authoritarian, consultative, collegiate)
- Speed of decision making
- Structure of NGO (hierarchical, decentralized)
- Ability to act and use information provided by VIs
- Regular presentation of information to the community on key decisions (reporting)
- Transparency in decision making
- Sensitivity of NGO staff
- Timeliness of support
- Quality and nature of technical and management support
- Participation of VI representatives in key policy decisions
- Ability to influence government operations and policies (lobbying)
- Attendance of VIs and NGOs at seminars and workshops with a decision-making focus at the district and state levels
- Program performance

As can be seen, these criteria relate to processes of decision making, the management style of AKRSP, reporting and acting on information, the nature of program support, and support in gaining access to external institutions and decision-making forums. This laid a good framework for evaluating the performance of AKRSP.

Ranking AKRSP as a Support Organization

In order to assess AKRSP's performance based on the above criteria, VIs were asked to rank AKRSP on each of the criteria through a matrix-ranking exercise. VIs were also asked to justify the ranking by recalling a critical incident that could support their decision. Thus, both quantitative and qualitative information was collected during the process. This information was used subsequently in external evaluation and in training AKRSP staff and VI officebearers. It was also used to take corrective action during subsequent planning and review exercises. An example of such a ranking is given in Table 16.1.

Some of the critical incidents recalled while ranking AKRSP's performance are as follows:

Table 16.1   Ranking of AKRSP as a Support Institution by Village
Institution in Bharuch District

Criteria	Rank*
Process of consultation	2
Management style	3
Relationship with VIs	2
Speed of decision making	1
Structure of NGO	3
Ability to act on information provided by VIs	2
Regular presentation of information on key decisions to community	4
Transparency in decision making	3
Sensitivity of NGO staff	2
Timeliness of support	1
Quality and nature of technical and managerial support	2
Participation of VIs in key decisions	3
Ability to influence government operations and policies	2
Attendance of VIs in decision-making forums of government	3
Program performance	2

* 1 = best; 2 = good; 3 = medium; 4 = poor.

Regular Presentation of Information to the Community on Key Decisions. AKRSP supported VIs in initiating a lift-irrigation cooperative and, through mutual discussion, agreed to support the management costs (the salary of a water distributor) on a progressively declining basis for the first three years of operation, to enable the cooperative to stabilize its operations. This agreement was made on the basis of estimates of additional income for members, evolved jointly by the VIs and AKRSP. The performance of the program was reviewed after the first two years. Studies undertaken by AKRSP showed that irrigation in some villages had resulted in a higher and more rapid increase in income than had been envisaged. AKRSP discussed this issue with some, but not all, the VIs and decided to reduce the amount of management support, providing it for only one more year. The decision was communicated to office bearers in an annual review meeting, and they were asked to tell their members.

Many members were surprised at this decision, since they had never been presented with the relevant information. They were not against the assessment of viability and the rationalization of management support but thought that AKRSP should have presented the information directly in the VI meetings. They felt that the decision had been made by AKRSP in its internal forum without adequate consultation with VI members. They also indicated that each VI required different support, and AKRSP should have made regular presentations to *all* VIs. After all, this was a key decision affecting the viability of the farmers' livelihoods.

Timeliness of Support. During one particular year, VIs were facing a drastic shortage of groundnut seeds in the *Kharif* season, since nearly all the stocks had been cornered by the Groundnut Growers' Federation. VIs were concerned that most members would not be able to sow good-quality seeds at the right time and would thus lose out on potential income in a good rainfall year. During one of the review meetings, they raised this as a concern and asked AKRSP to help. AKRSP approached the Groundnut Growers' Federation in Ahmedabad (the state capital) and asked whether it would be able to earmark a stock of seeds for the VIs supported by AKRSP. The federation requested a deposit of 20 percent of the value of the seeds as a precondition for reserving the stock. AKRSP knew from past experience that VIs had already collected deposits from their members. But to save precious time, AKRSP deposited the money itself and asked the VIs to reimburse it from their funds. Timely delivery of seeds was linked to a credit and marketing program planned by the VIs. The VIs got their seeds delivered on time and performed significantly better than other villages in the area. During a subsequent review exercise, they appreciated the speed of AKRSP's response and encouraged AKRSP to respond to similar contingencies in the future.

Institutional (Venn) Diagramming to Compare AKRSP Performance with That of Other Development Institutions

Since discussing relative performance is a sensitive issue, VI members are asked to represent institutions by circles (*chapatis*, in the Indian context) and indicate their relative performance by arranging them in different sizes and colors. They are also encouraged to develop criteria for assessing comparative performance and to indicate the closeness of the external institution to the VI by arranging the *chapatis* at different distances. Subsequently, this method was also used to enable VI members to evaluate the performance of the VI in relation to external institutions.

VIs were also asked to illustrate the levels of coordination and overlap between the different institutions with which they interacted. They were then asked to indicate any improvements required in the workings of these institutions in relation to the VI and to one another. In this process, AKRSP generated useful data on its performance vis-à-vis other institutions (including the government) and developed greater downward accountability by enabling VIs to compare AKRSP with other institutions.

Chapati diagrams revealed that there were a number of other informal institutions that provided support to the village community by enforcing rules and regulations about common property resource management (for example, in forest protection). AKRSP had not involved these institutions in the consultative process adequately during the initial stages and, in some cases, had provided incentives to VIs to set up parallel institutions, thus increasing the cost of management. VIs indicated that AKRSP should build on informal institutions and processes before catalyzing the formation of new ones. As a result, AKRSP now includes an assessment of indigenous institutions as an integral part of the participatory appraisal process.

AKRSP has also supported the development of an animal husbandry program for VIs. However, the quality and frequency of AKRSP support have been minimal, since it has not been able to recruit high-quality staff in this area. In one region, people indicated that the staff of the government animal husbandry department were very competent and provided good support to the VI in spite of resource constraints. The VI therefore suggested to AKRSP that it wind up its operations in animal husbandry and provide resources to the VI so that it could provide logistic and transport support to the government, enabling it to provide services to VIs in a timely manner.

Evaluation Workshops to Discuss Results of Ranking Exercises and Steps for Corrective Action

The results of the ranking process and institutional assessment were compiled jointly with VI representatives and presented to workshops, which discussed results and agreed on steps and mechanisms for corrective action in the future. These workshops were organized on a regional basis, with all VIs participating in smaller group discussions and indicating areas for corrective action through presentations to one another. AKRSP also made presentations on the action it would like to take based on the evaluation exercises. Decisions made at the end of the workshops included:

- A workshop to review AKRSP performance by VIs would be held every six months.
- AKRSP would make a presentation of its annual plan to the VIs in February and March.
- A group of VIs would undertake a performance audit of AKRSP.
- AKRSP would invite VI representatives to its strategic planning meetings on a rotating basis.
- VIs would be provided with training in program management and communication skills, to enable them to make presentations at external forums.

All these measures have contributed significantly to the enhancement of reciprocal accountability between AKRSP and VIs.

Participation of VIs in Strategic Planning Exercises Prior to External Evaluation

Before an external evaluation takes place, AKRSP now asks VIs to undertake an internal evaluation of their programs and of AKRSP (using some of the methods described earlier) and to present the results to the AKRSP management. They are encouraged to produce a document summarizing their findings in the local language, which is used as an important input to the external evaluation process. This document is also used as a guiding framework for strategic and annual planning exercises. This ensures that AKRSP seeks the opinion of VIs before any external evaluation is undertaken and that subsequent funding of AKRSP is based on feedback from VIs.

Development of Local Monitoring and Management Information Systems

VIs are in the process of developing their own federation and will assume more of the responsibilities currently handled by AKRSP. VIs have therefore been encouraged to develop local monitoring and information systems that enable them to develop accountability with external institutions and increase their capacity to provide feedback and communicate with members. These systems include the development of simple participatory methods to facilitate performance assessment in other agencies and the training of VI functionaries in using these methods. The methods have enabled the VIs to be proactive in evaluating AKRSP and other agencies. Some VIs do not wait for AKRSP to take the initiative in developing feedback mechanisms, but not all VIs are equally interested in evaluating the performance of AKRSP. AKRSP is working toward developing a core group of village leaders who can take the initiative in monitoring and evaluating the performance of external agencies (including government) and help change the direction of accountability (downward) in the long run.

Participation of VI Officers in Recruitment of NGO Staff, Training, and Performance Appraisal

This sort of involvement has been tried only on an experimental basis, since it is a sensitive step and should be taken only after careful consultation with all concerned. It ensures that VI leaders take more responsibility at the initial stage of a program and assume a proactive role in ensuring staff performance and accountability. It also ensures that AKRSP staff are oriented early on toward the concept of management by the VI. Subsequently, VIs are given a major role in training new staff who are attached to VIs. VIs are encouraged to provide feedback about the performance of staff, develop criteria for performance appraisal, and periodically assess their performance. These inputs are incorporated into the formal staff appraisal process used by AKRSP.

Problems Encountered

Of course, the use of participatory methods can lead to many problems. The major problem is the change in power relationships that VI participation implies. People working for AKRSP sometimes feel threatened and may be defensive because the methods cause uncertainty in their jobs and they must submit to evaluation by multiple stakeholders.

A second problem relates to changes in management style. Many issues raised in assessments by VIs lead to a transition from management styles based on hierarchy, inhibited communications, and command-and-control relationships to more organic styles that encourage lateral communication, collegial authority, and flexible rules and procedures. This transition is not easy.

A third problem relates to a common fear of making mistakes and a lack of suitable opportunities within NGOs to learn from experience. The use of participatory methods depends to a large extent on prioritizing learning as an objective in organizational development.

Fourth, these methods imply changes in program management and implementation procedures, particularly in resource allocation, financial decentralization, and decision-making mechanisms. Many institutions that start using participatory methods are not ready to make corresponding procedural, structural, and policy changes and thus are unable to sustain their use. The use, operationalization, and integration of new methods within both VIs and AKRSP is a long-term process that requires iteration and adaptation. Most NGOs, VIs, and donors lack the patience to introduce such a process and so continue to initiate programs without adequate consultation.

For NGOs and others who want to try to use participatory methods, the experience of AKRSP suggests the following lessons:

- Do not try to use these approaches on a large scale. They require a significant amount of iteration and experimentation. Pilot them first in a region or a group of VIs, discuss the results, and institutionalize lessons learned from experience.

- Spend enough time initially in explaining the purpose of the methods to key NGO staff members and office bearers from VIs. Seek the commitment of top management for using these approaches and sustaining their use.

- In the initial phase of introducing these methods, the results of any evaluation process should be delinked from financial support to VIs and incentives to staff members. This is essential to ensure that both VIs and NGO staff learn from the process. Subsequently, feedback can be used to make decisions about resource allocation for VIs and performance appraisal for NGO staff.

- It is important to involve VIs in the assessment process before seeking their feedback on performance. VIs are not interested in participating in the process if they have not been involved at the beginning.

- Participatory methods should be used only if the NGO is interested in changing its decision-making mechanisms and accountability structures.

Implications for Practice and Policy

The experience of AKRSP shows that participatory methods can be used by NGOs to develop reciprocal accountability to community institutions. We believe that there is a strong case for applying the same principles in other contexts, including in relations with Northern NGOs and donors. Building both upward and downward accountability requires major reversals in the mind-sets of donors, NGOs, and community institutions.

Any external evaluation by an external donor or a team composed of external professionals should be preceded by a reciprocal evaluation by the recipient of funds. The process should start with community institutions being evaluated by their members, followed by an evaluation by the institutions of the nature and performance of NGO support. Southern NGOs should have an opportunity to evaluate their donors (Northern NGOs or other aid agencies). Northern NGOs that raise funds from official agencies should develop similar processes. External evaluation should incorporate the results of these processes into outputs. In many cases, the role of the external evaluation itself becomes peripheral, perhaps limited to combining the outputs of the process at all these levels.

There is already considerable dissatisfaction with so-called experts and short-term consultants who spend very little time with programs and make recommendations based on their impressions, perhaps affecting the development process in an area significantly. We are not making a case for the eradication of external evaluation but believe that it should form a small part of the evaluation process and the process of accountability. NGOs should make more use of participatory methodologies for interactive learning and corrective action. Many NGOs continue to use hierarchical, top-down control systems to exert authority and demand accountability in their own institutions; in the process, they may become as bureaucratic as their counterparts in government. NGOs should also earmark increased time and resources to institutional development in the first two years of the program cycle, to enable the development of consultative and participatory evaluation mechanisms. Any overemphasis on financial accountability should be replaced by a process of joint decision making, evaluation, and governance.

Participatory methods can be an important step in introducing more appropriate accountability mechanisms. However, the use of these methods alone does not guarantee increased or reciprocal accountability. To do this, NGOs need to make major reversals in their own institutions and be prepared to carry out structural changes in the long run. The question is, will NGOs be proactive, or will they be forced to make such changes only under external pressure?

References

Carroll, T. F. 1992. *Intermediary NGOs: The supporting link in grassroots development*. West Hartford, Conn.: Kumarian Press.

Edwards, M., and D. Hulme. 1994. *NGOs and development: Performance and accountability in the "new world order."* Background paper for the SCF/IDPM Workshop on NGOs and Development, Manchester, June 27–29.

17

Transforming the Transnational NGOs

Social Auditing or Bust?

Simon Zadek and Murdoch Gatward

W/hat are the possible futures for NGOs? Are they to become little more than the organizational mechanism for an international welfare system, as Fowler (1994) fears? Is the level of co-option into state agendas through funding and joint initiatives as advanced and problematic as Farrington and Bebbington (1993) have intimated? Are they doomed to become the new "lords of poverty" despite Hancock's (1989) plea to the contrary? What will be the leading edge of local, national, and international "third-sector" organizations as we move into the twenty-first century? Will NGOs have the flexibility and efficiency they claim to underpin their effectiveness, and the vision they claim as their "specialty" (Clark 1991; Edwards and Hulme 1992)? Most important of all, will NGOs have the *legitimacy* to represent those they claim as their constituents, and forms of *accountability* that ensure effectiveness in relation to their needs?

These questions need to be considered in the broader context of development, which includes:

- Extensions in economic globalization.
- Continued environmental decay.
- Increases in material absolute and relative poverty.

Northern, or transnational, NGOs (TNGOs) face an additional set of issues specific to their current institutional situation:

Gradual Deoperationalization from the South. A pattern of change that, on the surface, has been welcomed and encouraged by Northern NGOs, as their Southern "partners" become increasingly effective and anxious to take on the operational roles previously filled by Northern NGOs. Beneath the surface, however, has been enormous resistance to this change from some Northern NGOs, many of which have evolved around an operational focus. Few of them have come firmly to grips with the enormous implications of these changes in terms of their future size, form, and relationships.

Decline in Income. This is partially attributable to economic recession, but it also marks a more fundamental shift that will eventually undermine traditional sources of NGO financing, requiring more radical changes in approach than traditional marketing perspectives can offer. One trend that may continue is a shift in public support from development to relief. Another trend is a reduction in state funding as bilateral links develop between Northern funders and Southern NGOs. The intermediary role that funded much of the institutional growth of the larger TNGOs during the 1980s will more or less disappear over time.

Concern over Accountability. Development NGOs in the North have acquired a habit of saying "we represent," but they do not do so in any clear sense. This habit is being increasingly challenged, partly as a consequence of the withdrawal of Northern NGOs from operational work in the South, partly because of the parallel growth in the international voices of Southern NGOs, and partly because of a changing environment in both the North and the South that will increasingly question the moral high ground that NGOs achieved during the 1980s.

Policy Inertia. NGOs have increased their national and international policy advocacy at an extraordinary rate over the last ten years. Increasingly, they are consulted by the major development institutions, which have responded to pressure by creating a complex maze of consultative forums. However, the actual successes of policy advocacy are few and far between; the effect of engaging in consultation is often limited, yet it requires costly uses of scarce time and money (Edwards 1993).

A Crisis?

Do these issues add up to an impending crisis? Casual evidence from our ongoing involvement with TNGOs and others in both North and South suggests that a combination of ideological ruptures, concern about personal futures, funding shortfalls, and broader institutional shifts is creating considerable disorientation within the NGO community. There is, of course, much thinking and planning going on in NGOs in order to cope with these issues. However, the disorientation is highly dissipated and therefore tends to emerge in the context of on-off "firefighting" or ubiquitous "reorganization" exercises. As Landry and Mulgan (1994) and others have argued, there is nothing resembling a strategic response, or even a long-term vision of how nonprofits should adapt.

One view of this situation is that there should be no generalized strategic approach, given the diversity of the NGO community and its culture of institutionalized pluralism. The "community" clearly has no single form, aim, or voice. It is certainly reasonable to expect—and desire—that it will continue to evolve in many different forms and different directions. This diversity does not, however, obviate the need for debate and policy and for the development of some cohesive common ground in terms of insight and direction. Indeed, such diversity makes the need for coherence all the more important.

At the same time, the dilemmas facing major parts of the NGO community and its constituents are rooted in patterns of social and economic upheaval that may not wait for quiet contemplation or piecemeal responses. NGOs need to forge new directions in the future if they are not to become increasingly impotent or, indeed, if they are not to become part of the problem.

Ways of Seeing

It can be difficult to see problems clearly, let alone ways to resolve them and move forward. This is not because of ignorance or malice. We often prefer to hang on to redundant utopias rather than risk letting go and falling free into the unknown. This is particularly relevant today, as much to social activists and intellectuals as to bureaucrats, politicians, and the business community. The certainties of what is wrong are not matched by the clarity of how to achieve what is right. This state of "perplexity," as Max-Neef (1991, 1) describes it, is the "outcome of a situation for which we cannot recognise a precedent, which has kept us in a dead-end alley and barred the road to imaginative, novel and bold solutions." The only route forward, Gorz (1989, 8) confirms, is to "find a new utopia, for as long as we are the prisoners of the utopia collapsing around us, we will remain incapable of perceiving the potential for liberation." As John Maynard Keynes similarly argued, there is no shortage of new ideas, just a problem in letting go of the old.

One way of letting go of the old and grasping the new is to look forward, to envisage what it might be like in the future. Many of us have had personal experience with this approach while working at the grassroots level in community-led planning processes. Community "visioning" is an established part of the toolbox of participatory research. Few of us, however, have tried the same techniques in planning our own future, or the future of the organizations for which we work. Looking forward to the future, or imagining ourselves looking back from that future, may be a useful way of thinking about the issue of NGO accountability. What might the NGO community look like if it continues along its current path, or if we make certain assumptions as to what might occur over the coming years?

Visioning has its limitations, however. It can cause us to become detached from what is really going on and from what is likely or possible. These pitfalls can lead to the kinds of unrealistic visions that give those with utopian leanings a bad name. It is equally important, therefore, to root vision in concrete processes, possibilities, and practice. In particular, what practical examples are there of attempts to evolve and institutionalize new forms of accountability?

Both visioning and practical examples can offer insights into the issue of NGO accountability. However, these are complements, not substitutes. Together, they root the analysis in practical possibilities, while seeking to evade the constraints of focusing purely on the past and present. This chapter explores both approaches simultaneously. In the left-hand column it sets out one possible future scenario in which to consider NGO accountability. This scenario extrapolates from the earlier analysis of the current situation, trying to find a middle path between utopian and dystopian leanings. In the right-hand column it sets out one particular example of a practical approach to increasing accountability that is currently being tried by a number of organizations with support from the New Economics Foundation, particularly the U.K.-based fair trading organization Traidcraft.

Looking Back from 2010: Forced Shifts in Accountability	Looking Forward from Now: A Practical Approach to Accountability

Context

It all came to a head in the second half of the 1990s, although the roots of the crisis have a far earlier origin. After a period of rapid growth, many of the larger NGOs found themselves in increasing difficulties. Money was seen to be at the heart of the problem, although it proved to be just the tip of the iceberg. When they had it (money, that is), there seemed to be more and more strings attached. When they did not have it, their enormous bureaucracies (and their many dependent subcontractors) grew hungry, angry, and frightened. A real addictive dependency had set in. More and more of the stuff was needed, even though it was clear that the more money the NGOs had, the more their values and other strengths were compromised by its use.

Context

Traidcraft is a public limited company registered in England and has some 3,750 shareholders. Its main activity is the purchase and resale of products produced by small companies and community enterprises in Africa, Asia, and Latin America. It currently trades with over 100 such organizations, covering a wide range of crafts, fashion and household goods, and foodstuffs. It has an annual turnover of about £6 million, about 60 percent of which arises from sales of goods from the South. This allowed payments of about £1.5 million in 1992–93 to its producer-suppliers in the South.

Though not an NGO, Traidcraft's objectives focus on benefits to people other than shareholders, particularly the small companies and

Looking Back from 2010: Forced Shifts in Accountability	Looking Forward from Now: A Practical Approach to Accountability

The Northern TNGOs had an additional set of problems. By the early 1990s, their Southern partners had outgrown their subordinate status and were demanding a more than equal share of the pie to make up for lost time and their sense of grievance. The TNGOs found themselves limited to an ever-diminishing set of activities. Funding from governments and international agencies flowed directly to the growing cadre of Southern NGOs. The Southern NGOs took the international stage by storm, insisting on direct representation rather than relying on the earlier indirect routes to power through their Northern colleagues. Some Southern NGOs launched their own fund-raising organizations in Europe and North America.

Most of all, however, the legitimacy of the TNGOs was challenged. At the liberal end of the spectrum, they were seen as bloated bureaucracies in which well-meaning ethical and political initiatives became buried under a snowstorm of paper and a sweaty morass of circular consultation. At the more cynical end, they were seen as a self-serving elite, unwilling to submit themselves to the very forms of accountability that they advocated for others.

These issues did not come to a single head, although some have pointed to the renowned 1994 Manchester Conference on NGO accountability as a key turning point. But it would be true to say that there was a wave of changes that started in the mid-1990s and took about a decade

community enterprises in the South from which it buys most of the products it trades. Traidcraft is also rooted in the Christian faith and places its ethical aims in that context. Thus, Traidcraft's "foundation principles" specify the overall objective of the company as being to establish a just trading system that expresses the principles of love and justice fundamental to the Christian faith.

Traidcraft, like most NGOs and a few commercial organizations, makes its ethical aims explicit in all its relationships. Thus, although it does not raise grants or sponsorship, it has raised investment capital and sells its products to consumers in the United Kingdom on the back of a commitment to trade "fairly" with producers in the South. Furthermore, its foundation principles commit the company to "fair" and "participative" relationships with staff, the network of representatives who sell products, and the shareholders.

By consciously placing itself in the trading sphere, Traidcraft seeks to demonstrate that such principles are compatible with sustainable economic activity. It is committed to working out, and being a working example of, a more just system of international trade between the North and the South. International trade is, however, a demanding discipline, even for those who do not bring to it an overriding set of ethical principles. As Traidcraft has felt more keenly the pressures of trying

Looking Back from 2010: Forced Shifts in Accountability	Looking Forward from Now: A Practical Approach to Accountability

to work themselves (more or less) fully through.

The changes that took place occurred largely *despite* the efforts of many NGOs, particularly the transnationals. There were a few cases of medium-sized NGOs moving toward new forms of accountability. But these cases had no real ripple effect because of the obstinacy of the largest NGOs, the so-called Seven Brothers. Unfortunately, this resistance meant that the first real changes came about because of the emerging crisis rather than because opportunities for change were grasped positively.

The crisis comprised a series of disclosures about malpractice, shoddy performance, and outright cynicism in high-profile TNGOs (quite unrepresentative disclosures, as many of those in the know have since argued). These disclosures led to a dramatic collapse of funding from state and public sources, as well as the withdrawal from a number of TNGOs of accreditation rights to major national and international policy forums.

Seeking Ways Forward

The TNGOs were in shambles, as a domino effect tore through their ranks. The Seven Brothers met in closed sessions, but because they were unaccustomed to real collaboration, they failed to reach any agreement on how to meet this challenge together. Parallel to this process, all the Brothers (as well as many of the smaller NGOs caught up

to run an effective business, it has seemed increasingly important to be able to measure social and ethical performance, as well as reporting on financial results. This is important if the company is to determine its effectiveness in relation to its aims and make adjustments where necessary. It is also critical to be able to show those to whom commitments were made—particularly producers, customers, staff, and shareholders—that Traidcraft's practice matches those commitments.

Traidcraft recognizes that its continued success depends on being able to demonstrate that it is trading "fairly" with these various groups. Without some proof, support will eventually fall away, and with it the sustainability of the company and the gains that it has achieved. Furthermore, the proof that ethical trade is possible is necessary if Traidcraft is to provide a demonstration that might give courage and direction to other businesses.

Seeking Ways Forward

In the early 1990s, Traidcraft explored possible routes for assessing social impact and ethical behavior and for communicating this information. The extensive experience of many organizations in the evaluation of development work provided a rich source of principles and methods. The whole "participative" paradigm, in particular, seemed to resonate with Traidcraft's own organizational culture and

Looking Back from 2010: Forced Shifts in Accountability	Looking Forward from Now: A Practical Approach to Accountability

in the crisis) were busy making bilateral deals in an attempt to survive (and, to be fair, to maintain the real quality of work they had achieved).

The main (and certainly most publicized) outcome of this process was a series of mergers between key TNGOs and Southern NGOs. Five of the Seven Brothers chose this route as a way of rebuilding their damaged reputations. Others attempted (with varied success) to transform themselves internally in such a way as to regain credibility. Some, including the other two of the Seven Brothers, tried to ride it out.

This strategy failed, as they found themselves subjected to predatory "asset stripping" of people, programs, and funding sources by other NGOs from the North and the South. Most of those with the "ride it out" philosophy eventually had to change tack, with a number doing so too late and having to close their doors for good.

These mergers and internal transformations were in most cases sufficient to move the new organizations onto a plateau of stability. However, in some cases, the basis for change took on more confrontational forms. The experiences in the mid-1990s of mass demonstrations against the General Agreement on Tariffs and Trade (GATT) in India and the uprising in Chiapas following the signing of the North American Free Trade Agreement (NAFTA) provided a model for one form of resistance to what was perceived as the high-handed approach taken by TNGOs.

aims. However, these approaches remained inadequate for Traidcraft's needs in a number of respects. In particular:

- Traidcraft wanted to take account of all its relationships, as far as was practical.

- Traidcraft wanted this to be a regular, institutionalized activity.

- Traidcraft wanted both the process and the outcome to be public.

- Traidcraft wanted the process and outcome to have the same weight (as far as possible) as the statutory financial audit.

- Traidcraft wanted the process to be usable by other trading organizations, particularly commercial companies.

Thus, although Traidcraft did not want to reinvent existing wheels, it needed to mold together elements of existing approaches to form a model that would fulfill the above criteria. To achieve this, Traidcraft approached the London-based research and lobbying NGO the New Economics Foundation (NEF) to assist in the development and testing of the method, as well as the dissemination of the lessons learned to a wider audience. Furthermore, a steering group was formed to provide critical inputs in the development of the method; members included representatives from business schools, campaigning and research organizations, and some of Traidcraft's stakeholders.

Looking Back from 2010: Forced Shifts in Accountability	Looking Forward from Now: A Practical Approach to Accountability

The embarrassment caused by these demonstrations, as well as the small-scale but well-publicized loss of lives of TNGO officials and demonstrators (particularly in that one awful case in which the officials at one office turned out to be armed and fired on a peaceful demonstration in a fit of fear), pushed those transnationals that were slow on their feet toward change more quickly.

Another factor in this transformation was the law. A number of legal cases against the TNGOs were launched by community organizations through the international courts. Most focused on the argument that TNGOs had expropriated personal and community-based information in order to raise money. Others argued that "false promises" had been made. Legal history was made in a number of cases in which peasant and urban communities made effective use of legislation originally intended to protect famous people and profitable trademarks. Many of these cases were settled out of court. However, the writing was on the wall for all to see, and legal precedents played a key role in the TNGOs' decisions to shift the on us of ownership (and, of course, legal liability) elsewhere.

Accountability and Ownership

The issue of accountability therefore became inextricably linked with the issue of ownership. It became widely accepted that the traditional

The outcome of this process was the Traidcraft social audit. Traidcraft is now in its third year of auditing. Other commercial companies are testing it or evolving their own methods; other versions relevant to community enterprises are being developed and tested in the United Kingdom, Tanzania, and South Africa; and interest has been shown by NGOs and international agencies for organizational and project-level assessments (Zadek and Evans 1993; Zadek 1994).

Social Auditing

Social Auditing offers a method of accountability that involves all stakeholders and is neither prescriptive nor bureaucratic. Buzzwords that are in vogue at the moment, such as "transparency" and "good governance," are easy to use but difficult to implement. How can NGOs or community businesses ensure transparency and measure themselves against something other than static objectives that, though out-of-date within six months of being introduced, become the yardstick of any future evaluation?

For any organization to have ownership of its outputs, the indicators by which it is measured must be relevant to everyone involved, not just to the key players, such as directors and senior management. Read any up-to-date management textbook, and the philosophy of taking decision making to the lowest

Looking Back from 2010: Forced Shifts in Accountability	Looking Forward from Now: A Practical Approach to Accountability

model of NGO ownership—which was basically no formal ownership at all, leaving effective ownership in the hands of unelected officials— was inadequate. In 1996, drawing partly from an in-depth, government-sponsored analysis of the voluntary sector in the United Kingdom produced in 1994, a Private Members Bill passed through English Parliament, marking the end of charitable status for all but a few (rather archaic) cases. This was soon followed by European legislation to the same effect. By the turn of the century, the whole notion of "non-governmental" as a form of (non) ownership was effectively over.

Forms of TNGO Accountability

It would be great to be able to say that a "new" form of ownership arose phoenix-like from the ashes to support appropriate forms of accountability for NGO-like organizations. This did not happen, although there was a period of intense and often creative innovation in new forms of accountability and ownership. Rather, a range of existing models of accountability were taken up by different NGO-like organizations.

Institutional-Federal Model. Probably the most common form adopted was what became known as the "institutional-federal" model. This approach tended to be quite similar to the model being adopted by the European Union at the time. Each part of the newly merged organizations

point will be preached. The same applies to the measurement of success or failure: the indicators must be set at the lowest point of the organization. By developing a methodology for social as well as financial auditing, an organization is able to set its own indicators and respond to changes within its social structure. All stakeholders have a say in the development of indicators as the methodology evolves, as well as in their application. Managers have regular access to information regarding both social and financial developments, which enables them to respond in a timely manner rather than when it is too late to do anything.

Key Stages of the Social Audit Process

Traidcraft's social audit was constructed on the basis of a carefully designed process of consultation across stakeholder groups. The key stages of this process are summarized below.

Identify Stakeholders. The first stage of the Traidcraft social audit is to identify key "stakeholder" groups. These groups included over 100 producer-suppliers, its thousands of customers, its 100-plus staff and 2,000 voluntary representatives, and, of course, its 3,000 shareholders.

Identification of Stakeholder Aims and Indicators. The second stage is to initiate a process of consultation with each stakeholder group that allows them to establish criteria against which they believe that

Looking Back from 2010: Forced Shifts in Accountability	Looking Forward from Now: A Practical Approach to Accountability

(often including parts of the old ones, following the" Europe of the Regions" philosophy) had a vote according to various possible measures of size. The more conservative organizations tended to opt for measures based on financial contributions, whereas the more radical organizations went for some measure of how many people each part represented. This federal structure was different from the decentralized model employed by some TNGOs in the 1990s, in that the heads of the parts (many of which were in the South) made up the board of directors.

Block-Vote Model. Some NGOs went for a variation of the block-voting formulas adopted by U.K. trade unions and other movements in an earlier era. World Plan (International), for example, created a voting structure that gave funder-stakeholders an aggregate block vote of 25 percent, community organizations (the intended beneficiaries) about 55 percent, and staff the remaining 20 percent. Although this should have given the community organizations effective control, the staff and funders managed from the outset to operate a divide-and-rule approach that gave them effective power. When this no longer functioned, the staff themselves organized a workers' buyout (with support from the funders), leaving WPI in its current well-known form as the only TNGO workers' cooperative. WPI now provides a range of services, in practice, doing a lot of cheap subcontract work for other NGOs.

Traidcraft's social impact and ethical behavior should be judged, and then to assess the organization's activities on this basis. Thus, the social accounts of Traidcraft reflect the aims and concerns of its key stakeholders, as well as its own stated social and ethical aims.

This stage requires consultative approaches tailored to the characteristics of each stakeholder group. Extensive face-to-face discussions are held with representatives of the shareholders and voluntary representatives. Following this, postal questionnaires are used to contact and solicit the views of each member of these two groups. Two rounds of discussions are held with staff— one to establish how they want to carry out the assessment, and another consisting of group workshops (based on their stated preferences). In addition, basic data on staff conditions (including wages and equal opportunities) are collected and analyzed. Finally, a sample of producers is selected for in-depth consultation, which in one accounting cycle involved spending several weeks with Traidcraft's Filipino producer-suppliers.

Production of Draft Social Accounts. The third stage is the production of draft social accounts. These are produced jointly by Traidcraft and NEF, discussed with the Traidcraft board, and circulated to some stakeholders for comments. In producing these accounts, it is difficult to compress the enormous amount of information generated into a small number

| Looking Back from 2010: | Looking Forward from Now: A |
| Forced Shifts in Accountability | Practical Approach to Accountability |

One-Person-One-Vote Model. Of the large TNGOs, TransFam adopted the most radical approach of all, a one-person-one-vote system for its 1 million members. This was not, sad to say, because it was the most radical organization prior to the period of change. It was TransFam, some may recall, that became the focal point of mass demonstrations in the late 1990s and that had to cope with the largest number of litigations. Eventually, faced with imminent bankruptcy, TransFam signed the famous Delhi Accord in 1999. The 3,000-plus closely typed pages of the accord boiled down to a relatively simple deal whereby TransFam would become owned by all those people who had directly received financial assistance through it over a specific period. In return, the various litigations were dropped, and the relatively widespread intimidation of TransFam officials ceased. It was quite a depressing affair at the time, seen as a low point in the collapse of the TNGO dinosaurs. It is somewhat ironic, therefore, that the TransFam model is now seen as the most radical to emerge from that period.

Many of the new forms of accountability and associated ownership described above arose from the survival instincts of the large TNGOs when faced with extinction. These changes were applauded by the more visionary people within these organizations. However, it would be inaccurate to suggest that this minority played a major role in catalyzing the changes.

of readable pages. This information includes not only statistics but also a vast body of qualitative data, often in the form of narratives about particular events or perspectives on Traidcraft. In selecting information and the format of presentation, it is necessary to get a balance between "hard" (objective) data (such as income to producers) and qualitative information that reveals the complex fabric of social and ethical issues relevant to constituents and to Traidcraft.

Auditing the Accounts. The penultimate stage in the social accounting process is to audit the accounts. It is NEF's role to "sign off" on the accounts, with whatever qualifications are deemed necessary. At the same time, NEF's involvement in both the development of the methodology and the drafting of social accounts means that there is a danger of a conflict of interest or simply the loss of objectivity. For this reason, NEF invites a group of people with some expertise to represent the various stakeholder concerns and interests in an audit group, to discuss and comment on the accounts, and to advise NEF on the appropriate position to take.

Publication of Accounts. The final step is to sign off and publish the accounts. Publication of the social and financial audits occurs concurrently, highlighting the importance of the former. All stakeholders receive a copy of the audit, and copies are available as a matter of public record for experts, traders, producers, and the media. Traidcraft is currently

Looking Back from 2010: Forced Shifts in Accountability	Looking Forward from Now: A Practical Approach to Accountability

The "NICs": Accountability and Organization

There was a group of organizations that voluntarily embraced radical transformations in accountability and ownership over that period, the so-called new internationalist conglomerates (NICs). Some of them were originally Northern NGOs that operated on the international scene but were rooted within their own communities and countries. This in itself gave them a different sense of accountability from the outset. Most of the NICs tended to be relatively smaller and younger than other NGOs. This meant that there was less change-constraining institutional inertia due to bureaucratization and internal vested interests. Also interesting was the fact that many of these NGOs were of the information age. Their main functions concerned the movement of information rather than the raising and disbursement of money. They were involved in development education, research, lobbying, and campaigning rather than funding projects that had physical manifestations. This gave them an altogether different organizational form, one that did not need to have the same patterns of hierarchical authority.

Their relationships with one another and the communities they related to tended to far more open-ended, involving less dependence, fewer reporting structures, and a generally far higher level of voluntarism. All these features supported

working on the 1994–95 audit, which will be published and can be compared with the previous year's results. The company is committed to undertaking a social audit annually.

Accountability and Effectiveness

Accountability does not equate with effectiveness and is not sufficient in itself. Social auditing is not, therefore, just about accountability. By undertaking social audits on an annual basis, an organization's objectives cease to be static and become more responsive.

The project evaluation cycle encourages measurement by someone else on behalf of a third party. Furthermore, it usually identifies problems out of context, in relation to outdated aims, and much too late. Social auditing, in contrast, is undertaken by an organization for its own benefit. The results are therefore owned by that organization and are taken on board as part of the strategic planning process.

Social auditing offers a form of accountability that is integral to ongoing planning. It recognizes the intimate relationship between stakeholders' participation and the effectiveness of decisions made and actions taken.

Conclusions and Lessons

Can social auditing really make an organization more accountable?

Looking Back from 2010: Forced Shifts in Accountability	Looking Forward from Now: A Practical Approach to Accountability

the transformation process.

There was a further subgrouping within the NICs known as the new international traders (affectionately known as the NITs). The main feature of these organizations was that they traded actively in goods and services.

The background to the changes that took place in this latter subgroup was equally, if not more, complex than that for the TNGOs, and it varied a lot among the organizations. One example is that of the ear, nose, and throat products organization Facing the World. Facing the World had grown to be an enormous, worldwide, franchise-based retail chain by the mid-1990s. Its reputation was based on good products and "fair trading" relationships with its suppliers. Facing some criticism for its secrecy, the organization agreed to undertake a social audit, a technique that was then at an experimental stage. But it was too late for such a conciliatory gesture. "Open season" was declared on Facing the World. Sales collapsed (a bit like with the water giant, Perrier, in the early 1980s), and the organization faced extinction.

It was at this stage that a deal was cooked up aimed at reestablishing a sound financial basis and rebuilding its public image. The organization issued shares to all its franchises and suppliers. The franchises had to pay according to their likely losses if the organization went under (and their likely profits if it did not).

The suppliers received free shares based on the level of the trading

After all, it does little more than make information available about what has happened in relation to those who are most affected by the organization's activities.

The case of Traidcraft suggests that social auditing *can* make a difference. To date, the social audits of Traidcraft have thrown up a range of issues about the way the company goes about its activities and the ways in which different stakeholder groups are affected as a result. Generating this information, recognizing the views of stakeholders, and publicizing the audit so widely have undoubtedly led to Traidcraft's refining and questioning the validity of key aspects of its approach, as well as developing new tools and processes for securing the interests of key stakeholders.

This success has, of course, depended largely on the receptivity of those who run Traidcraft, particularly the managers and the board. Traidcraft started on the route toward a social audit because these groups decided that they really did want to be accountable to stakeholders. Other organizations thinking about social audits need to ask the same question: do we really want accountability to stakeholders, and if so, which ones?

The social audit carries no statutory or mandatory weight, unlike the financial audit and some elements of the environmental audit. One day this may change, but not yet. The publication of the social audit can nevertheless create considerable

Looking Back from 2010: Forced Shifts in Accountability	Looking Forward from Now: A Practical Approach to Accountability

relationship. The existing shareholders retained a small proportion of the shares, about 10 percent. Given the extraordinary success of the renamed Facing Our World, which is now a well-known story, this small shareholding proved to be far more profitable than the original holding.

Conclusions and Lessons

The history of the last twenty years has been remarkable. Looking back, it seems obvious that the changes should have been expected. However, all the historical documents reviewed, as well as the extensive interview program underpinning this historical overview, confirm that it was all pretty unexpected. Even those who were most committed to change had gotten stuck in a visionless vision, one that was able to see what was wrong but just could not unravel what to do. Everyone seemed to be looking for the "big story" and missed the massive events that were unfolding on their own doorstep—that is, until these events stood up and slapped them in the face.

This story is a lesson for us all. We may be pleased at the changes that have taken place—the new forms of TNGOs, the NICs, and the NITs. But history challenges us all not to repeat the incredibly myopic behavior of the late-twentieth century. After all, it might have turned out very differently, and may still do so in the future.

pressure on the organization concerned to take note of its contents. This is particularly true for organizations whose continued existence depends in part on the belief by its individual and institutional supporters—including staff and volunteers—that it is ethical according to some set of explicit principles. However, even the more coldhearted commercial organizations cannot always ignore clear evidence of moral malpractice, even when it is entirely legal.

Social auditing is an approach, not a solution. It allows organizations to move toward new forms of accountability without major shifts in ownership and organizational structure. It allows for an evolutionary process of taking stakeholder interests more directly into account and having to report on activities according to those interests. Finally, through the information generated and its open publication, social auditing can be effective in reorienting an organization's activities toward stakeholder interests.

References

Clark, J. 1991. *Democratizing development: The role of voluntary organizations.* West Hartford, Conn.: Kumarian Press.

Edwards, M. 1993. Does the doormat influence the boot? Critical thoughts on UK NGOs and international advocacy. *Development in Practice* 3(3): 163–75.

Edwards, M., and D. Hulme, eds. 1992. *Making a difference: NGOs and development in a changing world.* London: Earthscan.

Farrington, J., and A. Bebbington, with K. Wellard and D. J. Lewis. 1993. *Reluctant partners: Non-governmental organisations, the state and sustainable agricultural development.* Non-Governmental Organisations Series. London: Routledge.

Fowler, A. 1994. NGOs and the globalization of social welfare: Perspectives from East Africa. In *NGOs and people's organizations in service provision in East Africa,* edited by A. Fowler. Unpublished manuscript.

Gorz, A. 1989. *Critique of economic reason.* London: Verso.

Hancock, G. 1989. *Lords of poverty: The power, prestige, and corruption of the international aid business.* New York: Atlantic Monthly Press.

Landry, C., and G. Mulgan. 1994. *The future of the charities: Themes and issues.* London: Demos.

Max-Neef, M. 1991. *Human-scale development: Conceptions, applications, and further reflections,* New York: Apex Press.

Zadek, S. 1994. Trading ethics, *Journal of Economic Issues* 27(2):631–45.

Zadek, S., and R. Evans. 1993. *Auditing the market: A practical approach to social auditing.* London and Gateshead: Traidcraft/New Economics Foundation.

18

The Primacy of the Personal

Robert Chambers

Experience with participatory rural appraisal (PRA) suggests that a reversal of the normally dominant behavior and attitudes of outsiders is crucial for participatory development. Personal behavior and attitudes have, however, been neglected in determining how to do better. The development enterprise has a North-South orientation due to patterns of dominance between "uppers" and "lowers," funding, pressures to disburse, and upward accountability. These patterns increasingly affect NGOs, which may then become more like government organizations in scale, staffing, hierarchical culture, procedures, and self-deception.

Policies, procedures, and organizational cultures are determined by individuals, especially those in positions of power. To stem and reverse trends of dominance and deception require personal change and action by them: to shift emphasis from upward to downward accountability; to resist pressures to disburse; to stress trust and to reward truthfulness and honesty; and above all, to enjoy giving up the normal exercise of power, enabling lowers to do more and take more responsibility. Participatory field experiences and training can help bring about these personal changes. These, in turn, require a new professionalism of training and, for some NGOs, a redefinition of roles. The question then is to what extent such changes would resolve the problems of performance and accountability that currently and correctly concern so many NGOs.

"Discovering" Behavior and Attitudes

In the early stages of the coalescing of approaches and methods that led to PRA and its relatives, participatory methods seemed to be the key: participatory mapping and modeling; matrix ranking and scoring; seasonal calendars; trend and change analysis; causal, linkage, and flow diagramming; wealth and well-being ranking; time-use analysis; the

241

identification and ranking of best bets; and so on. The failure for so long to recognize the capability of local people to conduct their own analysis, especially but not only visually, tended to be attributed to the fact that methods such as these, and their combinations in sequences, had previously been underdeveloped and little used by local people. In the early 1990s, however, field experience showed that the beliefs, behavior, and attitudes of outsiders explained more of this earlier failure than did the lack of methods.

The belief that such methods could be used only by outsiders was self-validating. When dominant outsiders did not believe that local people could map and diagram, the locals lacked the encouragement and occasion to find out for themselves that they could. When the incapacity presented by local people—"we do not know how to make a map"— fit the preconceptions of outsiders, it was not challenged but reinforced by acceptance; yet I know of no case in which local people, despite initial disclaimers, have been unable to map. The confidence that they could do it—that local people could map, diagram, list, estimate, compare, rank, score, prioritize, plan, act, monitor, evaluate, and themselves facilitate and train others—proved to be an enabling precondition for outsiders to facilitate activities that local people themselves often did not know they were capable of.

Outsiders' normal behavior also confirmed the incapacity of local people. Worldwide, when interacting with local people, outsiders tended to lecture, interrupt, criticize, suggest, and dominate both verbally and nonverbally. A key example was a PRA training exercise in Karnataka in 1990 where a participatory planning session was monitored. At that session, the villagers spoke for only eleven out of forty-five minutes and were interrupted forty-five times. The most difficult lesson for outsiders in PRA training was then understood to be learning to shut up: not to dominate, not to interview, and not to interrupt while local people were doing their own analysis. More and more, PRA field training exercises have come to stress outsiders' behavior and attitudes more than methods.

Necessary behavior and attitudes include outsiders sitting down, listening, and learning; relaxing and not rushing; handing over the stick (or pen or chalk); embracing error and failing forward; being transparently clear about who they are, their purposes, and what can and cannot be expected; and being nice to people (see Mascarenhas et al. 1991; Chambers 1994b, 1994d, 1994e). Rigid rules are replaced by using one's own best judgment at all times. Most recently, in late 1994, experience in Sri Lanka has added the principle of "ask them": asking local people not just what they know and how they would like to show it but also how they would advise outsiders to behave and to become better facilitators.

Table 18.1 North-South Upper-Lower Relationships

Dimension/ Context	North Uppers	South Lowers
Spatial	Core (urban, industrial)	Periphery (rural, agricultural)
International and development	International Monetary Fund, World Bank Donors Creditors	Poor countries Recipients Debtors
Personal ascriptive	Male White High ethnic or caste group	Female Black Low ethnic or caste group
Life cycle	Old person Parent Mother-in-law	Young person Child Daughter-in-law
Bureaucratic organization	Senior Manager Official Patron Officer Warden, guard	Junior Worker Supplicant Client Other rank Inmate, prisoner
Social, spiritual	Patron Priest Guru Doctor	Client Layperson Disciple Patient
Teaching and learning	Master Lecturer Teacher	Apprentice Student Pupil

Source: Chambers (1994c).

Normal North-South Dominance

These insights extend naturally into examining wider patterns of dominance and submission, seeing one dimension of social relations as being between uppers and lowers (Table 18.1) and then, by analogy with a magnetic field, as oriented North to South (Figure 18.1). The stronger the top magnets, the stronger the North-South orientation of the lower magnets. Any person can be an upper in some contexts and a lower in others; some are multiple uppers (male, old, senior, white, wealthy), and others are multiple lowers (female, young, junior, black, poor). Complete revolutionary reversals, as in Robespierre's France, Lenin's Russia, Mao's China, and Mengistu's Ethiopia, are "slot-rattling," retaining the patterns of dominance but putting different people in power. Democratic empowerment entails reversals that neutralize forces of dominance and liberate,

Figure 18.1 Dominance, Reversals, and Freedom

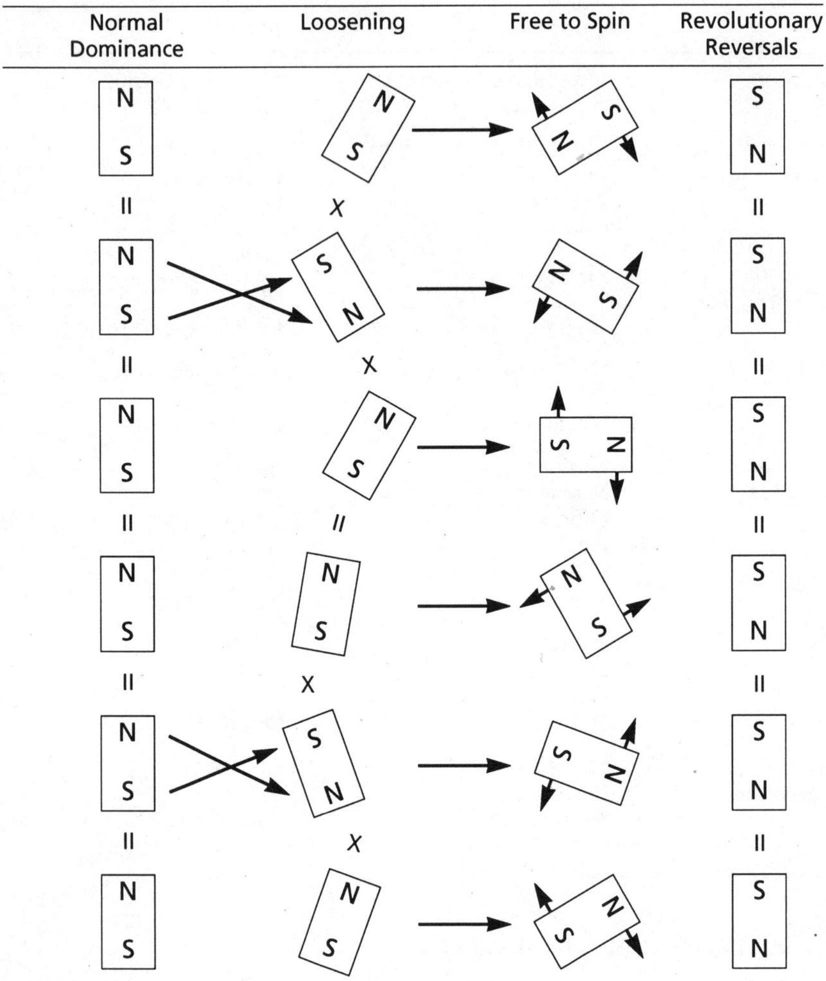

	Normal Dominance	Loosening	Free to Spin	Revolutionary Reversals
Who holds the stick?	Uppers	⟶	All	Lowers (who become uppers)
Teaching/ learning	From above	⟶	Lateral, below, above	From above (= old below)
Whose reality counts?	Uppers	⟶	All, multiple, diverse	New uppers (= old lowers)

Source: Chambers (1994c).

allowing freedom for relationships in all directions ("free to spin" in Figure 18.1). For this to happen requires changes in the behavior and attitudes of uppers, in how they relate to lowers, and in how they encourage lowers to be and to behave.

Contemporary Change in NGOs

Participatory rhetoric notwithstanding, the whole enterprise of development can be seen as being oriented by this metaphorical North-South magnetism of dominance, with uppers and lowers. In the internal hierarchies and external relations of funding agencies such as the World Bank, multilaterals, bilaterals, and Northern NGOs (NNGOs) that provide funds, and in the organizations of the South that receive them, the relationships are repeated and reinforced downward. Four dimensions stand out.

First, pressures to disburse drive donor staff to dominate. The cultures of large multilaterals such as the World Bank, the European Union, and the Asian Development Bank encourage and reward the commitment and disbursement of large sums of money. In donor-speak, the "absorptive capacity" of recipients is a constraint that hinders and delays expenditures. In Sri Lanka in 1994, the directors of three International Fund for Agricultural Development (IFAD) projects were said to be subject to meetings every quarter at which their expenditure records were reviewed. Nor are bilaterals and NNGOs always free from these pressures. When NNGOs raise large sums, they are reluctant to hold surpluses in the bank, fearing criticism from their supporters for the slow use of their contributions. As is so often the case with large donors, and sometimes with small ones, Northern staff on a mission are impatient and insistent. The incentives are to spend, and for uppers to pressure lowers to spend more and faster.

Second, rushing reinforces dominance. Participation takes time, but time is always short. For convenience, field visits are brief. Projects are appraised and prepared in a hurry. The more the rush, the less the consultation and the greater the imposition of the reality of the uppers (donor agency and senior staff) on that of the lowers (field staff and local people).

Third, demands for accountability upward are believed to require systematic planning. Rightly or wrongly, those who receive funds are not trusted to plan well. So donors demand the use of logical framework analysis and its subspecies GOPP (GTZ 1988), and ZOPP (objective-oriented planning) and the like. Whatever the participatory rhetoric, it is rare indeed for poor local people to be involved in these processes.[1] But, as has been documented, what outsiders think people want or will be good for them is often not what they want and need (see Leach and Mearns 1988; Starkey 1988; Bernados 1991; Porter, Allen, and Thompson

1991; SPWD 1992). To take a recent example, when an IFAD project in the north central zone of Sri Lanka used PRA approaches, it emerged that people wanted cattle, not the goats prescribed by a consultant economist. When it is preceded by top-down planning, however logical, participation becomes submissive: "they" participate in "our" project. Even when monitoring and evaluation are demanded to ensure that the money has been well spent and impacts have been good, the criteria and methods used are determined from above. Logic forces the local to fit its imperious frame.

Fourth, power deceives. The patronage of funds, pressures to disburse, rushing, logical framework analysis, and accountability upward all strengthen North-South hierarchies. They also give rise to top-down standardization and packages, with misfits between central programs and local needs. Prudent staff then provide misleadingly positive feedback.[2] The more the need or desire for funds, the greater the danger of deception. NGOs with savings and lending programs for the poor report ever better repayment rates, competing with others in reporting figures that constantly improve. The deceiving and self-deceiving state has long existed; it is now being joined by the deceiving and self-deceiving NGO.

As bilateral and multilateral donors divert more of their funds to NGOs, and as higher proportions of NGO funding come from these official sources,[3] NGOs become more prone to these influences. It is a commonplace that a top-down disbursement drive impedes and negates participation. The cultures and procedures of organizations are affected. As NGOs become bigger and undertake more of the service functions previously performed by governments, they become more like hierarchical government organizations. This threatens the loss of some of the real and supposed comparative advantages of NGOs, including sensitivity to local conditions, commitment to the poor, honest reporting, ability to vary actions according to needs, and staff with the will to serve and to work hard and long hours.

Personal Choice

Many prescriptions for development state that people in power—uppers—should do something different. It is embarrassing to make such an obvious point. Yet we are so trapped in the search for universals that fit normal concepts and criteria and that are part of our professional tools of trade, that we easily can not notice or not discuss what stares us in the face. This is the fact that individual personal choice of what to do and how to do it mediates every action and every change. Policy, practice, and performance are all outcomes of personal actions. What is done or not done depends on what people choose to do and not to do, and especially on the choices and actions of those with power.

If, for example, all managers and staff in all multilateral and bilateral agencies, NGOs, and grassroots organizations abandoned their North-South orientation tomorrow, adopted a participatory philosophy and behavior, and supported one another in these changes, the world of development would be transformed. The drive to disburse, the rushed visits, top-down logical planning, upward accountability, and many deceptions would diminish or disappear. Each level would empower and trust the levels below to exercise discretion, to foster diversity, and to learn from mistakes. Or, to take another example, if all development professionals were tomorrow to become aware, committed, honest, and courageous in serving and empowering the poor, and enabling others to do the same, most field programs would be transformed.

Homeostasis

What stops changes like these are "the system" and the self. The system includes organizational cultures, inertia, procedures, precedents, punitive management, criteria for promotions, confidential reports, and corruption. The self is ego, ambition, family-first motivation, and the illusion of impotence. The individual appears powerless. One person cannot change, it is said, unless others change, unless the whole system changes.

This is a convenient but false position. In reality, every person always has *some* room to maneuver; every upper can make space for lowers. Alliances can be formed upward, downward and laterally with others who are like-minded both inside and outside an organization. By expanding and exploiting spaces, by seeking and supporting allies, many brave people have had the vision and courage to make changes and to help others change.

The mystery is that such obvious points need to be made at all. Personal beliefs, behavior, and attitudes are an odd blind spot in development. Training (now graced with the ungainly economists' label of "human resource development") is given prominence, but it is more designed to teach, to impart knowledge and skills, than to provide opportunities for experiential learning. Training is usually didactic, in a top-down transfer of technology mode. The trainer is an upper who is presumed to know; those taught or trained are lowers who are presumed not to know. The teacher or trainer transfers to the trainees not only knowledge and skills but also the upper-lower orientation. So trainees leave their courses to become uppers. Armed and authorized by their certificates, they then transfer knowledge and technology to new lowers. Training thus reproduces and reinforces the North-South field.

In contrast, when training is itself participatory—a process of helping people to learn through experience and to find things out for themselves, enabling personal change toward egalitarian, democratic relationships—the North-South field can be expected to weaken. Options for more trust, freedom, and choice in relationships and actions will open up, allowing and encouraging more local and individual diversity.

Reasons for Neglect

The neglect of the personal may be partly explained as follows:

Academic Values. Any discussion of personal change risks the charge of evangelism. Academics abhor moralizing. They tend to reward appearances of dispassionate scientific detachment, rigor, and objectivity.

Fear of Hypocrisy. Almost all development professionals (myself included) are hypocrites, and at some level, many know it. But we do not like to parade our hypocrisy too publicly by saying what ought to be done at the personal level, because we know that we will not do it ourselves.

Missing Disciplines. Psychology is a missing discipline in development. Psychologists are rare among development professionals, and when they are found working in development, it is often not as psychologists but in some other capacity.

Low Caliber and Commitment of Training Staff. Many staff are posted to training institutes as punishment or in the hope that, in a training position, their incompetence or indolence will do less harm.[4] As a consequence, few trainers are willing or able to innovate by conducting training for personal change or to work outside office hours.

The Challenge of Participatory Training. Participatory training is not easy. Helping people to learn for themselves rather than teaching them in a North-South manner often requires personal reorientation by the trainer, plus risk taking, effort, long hours, sometimes discomfort, and the toleration of uncertainty. The dominant mode of teaching and training, in contrast, is the lecture or lecture and discussion, where the instructor maintains control and implements a closed-ended blueprint instead of facilitating an open-ended process, allowing him (most are men) to go home at 5 P.M., if not earlier.

Even after these explanations, a mystery remains: why are personal change and training that is concerned with behavior and attitudes such Cinderellas of development, when they are such potent and universal variables amenable to change?

An Agenda for Personal Action

If policy, practice, and performance depend on personal action, and if personal action depends on personal experience, learning, and commitment, an agenda for action can be sought. Many actions imply reversals of the conditions normally found. Here is a list:

- Accountability: shifting emphasis from upward to downward accountability for performance.

- Behavior: respecting, listening to, learning from, "handing the stick over to," and empowering one's lowers, and encouraging and enabling them to do the same.

- Management: instituting and supporting democratic and participatory management.

- Disbursements: refraining from disbursing, and resisting pressures to disburse, big sums fast; changing procedures, values, indicators, and rewards to stress quality, participation, and sustainability.

- Trust, error, and truth: trusting lowers to exercise responsible judgment, encouraging them to fail forward, acknowledging and reporting error, and valuing unpalatable truths as opportunities to learn and to do better.

- Diverse experience: deciding where it is best to work and seeking a mix of locations, posts, responsibilities, and experiences (South and North, lower and upper, periphery and center) in the interest of learning, improving judgment, and seeing what is best to do.

- Experiential learning: seeking opportunities for experiential learning for oneself and for one's lowers.

- Reversals of power: learning (as an upper) to enjoy giving up power and (as a lower) to enjoy accepting and exercising responsibility.

An Agenda for Experiential Learning

The thrust of this argument is that personal learning and development should be high on the agenda for all development professionals, with scope for evolution and change in beliefs, behavior, and attitudes. Much of this concerns helping uppers learn how to learn from lowers, and helping lowers to learn from and with one another. These elements have been amazingly neglected. Most university staff still lecture and know little about participatory learning. Since the time they took up their posts, most donor agency staff have spent no unconstrained, unrushed, unofficial time exposed to and learning about field realities, if they have ever done so. Many NGO staff believe that they can speak for the poor, but few have facilitated participatory analysis by poor people; or if they have, they tended to dominate without realizing the misleading effects of their dominance.

The power and the potential of the family of approaches and methods now known as PRA must not be exaggerated. PRA, like any other

Figure 18.2   Group Visual Synergy in PRA

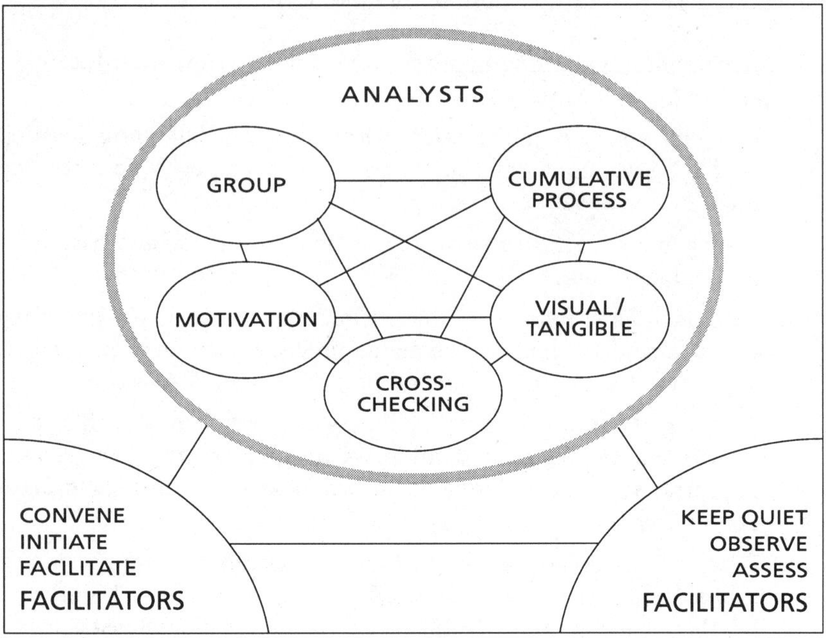

participatory approach, can be done badly, and it is being done badly on a growing scale. But where PRA has been done well, it has often brought personal change for those who facilitate it. Those who have managed to alter their normally dominant behavior, to hand over the stick, to facilitate, to take time, to sit down and listen, and not to dominate have found, quite simply, new pleasures, satisfactions, insights, and interests. In short, they have found that they enjoy and learn from the experience, and that things change for them.

Several elements have proved powerful: living and sleeping in villages; taking the role of novice in learning and performing village tasks; watching video feedback of personal behavior; facilitating and observing group visual synergy, which shows how well "they" can do it (Figure 18.2); sharing food; and undertaking personal and group reflection. All this suggests a four-point agenda for experiential learning and change:

1. *New policy and practice in agencies.* This means rethinking and reorganizing by uppers in NGOs, governments, and donor agencies to provide field learning experiences for themselves and their lowers, and setting aside time for these activities. This is not a new idea. It has already been pioneered by the German organization Justitia et Pax (Kochendörfer-Lucius and Osner 1991; Osner et al. 1992).

2. *Multiplying, supporting, and releasing good trainer-facilitators.* More good participatory trainer-facilitators are needed. The PRA experience is that this is a specialized activity requiring a special personal orientation and stamina. Most of the PRA training expertise is in the South. But there is a danger in North and South alike of getting trainers who are not right for the job. Some good PRA trainers in the South have been and are being enabled within their organizations to devote more time to participatory training. Others, sometimes frustrated by line responsibilities, have left to become full-time independent trainers or to found their own NGOs. Given current demand and need, the case is strong for supporting and releasing good trainer-facilitators wherever they are. For all concerned, the question of quality of training and learning remains.[5]

3. *Organizations for learning experience (OLEs).* New organizations, or changes in existing organizations, are needed to provide interactive learning environments and experiences (Pretty and Chambers 1993). In other fields, such as humanistic and Gestalt psychotherapy, such organizations exist. The difference in development is that the best interactive learning environment is the village or slum, which poses both ethical and logistical problems. The challenge is to found, expand, and multiply such organizations, and for them to gain and share more experience.

4. *New approaches and methods.* Scaling up requires the discovery, development, adoption, sharing, and spread of effective approaches and methods for behavior and attitude change. Many exist in diverse fields and could be brought together. More could and should be invented specifically for the development context.

These four directions imply a new professionalism, with reversals of the normal top-down, center-outward, and upper-to-lower tendencies. Instead, the balance of the new directions is bottom-up, periphery to center, and lower to upper. These reversals also turn the normal North-South donor-recipient relationship on its head. More and more development professionals in the North are requesting PRA experience and training for themselves in the South. Demand exceeds supply. The South already has a donor role in enabling those from the North to gain more general development experience. This could be extended and deepened by providing more people from the North with PRA-type learning experiences in the field, contributing more balance and reciprocity to South-North and North-South relationships, with the South being the donor.

The final questions refer back to the challenges faced by NGOs. Does the personal provide a point of entry that is as obvious as it is relatively neglected? If those working in NGOs pursued an agenda of personal and institutional change, with alliances and mutual support by uppers and lowers alike, would the practical and ethical problems of management be reduced? If primacy were accorded to the personal, would the problems of performance and accountability be resolved?

Notes

I am grateful to Jenny Chambers for discussions and insights that contributed to this chapter and to Charity Kabutha and Mallika Samaranayake for comments on a draft. Responsibility for opinions and errors is mine.

1. No doubt there are other cases, but I know of only one in which local people have been involved. This is in Urapulayagama Village, Kurunegala District, Sri Lanka, where, as part of a program of the National Development Foundation, supported by the Self-Help Support Programme of Intercooperation, the village displayed a logical framework chart and monitored implementation against a bar chart for activities. The normal practice outlined in the GTZ manual (GTZ 1988) is not only pathologically reductionist (forcing analysts to identify just one core problem, one overall goal, and one project purpose) but also top down: the five ZOPP exercises (GTZ 1988, 27) do not involve those who are described as "the target group."
2. For evidence and elaboration, see Chambers (1988, 1992, 1994a).
3. NNGOs committed to long-term programs but with volatile income from the public are continually tempted into heavier reliance on official funding.
4. There are outstanding exceptions, and at least half a dozen could be named in India alone; but I believe this to be sadly true for most training institutes.
5. See IDS/IIED (1994), a statement by some twenty practitioner-trainers of suggested principles and precepts, available free from PRA, IDS, University of Sussex, Brighton BN1 9RE, UK.

References

Bernadas, C. N. Jr. 1991. Lessons in upland farmer participation: The case of enriched fallow technology in Jaro, Leyte, Philippines. *Forests, Trees and People Newsletter* no. 14 (October): 10–13.

Chambers, Robert. 1988. Bureaucratic reversals and local diversity. *IDS Bulletin* 19(4):50–56.

———. 1992. The self-deceiving state. *IDS Bulletin* 23(4):31–42.

———. 1994a. All power deceives. *IDS Bulletin* 25(2):14–25.

———. 1994b. The origins and practice of participatory rural appraisal. *World Development* 22(7):953–69.

———. 1994c. *Paradigm shifts and the practice of participatory research and development.* IDS Working Paper no. 2. Sussex: Institute of Development Studies.

———. 1994d. Participatory rural appraisal (PRA): Analysis of experience. *World Development* 22(9):1253–68.

———. 1994e. Participatory rural appraisal (PRA): Challenges, potentials and paradigm. *World Development* 22(10):1437–54.

GTZ. 1988 *ZOPP (an introduction to the method)*. Frankfurt am Main: Gesellschaft für Technische Zusammenarbeit (GTZ).

IDS/IIED. 1994. *Participatory methods and approaches: Sharing our concerns and looking to the future*. London: Institute of Development Studies, University of Sussex, and International Institute for Environment and Development.

Kochendörfer-Lucius, G., and K. Osner. 1991. *Development has got a face: Lifestories of thirteen women in Bangladesh on people's economy*. Results of the International Exposure and Dialogue Programme of the German Commission of Justice and Peace and Grameen Bank in Bangladesh, October 14–22, 1989. *Gerechtigkeit und Frieden Series*. Bonn: Deutsche Kommission Justitia et Pax.

Leach, Gerald, and Robin Mearns. 1988. *Beyond the woodfuel crisis: People, land and trees in Africa*. London: Earthscan.

Mascarenhas, James, Parmesh Shah, Sam Joseph, Ravi Jayakaran, John Devavaram, Vidya Ramachandran, Aloysius Fernandez, Robert Chambers, and Jules Pretty. 1991. *Proceedings of the February 1991 Bangalore PRA trainers workshop. RRA Notes 13*. London: IIED; Bangladore: MYRADA.

Osner, Karl, Gudrun Kochendörfer-Lucius, Ulkie Muller-Glodde, and Claudia Warning. 1992. *Exposure und Dialogprogramme: Eine Handreichnung für Teilnehmer unter Organisatoren*. Bonn: Justitia et Pax.

Porter, Doug, Bryant Allen, and Gaye Thompson. 1991. *Development in practice: Paved with good intentions*. London and New York: Routledge.

Pretty, Jules, and Robert Chambers. 1993. *Towards a learning paradigm: New professionalism and institutions for agriculture*. IDS Discussion Paper 334. Brighton: Institute of Development Studies, University of Sussex.

SPWD. 1992. *Field methods manual. Vol. I. Diagnostic tools for supporting joint forest management systems*. Prepared for the Joint Forest Management Support Program, Society for Promotion of Wastelands Development, New Delhi.

Starkey, Paul. 1988. *Perfected yet rejected: Animal-drawn wheeled toolcarriers*. Braunschweig and Wiesbaden: Friedrich Vieweg & Sohn.

---------- **19** ----------

Beyond the Magic Bullet?

Lessons and Conclusions

Michael Edwards and David Hulme

A huge amount of information and experience from a wide range of contexts has been reviewed by the contributors to this book. Clearly, any attempt to identify common conclusions and implications runs the risk of overgeneralization, particularly given the difficulty of disentangling the effects of official aid and the New Policy Agenda from preexisting or other related influences. It is clear from the pictures painted by the contributors that NGO and grassroots organization (GRO) performance, accountability, and legitimacy are tremendously complex areas. The situation of Sudanese migrant associations described by Pratten and Ali Baldo in their chapter provides a particularly good example of these complexities, with all sorts of "checks and balances" between GROs and their members mediated by history and culture and dependent on "contemporary reconstructions of community identity." Nevertheless, there are some clear and common threads that run through the chapters and seem to indicate that similar influences are at work. At least five sets of conclusions present themselves.

Influence of the New Policy Agenda: Real or Imagined?

There is certainly evidence from the case studies in this book that official aid to NGOs and the roles adopted by NGOs under the New Policy Agenda can distort accountability upward and overemphasize linear approaches to performance measurement, with damaging effects on the ability of NGOs to be catalysts for social change. Desai and Howes's account of Apnalaya in Bombay and the chapters by Gariyo (on NGOs in East Africa) and Hashemi (on NGOs in Bangladesh) provide such evidence, but in each case, the influence of official aid and external agendas is only one of many factors at work. With or without the New Policy Agenda, strategic accountability is nearly always weaker than functional accountability, and downward accountability is nearly always weaker than upward accountability. Even among very large NGOs (Southern or Northern) there is only limited empirical evidence of a significant falloff in quality as a result of the growth of official funding or an incompatibility between service provision, advocacy, and "development as empowerment." Certainly, there are individual examples of negative trade-offs (Perera forthcoming), but perhaps as Howes and Sattar (1992, 117) put it for the Bangladesh Rural Advancement Committee (BRAC), "when attention is given to building organisational capacities to support programme expansion, there is no inherent contradiction between quality and scale. Bigger can be better."[1] Such conclusions may simply reflect the fact that we still have insufficient evidence of the impact of current trends to conclude very much at all, or that the New Policy Agenda constitutes a *potential* threat to NGO performance and accountability whose real influence is yet to be fully felt, or that it is in other areas (such as broader state-society relations) that the real issues will emerge (Hulme and Edwards, forthcoming). But the evidence we do have suggests that there are certainly no universal relationships between official funding and the "corruption of NGOs," nor are there any necessary correlations between NGO size, growth, function, and funding.

Overall, the case studies show that it is the *quality of the relationships* between GROs, NGOs, donors, and governments that determines whether patterns of funding and accountability promote or impede the wider goals of all these organizations in development. Issues of quantity and size are less important (Fowler 1991). A partnership approach, which emphasizes participation, learning, reciprocity, and transparency, may permit the problems that accompany organizational growth and donor funding to be managed: GRO-NGO performance, legitimacy, and accountability need not be eroded. Donors (whether official or Northern NGO) must therefore be encouraged to move toward funding arrangements that provide stability and predictability in the long term, and timeliness and flexibility in the short term (Van der Heijden 1987). Long-term institutional support requires a "continual dialogue about objectives and strategies, rather than simply a specification of outputs and targets" (Carroll 1992, 164) and hasty evaluations by overseas consultants. This is very different from the cut and thrust of the contract culture that (contrary to current thinking in official agencies) may ultimately disable organizations and compromise long-term quality of impact. It may be better to channel official donor funds to NGOs and GROs via an independent public institution that can protect them from undue donor influence, as recommended in the United States (Hellinger, Hellinger, and O'Rogan 1988, 114) and in other countries (Smillie 1993; Baron 1993), or via local NGO networks that can ensure quality control through self-regulation and peer pressure, as in the Philippines (Constantino-David 1992). Official donors, such as the European Union, the Canadian International Development Agency (CIDA), and the Overseas Development

Administration, that are considering more direct funding of NGOs and GROs in the South need to reflect on the alternatives available to them in this respect, rather than simply expanding their own offices in Southern capitals (Crombrugghe, Douxchamps, and Stampa 1993).

The Importance of Negotiation

One of the most striking conclusions to emerge from earlier chapters is the emphasis that so many place on *negotiation among stakeholders* as a guiding principle for improving NGO accountability in the future. Indeed, Fowler, Shah and Shah, Biggs and Neame, and others make it clear that there can be no improvements without such negotiations, supporting Marsden, Oakley, and Pratt's (1994, 1) earlier understanding of evaluations as "negotiating points in the process of development." Increasing the involvement of grassroots constituencies (beneficiaries and supporters) is the only way to correct the weakness of downward accountability, which is such a common characteristic of the case studies in this book. "Structured involvement" of a wider range of stakeholders can help resolve many of the dilemmas facing NGOs and GROs in performance assessment and accountability, though it will not make these dilemmas disappear. As Parmesh and Meera Shah show in their chapter, increasing the involvement of grassroots stakeholders also opens up the prospect of major changes in roles, responsibilities, and accountabilities and should not be undertaken by agencies that have no serious commitment to reform in their own institutions and structures. But wherever there are multiple constituencies, negotiation may be the only way to deal with differences over performance standards, "bottom lines," and evaluation results. Since the short-term objectives of different stakeholders are likely to differ, such negotiations should focus on long-term aims and mission if any consensus is to be generated (Drucker 1990, 110). The concept of "stakeholders" is not, of course, uncontroversial. Poor people's development is "their" process, which they must control; to this extent, they are "shareholders" in development, not "stakeholders"—a situation analogous to Tandon's distinction (see chapter 3) between the legitimate involvement of donors in NGO accountability but not in NGO governance.

A related conclusion concerns the importance of informal mechanisms in maintaining legitimacy and accountability. As the chapters by Pratten and Ali Baldo, Uphoff, and others show, these mechanisms can often be very effective—more so than formal (democratic, representative) mechanisms introduced from the outside. This resonates with Carroll's (1992) conclusion that an open, collegial style and attitudes that encourage bottom-up participation can help build organizations that are responsive and accountable to grassroots constituencies, even when they are not formally membership organizations. The possible erosion of such indigenous and informal systems by foreign aid (a danger cited by Gariyo and Hashemi in their chapters) is therefore very worrying.

As Biggs and Neame point out in their chapter, the key issue for NGOs in the New Policy Agenda is not how to preserve a "mythical autonomy" but how to strengthen multiple accountabilities and "room to maneuver" so that they can negotiate more effectively. The "social audit" methodology described by Zadek and Gatward, the Aga Khan Foundation's participatory monitoring and evaluation framework presented by Shah and Shah, and the checks and balances analyzed by Covey in her chapter on policy alliances are practical mechanisms for promoting stakeholder involvement in performance assessment and for strengthening downward (and sideways!) accountability. Their example deserves to be followed by other NGOs, governments, and official aid agencies.

The "Baby and the Bathwater"

It is impossible to read the chapters in this book without being fully appraised of the sheer complexity of NGO performance assessment and accountability. Clearly, this is an area that is full of difficulties: the problems of identifying impact when individual NGOs and projects are such a small part of the overall picture, how to measure qualitative changes in the strength of institutions or the awareness of individuals, how to deal with the many and often conflicting pressures for different forms of accountability from different directions, and so on. Faced by such a daunting range of problems, there is sometimes a tendency (reflected in some of the chapters in this book) to abandon the search for more rigorous performance measures or to establish more sophisticated systems for tracking impact. In our view, this is a mistake, equivalent to "throwing the baby out with the bathwater and refusing to take the issue of professionalism seriously" (Smillie, Chapter 14 of this volume). Despite the complexities and uncertainties involved, all agree that the current state of NGO and GRO accountability is unsatisfactory. The search for improvements must go on, even if, as Rondinelli (1993) concludes, accountability has to be restricted to the ways in which NGOs and others use their resources rather than the long-term impact of resource use on development. This poses particular problems for "strategic accountability" as defined in our introduction, an area that the case studies in this book show to be particularly (and unsurprisingly) weak.

Finding accurate links between causes and effects is a problem for all development agencies, not just NGOs. Indeed, it poses a dilemma for social science as a whole as it struggles to emerge from the limitations of its positivist, Newtonian paradigm (Uphoff 1992). But even if individual NGOs find it impossible, for good reason, to measure the long-term impact of their work on broad development trends, they can still

improve significantly on their current performance in evaluating learning, institution building, levels of participation, gender equity, and so
on. As Desai and Howes conclude in their chapter, "it may be difficult
to prove success conclusively, but the easier task of demonstrating
that . . . [NGOs have] not failed in key areas would in itself represent a
considerable improvement on the present state of affairs." There is certainly no room for complacency. If NGOs do not improve significantly
in this area, they run the risk of being "sidelined to a backwater of carp-
ing utopianism . . . [to be avoided only if they] . . . further develop their
capacity to identify concrete steps and achievable targets, and to agree
on reasonable ways in which these can be measured" (German and
Randel 1994). Drucker's (1990, 60) advice—to "always ask how can we
do what we already do better"—is a useful reminder of the need to look
for practical and incremental improvements even where reality is contingent and impact is so difficult to establish.[2]

Accounting for What?

Although functional specialization is clearly not essential for efficiency, some of the problems concerning NGO performance and accountability identified in earlier chapters seem to be related to an inability
among NGOs to decide what they really want to do, or to a mix of functions and tasks that may conflict with one another. The potential contradiction between the organizational characteristics required to perform
effectively as a service provider and those required to perform as a cata-
lyst of social change and institutional development was highlighted in
our introduction. Similar conflicts may exist between accountability and
effectiveness in policy alliances (as Covey shows in Chapter 15). Equally,
however, there may be no contradiction but rather mutually supporting
functions, given the need for empowerment approaches to bringing
material benefits if people's interest is to be sustained. The chapters in
this book by Ramesh (on the Working Women's Forum in India) and
Karim (on Proshika in Bangladesh) provide good illustrations of how different functions can be married successfully. The same is true for NGOs
that need to have solid field experience related to their lobbying issues if
they are to remain authoritative and credible (Edwards and Hulme 1992).
This is the key to what Fowler (1993, 334–35) calls the "onion-skin
approach"—an "outer layer of welfare-oriented activity that protects
inner layers of material service delivery that act as nuclei for a core strategy dedicated to transformation." Whether such an integrated strategy
would be openly supported by donors or tolerated by governments is
another matter, with important implications for the degree of transparency afforded to different accountabilities. Such combinations of
functions are explored in more depth later in this conclusion, but they

clearly complicate the issues of performance and accountability for NGOs.

The Management of Accountability

Because stakeholder perceptions inevitably differ and NGOs are subject to so many conflicting pressures, the dilemmas of accountability identified above cannot be solved—they have to be *managed*. For example, Northern NGOs will always remain accountable to their donors and supporters, as well as to their partners and (to some extent) the beneficiaries of their work. As the example of Apnalaya in Bombay shows, managing multiple funding sources and therefore accountabilities is already normal practice in many NGOs (see Chapter 7). Official aid agencies, although they may move toward less linear approaches to development, will have to satisfy the demand for results that comes from their political paymasters. Many NGOs *choose* to work across national boundaries, sectors of work, service delivery, and other approaches to development; they do not see these choices as mutually exclusive. In other words, these are management issues rather than issues of principle. As Commins (forthcoming) puts it, "it is possible to remain operationally accountable to governments in terms of use of funds and yet remain accountable to the low-income communities where the NGO is carrying out programmes." Chief among the factors that enable NGOs to manage these dilemmas effectively are a strong sense of mission and attachment to values and principles; effective learning and action research (Hasan 1993; Wils et al. 1993); local-level institution building and high levels of participation (Riddell and Robinson 1992); effective management, strategic planning, and accountability mechanisms; skilled and committed staff; and a favorable external environment (progressive donors, open governments, and strong links with other NGOs). This, in turn, requires organizational structures and cultures that encourage learning, accountability, and experimentation—organically structured, decentralized organizations that are problem-solving and task oriented (Wierdsma and Swieringha 1992; Fowler 1988; Edwards 1994; Beets, Neggers, and Wils 1988). Underlying these characteristics are some deeper traits, including a willingness by NGO staff to hand over more control to partners and beneficiaries and an ability to live with nonstandardized responses and procedures in order to promote flexibility and experimentation— the open-systems approach to development work recommended by Chambers, Uphoff, Fowler, and others in this book. With these features in place, NGOs can analyze strategic choices about cooperation with donors or governments—or any decision on programming—and identify those that are likely to weaken their comparative advantages or relations with beneficiaries (Fowler 1988, 22). They will also be in a better position to prevent a "law of diminishing" returns from setting in when increasing bureaucracy threatens to reduce the value added by each increment in funding.

The Future of NGOs

What implications do these findings have for the future of NGOs and their role in development? The first point to make is that, without effective performance assessment and strong, multiple accountability mechanisms, no NGO is likely to be able to find its way through the increasingly complex maze constituted by the world of development assistance, nor find and maintain the right balance between the opportunities and dangers afforded to NGOs as the "favored child" of official aid. Weak or distorted accountability and an inability to demonstrate impact and effectiveness in a reasonably rigorous manner (where this is possible) are likely to leave NGOs more vulnerable to co-optation into the agendas of others, or simply to lead them into areas where they are not doing much that is useful. Improving performance assessment and accountability is not an "optional extra" for NGOs; it is central to their continued existence as independent organizations with a mission to pursue. However, judging by the meager level of resources devoted to organizational development in these areas and the reluctance of NGOs to innovate, an independent observer would have to conclude that most NGOs were not seriously concerned with accountability at all. Despite record increases in income between 1984 and 1994, very few NGOs (Northern or Southern) have invested sufficiently in evaluation, learning, research, and dissemination; nor have they become more transparent or accountable to their different constituencies. This is true despite the fact that their "continued existence depends on the belief by staff and supporters that they are ethical according to explicit values and principles" (Zadek and Gatward, Chapter 17 of this volume).

Second, many of the problems facing NGOs in this field (less so GROs) arise because NGOs are *problematic organizations*. By their very nature, NGOs must live and work in situations of necessary ambiguity. Some of these ambiguities are the result of the characteristics of NGOs as a form of organization—accountable to trustees in one country but working with communities in others; committed to fundamental reforms but funded by donors and supporters who (by and large) demand short-term results; wanting to democratize development but forbidden from entering formal politics. Others are a matter of choice, for example, when an NGO decides to work across a range of approaches embracing service delivery, institutional development, and advocacy, each of which may require different funding mechanisms, organizational structures, skills, and timescales. Faced by these potential contradictions, it has become fashionable to conclude that NGOs must choose to be one thing or another—they are either "public service contractors" or "citizens' movements" (Korten 1990); a "first force" that "harnesses independent energy for a moral purpose" or a "third force" acting as subcontractors to the state (Knight 1993); organizations that are "market-led" or "values-based" (Robinson forthcoming).

There is good reason to believe, however, that such conclusions are misplaced, though no doubt certain NGOs will fall clearly and consciously into one category or another. Social justice requires that people be liberated from the conditions of material poverty as well as have the ability to organize themselves to defend their rights. Different sorts of organizations will be more, or less, effective in promoting these goals according to context and circumstance. The scale of material poverty and the size of gaps in access to basic services in many of the world's poor countries require that NGOs continue to play a significant role in service provision and "welfare," although clearly they cannot permanently substitute for the state if progress is to be equitable and sustainable. At the same time, it is perfectly possible (though perhaps increasingly difficult) to innovate and to retain a sense of mission, a high level of independence, and an attachment to values and principles. There are many NGOs that play a major role in social organization, consciousness-raising, and advocacy, just as there are many GROs that aim to support material improvements in their members' lives. Indeed, there are strong arguments (some outlined above) that these functions are best combined. If this is true, then the future of NGOs and GROs may be dominated by two developments: the rise of the "legitimate hybrid," to use Korten's (1990, 105) term; and the evolution of national and international networks, alliances, and federations in which organizations with different roles and characteristics work synergistically to achieve common long-term goals.

In this sense, the future of Northern NGOs may resemble the "new internationalist conglomerates" envisioned by Zadek and Gatward in Chapter 17. The lessons generated by the Institute for Development Research's work on international policy alliances, and the importance of the "bridging role" for NGOs that such research highlights, are extremely relevant here (see Chapter 15). This does not mean that difficult questions of legitimacy and accountability can be ducked. Differences in these areas between (for example) membership and nonmembership organizations will remain, and the dilemmas of performance and accountability highlighted earlier will still have to be managed. However, variations in needs, context, funding sources, organizational competencies, legal and regulatory systems, supporter profiles, donor attitudes, tradition, and politics point to a necessary focus on partnership, effectiveness, and learning rather than on particular organizational forms that are deemed right or wrong, good or bad. The chapters in this book by Covey, Béjar and

Oakley, Zadek and Gatward, and others point in this direction. As Nielsen (in Keating 1994, 73) puts it, "the landscape of the third sector is untidy but wonderfully exuberant. What counts is not the confusion, but the profusion."

These observations do not mean that all is well in the world of NGOs, particularly NGOs based in the North. Far from it: criticisms of Northern NGO performance and accountability surface regularly throughout this book, and they cannot be ignored. The complacency born of ten years of relatively easy fund-raising between 1984 and 1994 must give way to more serious reflection and openness to change. As Southern NGOs grow in number and authority (opening their own offices "overseas," as BRAC has done in Kenya and as Filipino and African NGOs are doing in Washington), and as an increasingly integrated global economy throws up new challenges to NGOs in their own "backyard," Northern NGOs are bound to come under increasing pressure to take partnership and accountability more seriously. As Bebbington and Riddell (forthcoming) put it, the challenge to NGOs in the North is to "define a role that can help to enhance the impact of the work of their Southern partners, and define it *with them.*" Joint advocacy, fair trading, facilitating access to specific expertise and information, and domestic development work are examples of what these roles might be, redirecting Northern NGOs to address those parts of the global problematic of exclusion that they can tackle most effectively. As Béjar and Oakley (see Chapter 6) put it, the key task is to "abandon unequal relationships between donors and recipients in favor of an effective South-North dialogue around common and practical tasks: to move from accountability to shared responsibility." Much more effort must go into support of local fund-raising and other means of promoting the financial independence of NGOs in the South, which Karim, Biekart, and other contributors to this book see as central if legitimacy and accountability are to be strengthened in the longer term. As in all open systems, to achieve real impact, NGOs must focus more on changing relationships between people and institutions (and the values on which they are based) and less on shifting (small but growing) amounts of funding from one part of the world to another. The changes implied by such a shift will be slow and difficult, not least because of the need to bring Northern NGO constituencies along to provide consistent and independent support to this transition. If Northern NGOs have not already started to do this (and most have not), then they need to do so *now*.

In this process, the questions of *legitimacy, identity, and governance* take center stage; these questions are even more demanding than issues of performance and accountability, for they go right to the heart of the NGO and its mission: most obviously, *what are NGOs for in the twenty-first century?* Clearly, there can be no one answer to this question, but thus far, few Northern NGOs have faced the question itself, preferring instead to decentralize their management functions within existing, Northern-controlled structures of governance. Of course, NGOs will adapt to the demands of a changing world, as they have done in the past, but will they adapt *enough*? Unless Northern NGOs begin to face up to the challenges of a new millennium quickly, unless they begin to redefine a role for themselves that recognizes what is happening in the world around them, and unless they begin to take accountability much more seriously, they are likely to be bypassed in the future by governments, official agencies, citizens' movements, and perhaps even their own supporters. NGOs have spent too much time criticizing others and not enough time putting their own house in order. Despite their rhetoric, no Northern NGO is seriously trying to "work itself out of a job," and sadly, most give the impression that only a financial crisis will force fundamental changes in this direction. No matter how effective NGOs are *technically* in monitoring and evaluation, strategic planning, or managing multiple accountabilities, hard decisions still need to be made about future roles and responsibilities. Moving away from operational work (and the large official grants that come with it) will inevitably mean a reduction in income for Northern NGOs. But perhaps a recognition of the limits to growth is not a bad thing, if it provides Northern NGOs with the room they seem to need for more profound reflection on their future, a greater commitment to issues of quality in their work, and the courage and vision to rethink and reform their roles into the twenty-first century.

In this task, *personal accountability* is going to be essential, given the inertia that characterizes all large NGOs, the resistance they put up to change, and the temptations for NGO managers that accompany organizational growth and the status of size. All organizations, and all individuals within them, possess some room to maneuver that can be used to promote incremental reform, transparency, learning, and sharing. As Chambers (Chapter 18) puts it, "if primacy were accorded to the personal, would the problems of performance and accountability be resolved?" Perhaps not (given the problems that face NGOs and the inherent difficulties of measuring performance and managing multiple accountabilities), but without an acceptance of personal responsibility and the determination to be accountable individually, there will be no resolution of these problems and certainly no improvement in NGO performance. Moves in this direction, toward the open-systems mode of thinking and acting recommended by Uphoff and others in this book, would be in the very best NGO tradition of innovation, solidarity, and humility.

The focus of this book on the New Policy Agenda and the influence of official aid may have led us to underestimate the influence of endogenous factors and to overestimate the negative impact of donor funding. But it is on this basis that we posit that the modes of programming of NGO and GRO operations, of defining performance indicators, of claiming legitimacy, and of accounting for achievements are being reshaped. From a neoliberal perspective, the emergence of NGOs and GROs is desirable for its contribution to economic efficiency and political pluralism, though it may only be transitional as the commercial sector evolves and effective interest groups crystallize. From a radical perspective, it may be cooptation: the abandonment of a mission for social transformation to become the implementer of the New Policy Agenda. If this *is* what is happening, then perhaps the best that can be hoped for is that the bubble will burst and NGOs and GROs will return to their former position—smaller and less lauded, but more independent and effective as agents of social change. The present popularity of NGOs with donors will not last forever: donors move from fad to fad, and at some stage, NGOs—like flared jeans—will become less fashionable. When this happens, the developmental impact of NGOs, their capacity to attract support, and their legitimacy as actors in development will rest much more clearly on their ability to demonstrate that they can perform effectively and that they are accountable for their actions. It is none too soon for NGOs to get their houses in order. Rethinking and reforming accountability—moving "beyond the magic bullet"— are central to this challenge.

Notes

1. In reality, it is difficult to know whether such conclusions are accurate, since independent empirical evidence is scarce. There is anecdotal evidence that the credit repayment rates and other impact indicators publicized by large NGOs in South Asia (including BRAC) are exaggerated, but insufficient evidence exists to confirm this view. Independent evidence in this area is urgently needed.
2. The key here is to experiment in practice with a wide range of different techniques for monitoring and evaluation and to learn from these experiences. Save the Children–U.K. recently published a "tool kit" on assessment, monitoring, review, and evaluation that provides a useful foundation for such a process.

References

Baron, B. 1993. *Innovation and future directions in East Asian philanthropy: Strengthening the public/private interface.* San Francisco: Asia Foundation.

Bebbington, A., and R. Riddell. Forthcoming. New agendas and old problems: Issues, options and challenges in direct funding of Southern NGOs. In *Too close for comfort? NGOs, states and donors*, edited by D. Hulme and M. Edwards. London: Macmillan.

Beets, N., J. Neggers, and J. Wils. 1988. *Big and still beautiful: Enquiry in the efficiency and effectiveness of three big NGOs (BINGOs) in South Asia.* Programme Evaluation NR32. DGIS/NOVIB.

Carroll, T. 1992. *Intermediary NGOs: The supporting link in grassroots development*. West Hartford, Conn.: Kumarian Press.

Commins, S. Forthcoming. Too close for comfort? In *Too close for comfort? NGOs, states and donors*, edited by D. Hulme and M. Edwards. London: Macmillan.

Constantino-David, K. 1992. The Philippine experience in scaling-up. In *Making a difference: NGOs and development in a changing world*, edited by M. Edwards and D. Hulme. London: Earthscan.

Crombrugghe, G., F. Douxchamps, and N. Stampa 1993. *Evaluation of EC-NGO co-financing in relation to institutional support for grassroots organisations in developing countries*. Brussels: COTA.

Drucker, P. 1990. *Managing the nonprofit organization: Principles and practices*. New York: HarperCollins.

Edwards, M. 1994. NGOs in the age of information. *IDS Bulletin* (Spring).

Edwards, M., and D. Hulme, eds. 1992. *Making a difference: NGOs and development in a changing world*. London: Earthscan.

Fowler, A. 1988. *NGOs in Africa: Achieving comparative advantage in relief and micro-development*. IDS Discussion Paper 249. Sussex: IDS.

Fowler, A. 1991. The role of NGOs in changing state-society relations: Perspectives from eastern and southern Africa. *Development Policy Review* 9:53–84.

Fowler, A. 1993. NGOs as agents of democratization: An African perspective. *Journal of International Development* 5(3):325–39.

German, T., and J. Randel. 1994. Trends in official aid and the implications for NGOs. Paper presented to the SCF/IDPM Workshop on NGOs and Development, Manchester, June 27–29.

Hasan, A. 1993. *Scaling-up the OPP's low-cost sanitation programme*. Karachi: Orangi Pilot Project.

Hellinger, D., S. Hellinger, and F. O'Regan. 1988. *Aid for just development*. Boulder, Colo.: Lynne Rienner.

Howes, M., and M. Sattar. 1992. Bigger and better? Scaling-up strategies pursued by BRAC 1972–1991. In *Making a difference: NGOs and development in a changing world*, edited by M. Edwards and D. Hulme. London: Earthscan.

Hulme, D., and M. Edwards, eds. Forthcoming. *Too close for comfort? NGOs, states and donors*. London: Macmillan.

Keating, M. 1994. North America's independent sector. In *Citizens strengthening global civil society*. Washington, D.C.: CIVICUS.

Knight, B. 1993. *Voluntary action*. London: CENTRIS.

Korten, D. C. 1990. *Getting to the 21st century: Voluntary action and the global agenda*. West Hartford, Conn.: Kumarian Press.

Marsden, D., P. Oakley, and B. Pratt. 1994. *Measuring the process: Guidelines for evaluating social development*. Oxford: International NGO Training and Research Centre.

Perera, J. Forthcoming. The case of Sarvodaya. In *Too close for comfort? NGOs, states and donors*, edited by D. Hulme and M. Edwards. London: Macmillan.

Riddell, R., and M. Robinson. 1992. *The impact of NGO poverty-alleviation projects: Results of the case-study evaluations*. ODI Working Paper 68. London: Overseas Development Institute.

Robinson, M. Forthcoming. NGOs as public service contractors. In *Too close for comfort? NGOs, states and donors*, edited by D. Hulme and M. Edwards. London: Macmillan.

Rondinelli, D. 1993. *Strategic and results-based management in CIDA: Reflections on the process*. Ottawa: Canadian International Development Agency.

Smillie, I. 1993. *From partners to stakeholders: The CIDA-NGO challenge*. Unpublished mimeo.

Uphoff, N. 1992. *Learning from Gal Oya: Possibilities for participatory development and post-Newtonian social science*. Ithaca, N.Y.: Cornell University Press.

Van der Heijden, H. 1987. The reconciliation of NGO autonomy and operational effectiveness with accountability to donors. *World Development* 15(suppl):103–12.

Wierdsma, A., and J. Swieringha. 1992. *Becoming a learning organisation*. London: Addison-Wesley.

Wils, F., V. Maddin, K. Alexander, and N. Sohoni. 1993. *AWARE and its work with tribals and Harijans in Andhra Pradesh*. The Hague: Institute of Social Studies.

About the Contributors

Michael Edwards has spent the last fourteen years working for development NGOs. From 1984 to 1988, he was Oxfam-U.K.'s regional representative in Lusaka; he then spent two years as director of the PRASAD Foundation in India. Since 1990, he has been head of information and research for The Save the Children Fund–U.K., based in London, and is currently undertaking research on the future of external intervention in development, funded by fellowships from the Leverhulme Trust and Simon Fund. He coedited (with David Hulme) *Making a Difference: NGOs and Development in a Changing World* (London: Earthscan, 1992).

David Hulme is professor of development studies and director of the Institute for Development Policy and Management, University of Manchester (U.K.). He has worked and conducted research in Papua New Guinea, Sri Lanka, Bangladesh, Malaysia, Malawi, and Kenya and has particular interest in rural development, antipoverty policies, microfinance, and civil service reform. His publications include (with Michael Edwards) *Making a Difference: NGOs and Development in a Changing World (London: Earthscan, 1992)* and *Too Close for Comfort? NGOs, States and Donors* (London: Macmillan, forthcoming).

Suliman Ali Baldo is director of studies for the Al Fanar Centre for Development Services, an independent research and consultancy group based in Khartoum, Sudan. A founding member of a leading Sudanese NGO, the Sudanese Popular Committee for Relief and Rehabilitation, he was also the country representative for Oxfam (U.S.) between 1988 and 1992.

Héctor Béjar is the founder-director of the Centre for the Study of Development and Participation (CEDEP) in Peru. He is also a member of the board of El Taller and a member of CIVICUS (the World Alliance

267

for Citizen Participation). He is a consultant, analyst, and writer in the areas of civil society, the reform of state, rural development, people's participation, and NGOs. He attended the Copenhagen Social Summit Conference as a member of the Peruvian NGO delegation.

Kees Biekart is a political scientist and research fellow at the Transnational Institute (TNI) in Amsterdam, working in its Latin America program. He is currently involved in a TNI research project on Northern NGOs and democratization in Central America. He is the coeditor (with Martin Jelsma) of *Peasants beyond Protest: Challenges for ASOCODE and Strategies towards Europe* (Amsterdam: Transnational Institute, 1994).

Stephen D. Biggs is a senior lecturer in the School of Development Studies, University of East Anglia (U.K.). He has worked for the Ford Foundation in Bangladesh and for the International Wheat and Maize Improvement Centre (CIMMYT), based in Delhi. He has been a member of advisory committees in Oxfam, the Intermediate Technology Development Group (ITDG), the Overseas Development Institute (ODI), and the Overseas Development Administration (ODA).

Robert Chambers is a Fellow of the Institute of Development Studies at the University of Sussex (U.K.). He has worked on rural development in sub-Saharan Africa and South Asia and is currently concentrating on the development and spread of the approaches and methods of participatory rural appraisal (PRA). He is the author of *Rural Development: Putting the Last First* (Harlow: Longman, 1983) and *Challenging the Professions: Frontiers for Rural Development* (London: IT Publications, 1993).

Jane G. Covey is executive director of the Institute for Development Research (IDR), an international research and education center in Boston that works in partnership with NGOs to support just and sustainable development. Her consulting and research activities include NGO strategic planning and NGO influence on national and international policy making. She serves on the NGO–World Bank Committee and on the Executive Committee of InterAction, a consortium of U.S. private voluntary organizations.

Vandana Desai is a fellow at the Institute of Development Studies, University of Sussex (U.K.), where she is currently involved in research on community participation, urban problems, slum housing, and evaluating the effectiveness of urban NGOs. She completed her doctorate in sociology at the University of Oxford and has extensive experience working with NGOs in the slums and squatter settlements of Bombay. She is the author of *Community Participation and Slum Housing* (Delhi: Sage Publications, 1995).

Alan F. Fowler is a consultant, analyst, and writer specializing in nongovernmental development organizations, with which he has worked for the past seventeen years, mostly in sub-Saharan Africa. Cofounder, in

1991, of the International NGO Training and Research Centre (INTRAC) based in Oxford, he has also been a visiting fellow at the World Bank in Washington D.C., advising on people's participation. His present work focuses on NGO effectiveness and organizational change.

Zie Gariyo is a research fellow at the Centre for Basic Research in Kampala, Uganda. Since 1989, he has researched and written on appropriate technology in peasant agriculture, press freedom in Uganda, and NGOs and development in East Africa.

Murdoch Gatward is currently director of Traidcraft Exchange's Africa program (based in Newcastle, U.K.), with particular responsibility for developing activities in South Africa and Tanzania. The subject of his chapter in this book, social auditing, is rapidly becoming a key tool to enable Traidcraft to assess the social and ethical profile of its own work, as well as that of actual and potential partners in the South.

Syed M. Hashemi teaches in the Department of Economics in Jahangirnagar University, Bangladesh. He received his doctorate in economics from the University of California (Riverside). Currently, he is on leave from his university post to act as director of the Grameen Trust's Programme for Research on Poverty Alleviation. For the past several years, he has been involved in research on targeted credit programs and the transformation of the lives of poor women in rural Bangladesh.

Mick Howes is a social anthropologist and a fellow of the Institute of Development Studies, Sussex (U.K.), where he has mainly been concerned with rural development issues. He has a particular interest in the participatory planning, monitoring, and evaluation of NGO activities and is currently engaged in research on the role of NGOs in strengthening membership organizations.

Mahbubul Karim has been working with the Bangladeshi NGO Proshika since its foundation in 1976. Currently, he is the director of programs of the organization and head of its Institute for Development Policy Analysis and Advocacy (IDPAA). Before joining Proshika, he worked with the Bangladesh Rural Advancement Committee (BRAC) for three years as a development journalist. Between 1992 and 1993, he served as director of the Association of Development Agencies in Bangladesh (ADAB).

Arthur D. Neame is senior program officer (Southeast Asia) at Christian Aid in London and a director of the Philippine Resource Centre, an NGO involved in development education in both the Philippines and the United Kingdom. He worked for NGOs in the Philippines for four years. While there, he studied community organization and was involved in socioeconomic projects with trade unions, people's organizations, and church-based communities.

Peter Oakley was a senior lecturer in the Agricultural Extension and Rural Development Department, University of Reading (U.K.), from

1976 to 1991. Since 1991, he has been head of the regional office for Latin America and the Caribbean for The Save the Children Fund–U.K., based in Bogota, Colombia. He is the author of *Projects with People* (Geneva: International Labor Organization, 1991) and coauthor (with David Marsden and Brian Pratt) of *Measuring the Process: Guidelines for Evaluating Social Development* (Oxford: International NGO Training and Research Centre, 1994).

David T. Pratten works for SOS Sahel, an NGO based in London. He coordinates the agency's research program on rural-urban linkages and local institutional development in Sudan, Ethiopia, and Mali. He is also conducting Ph.D. research at the School of Oriental and African Studies, University of London.

Janaki Ramesh is the manager of the Indian Cooperative Network for Women (formerly the cooperative arm of the Working Women's Forum). She holds a master's degree in communication from the University of Madras.

Meera Kaul Shah has experience working with governments and NGOs in the development of local, and specifically women's, institutions concerned with natural resource management. She is currently working as a trainer and consultant and providing support for the development of participatory approaches among governments, NGOs, and donors in India, Morocco, and Zambia.

Parmesh Shah has worked with both government and NGOs in India promoting participatory processes, local institutions, and development programs related to the management of natural resources. He is currently based at the Institute of Development Studies in Sussex (U.K.), working on his doctoral dissertation and as a trainer and consultant providing support for developing participatory processes and institutions in India, Zambia, and Vietnam.

Ian Smillie, author of *Mastering the Machine: Poverty, Aid and Technology* (London: IT Publications, 1991), is a founder of Inter Pares and a former executive director of CUSO (Canada). He is also the author of *The Alms Bazaar: Nonprofit Organisations and International Development* (London: IT Publications, 1995). He works as an Ottawa-based development consultant.

Rajesh Tandon is executive director of the Society for Participatory Research in Asia (PRIA), New Delhi, India; chairperson of the Voluntary Action Network India (VANI); president of the Asian/South-Pacific Bureau of Adult Education (ASPBAE); and a founder and board member of CIVICUS (the World Alliance for Citizen Participation). He has written extensively on participatory research, training, NGO management, and the role of civil society and voluntary development organizations in development.

Norman Uphoff is director of the Cornell International Institute for Food, Agriculture and Development and professor of government at

Cornell University, Ithaca, New York. He has worked on problems of rural development for more than twenty-five years, with special concern for participatory approaches and local organizations, predominantly in Ghana, Nepal, Sri Lanka, and Indonesia. He is the coauthor (with Milton Esman) of *Local Organizations: Intermediaries in Rural Development* (Ithaca, N.Y.: Cornell University Press, 1984) and author of *Learning from Gal Oya: Possibilities for Participatory Development and Post-Newtonian Social Science* (Ithaca, N.Y.: Cornell University Press, 1993).

Frits Wils is associate professor at the Institute of Social Studies (ISS) in The Hague, Netherlands. Through teaching, advisory work, and publications, he is involved in NGO work in Latin America and South and Southeast Asia, with a focus on organization, NGO–government relations, and economic development strategies. He helped coordinate a series of studies by ISS on large NGOs in Asia and Latin America and has worked extensively on NGO evaluations with the Dutch NGO NOVIB and the Netherlands Ministry of Development Cooperation.

Simon Zadek is the research coordinator of the New Economics Foundation (NEF) in London and heads the foundation's social audit work with community enterprises and NGOs and in the corporate sector. Social auditing is one of a number of NEF programs dedicated to promoting a more ethical and environmentally sane approach to economics and broader social processes. He is the author of *An Economics of Utopia: Democratising Scarcity* (Aldershot: Avebury Press, 1993).

Index

Accompanied evaluation *(Evaluación acompañada)*, 97–98

Accountability, 4, 8–15, 93, 226, 254, 256–60; Apnalaya mechanisms for, 104–13; of Bangladeshi NGOs, 123, 127–31, 132, 134, 138–39; of decision making in migrant associations, 148; downward *see* Downward accountability; evaluation of, 31–36; functional and strategic *see* Functional accountability, Strategic accountability; issues of for Uphoff, 27–31; and justification of aid cuts, 188; of Latin American NGOs, 93–94, 98–99; and legitimacy, 153; measured by social auditing, 237–39; models of in envisioned future, 234–37; in multiactor programming, 72; under New Policy Agenda, 48–50, 101, 254–56; of NNGOs toward Central American partners, 87, 88; participatory approach, 215–25; of policy alliances, 199–201, 209–11, 212; relationship to governance, 53–62; relationship to scaling up and mainstreaming, 67–68, 75–77; role in future of NGOs, 260–64; and sector analysis of NGOs, 23–31; and social science orientations, 35–36; upward *see* Upward accountability; ways of looking at: practical examples as, 228–39; visioning as, 228–40; WWF's strategies for, 114, 117–19, 122

ACORD (NNGO), 149

ADAB (Association of Development Agencies in Bangladesh), 124, 127, 132, 133; code of ethics, 134–35, 140n1

ADAR (Peruvian NGO), 94

Administrative (Public) sector, 23–27, 41–42, 43, 48, 74

Advocacy, 1, 36n5, 86, 90n17, 198–99, 261; role in policy reform, 198–99, 200, 203; WWF programs, 114. *See also* Policy alliances

Africa, 56, 7, 16n3, 156–65, 212, 229, 233; CBOs, 142; mainstreaming strategy, 73; NGOs, 179, 199. *See also individual countries*

African Charter for Popular Participation, 157–58

Aga Khan Rural Support Programme (AKRSP), 50n1, 183n3, 215, 217–24, 257

Agency for International Development, U.S. (USAID), 7, 107, 130

AGRARIA (Chilean program), 71

Agrarian Research and Training Institute, Sri Lanka, 29–31

Agricultural Bank of Sudan, 152, 154n10

Agriculture, 11, 45–46, 73, 158–59, 196; programs supported by AKRSP, 217, 219–20; in Sudan, 148, 151–52, 154n7

Aid, official. *See* Official aid

AIDS and HIV programs, 130, 188; provided by Apnalaya, 104, 107, 112

Akriti Sansthan (Indian NGO), 57

AKRSP (Aga Khan Rural Support Programme), 50n1, 183n3, 215, 217–24, 257

Al Barkal Union (migrant association), 150

Ali Baldo, Suliman, 142–55, 254

Al Maghawir students' association, 146–47, 151

Amateurism, of NNGOs as governmental concern, 195–96

Andhra Pradesh, state, India, 42, 44, 75, 114, *table* 116

Animal husbandry programs, 217, 221

Apex NGOs, 159–61, 164n1. *See also* Networks; NGOs; Southern NGOs

Apnalaya (Indian NGO), 101, 102–13, 254, 259

Arabism, in Sudan, 145, 151

Asia, 229; NGOs, 73, 199, 212. *See also* South Asia; *individual countries*

ASOCODE (Central American network of peasant organizations), 88, 89n9

273